PRESENTED TO:

....

FROM:

....

DATE:

....

The Invitation

to INTIMACY *with* GOD

MyDaily DEVOTIONAL

COUNTRYMAN®

A Division of Thomas Nelson Publishers

THOMAS NELSON
Since 1798

Published in Nashville, Tennessee, by Thomas Nelson. Thomas Nelson is a registered trademark of HarperCollins Christian Publishing, Inc.

Unless otherwise noted, Scripture quotations are taken from the Holy Bible, New International Version®, NIV®. Copyright © 1973, 1978, 1984, 2011 by Biblica, Inc.™ Used by permission of Zondervan. All rights reserved worldwide. www.zondervan.com. The "NIV" and "New International Version" are trademarks registered in the United States Patent and Trademark Office by Biblica, Inc.™

Scripture quotations marked AMP are from the Amplified® Bible, copyright © 1954, 1958, 1962, 1964, 1965, 1987 by The Lockman Foundation. Used by permission. (www.Lockman.org)

Scripture quotations marked ESV are from the ESV® Bible (The Holy Bible, English Standard Version®), copyright © 2001 by Crossway, a publishing ministry of Good News Publishers. Used by permission. All rights reserved.

Scripture quotations marked HCSB are from the Holman Christian Standard Bible®. Copyright © 1999, 2000, 2002, 2003, 2009 by Holman Bible Publishers. Used by permission. HCSB® is a federally registered trademark of Holman Bible Publishers.

Scripture quotations marked KJV are from the King James Version of the Bible. Public domain.

Scripture quotations marked NASB are from the New American Standard Bible®, Copyright © 1960, 1962, 1963, 1968, 1971, 1972, 1973, 1975, 1977, 1995 by The Lockman Foundation. Used by permission. (www.Lockman.org)

Scripture quotations marked NCV are from the New Century Version®. © 2005 by Thomas Nelson. Used by permission. All rights reserved.

Scripture quotations marked NET are from the New English Translation, NET Bible® copyright ©1996–2006 by Biblical Studies Press, L.L.C. http://netbible.com All rights reserved.

Scripture quotations marked NKJV are from the New King James Version®. © 1982 by Thomas Nelson. Used by permission. All rights reserved.

Scripture quotations marked NLT are from the Holy Bible, New Living Translation. © 1996, 2004, 2007, 2013 by Tyndale House Foundation. Used by permission of Tyndale House Publishers, Inc., Carol Stream, Illinois 60188. All rights reserved.

Scripture quotations marked WEB are from the World English Bible™. Public domain.

ISBN-13: 978-1-4041-0704-5

Cover and interior design: Kristy Edwards
Original package design © Thomas Nelson

Printed in China

18 19 20 21 22 DSC 5 4 3 2 1

The Invitation

to INTIMACY *with* GOD

MyDaily DEVOTIONAL

Introduction

The Invitation was created by fifty-one women as a reminder of God's love and grace. Nothing we say or do goes unnoticed by the Father. He is attentive to our needs—in fact, He never takes His eyes off of us.

Living in a fast-forward culture, it's easy for us to feel overlooked, forgotten, or uninvited. We long to be recognized, hunger to be included and to feel valuable as well as to be a part of something greater than ourselves. The good news is, through God's Word and moments alone with Him, we can discern our worth and discover our value.

It is our prayer that this devotional will help you see how important you are to the Father. He wants you to feel accepted and affirmed. He is inviting you to experience the depths of His love and mercy.

Tracey Mitchell

Tracey Mitchell, Hon. D.D.
Author, Speaker, TV Host
Dallas, Texas

Contents

Live and Love Fiercely

"Have I not commanded you? Be strong and courageous.
Do not be afraid; do not be discouraged, for the LORD
your God will be with you wherever you go."

JOSHUA 1:9

One night at a conference a woman came forward and asked if I could pray with her. I quickly agreed, and she leaned forward to whisper her prayer request. Before she could get the words out of her mouth, I gently stopped her and said, "I already know what's on your heart."

Looking confused, she asked, "How can you know what I am about to say?"

I said, "The grief is written on your face."

Tears formed as she collapsed in my arms. Over the years I've discovered most women silently suffer from things no one knows about, even though sharing their issues with a sister would have brought them healing. Sometimes the private struggles we face spill out in ways we least expect.

No one claws through the trenches of faith without coming out soiled. Daughters listed on God's highlight reel of faith weren't the spoiled kind, rather the soiled kind. They were women just like you and me, who were brave enough to deal with private issues of infertility, insecurity, anxiety, abortion, addiction, adultery, and other concerns that would steal our healing. Our awkward stabs at trying to be perfect leave no great impression on God. But when He sees us weak-kneed and clawing forward, His eyes remain glued on our situation, and we find hope for healing.

Father, help me live courageously. Let me be vulnerable
and rely on the strength of my sisters.

Tracey Mitchell, Dallas, TX

Make Something Beautiful of Your Scars

The LORD will accomplish that which concerns me; Your
[unwavering] lovingkindness, O LORD, endures forever—
do not abandon the works of Your own hands.

PSALM 138:8 AMP

While praying with a lady at a women's conference, I noticed a tattoo on her arm and asked about its meaning. Tears filled her eyes as she whispered, "This is God's personal promise to me. During the depth of my addiction, these words brought hope and freedom. Inked in my handwriting, I designed it to cover the scars of where I once cut myself. Now the trace marks of destruction have been replaced by promises of fatherly acceptance." Engraved in a loopy script was Psalm 138:8.

Most people have experienced seasons in their lives that they would rather not remember or would like to simply blot out entirely. Maybe it was a time when you made a terrible decision, did the wrong thing to get ahead, or turned your back on your faith. Although you wish you could erase those choices and forget how you messed up, those memories don't just go away. The good news is that God can turn those hurtful mistakes into something beautiful. Just as He did with this woman who had been caught up in addiction, He can turn our horrors into a testimony that will honor Him.

If you are finding it difficult to let go of past mistakes, begin to agree with God's promises for your life. He is a compassionate Father who longs to move you into a place of victory and blessing.

Jesus, please redeem the mistakes of my past and
engrave Your promises on my heart.

Step into Something New

"Lord, if it's you," Peter replied, "tell me to come to you on the water."
"Come," he said.
Then Peter got down out of the boat, walked on
the water and came toward Jesus.
MATTHEW 14:28–29

*A*re you ever tempted to take the easy route around a sticky situation? At times it has seemed like a good option for me. But I knew if I made the decision to do what was convenient and comfortable, I would regret it. Thankfully, I received wise counsel from friends who encouraged me to take the longer route and wait on God's best.

The enemy doesn't always set traps to make us feel uncomfortable. Sometimes the trap is to make us comfortable in places we should never settle down. We grow roots when we should be growing wings.

Not everything that entices us away from God's perfect plan appears evil. Sometimes the trap is set in a way that appears neither good nor evil . . . but simply comfortable.

When I think of dangerous situations like this, my imagination drifts to the disciples on the stormy lake. While waves crashed, Jesus invited them to get out of the boat and walk on the water. I want to be like Peter, who was the only disciple to get out of the boat. It must have been frightening, but he took a chance and answered Jesus' call. When we step into something new, we open ourselves up to wonders that we never would have experienced if we had stayed comfortably seated.

So take the risk: leap out of the boat and into the arms of the One who says, "Come."

....

Father, give me the courage to leap into the supernatural.

Tracey Mitchell, Dallas, TX

Obey His Gentle Whisper

In their hearts humans plan their course, but the LORD establishes their steps.
PROVERBS 16:9

Years ago I experienced a falling-out with a close business associate. Though I was surprised at how things ended, I can't say I didn't have any warning. If I had been paying closer attention to the inner nudge of the Holy Spirit, I would have never entertained that person's business proposal. But the truth was, I made a decision when I was exhausted and without prayerful consideration. But God's goodness and grace helped me out of a potentially damaging deal.

I understand what it's like to let your heart lead you down unhealthy paths. It would be hard to list the times I've had to crawl out of pits I should have never fallen into. If I would have kept to the path and obeyed the gentle whisper of the Spirit, I would have stepped around things I couldn't see in the dark. These aren't the big, obvious things that we know are wrong. Rather the Spirit waves a caution flag in more subtle situations because He wants to help us avoid a painful outcome.

Maybe you have felt an inner nudge asking you to take a closer look at a situation before you make a decision. If so, set aside time to pray and seek out wisdom from trusted men and women of God. Remember, patience pleases God. When you take time to acknowledge Him, He will show you which way to go. He will work behind the scenes to make sure your dreams don't fall into the hands of the wrong people. The things you couldn't make happen in your own strength, He can make happen in His endless power.

....

Father, when my own plans are leading me
astray, teach me to wait on You.

Lasting Change

If anyone is in Christ, the new creation has come:
The old has gone, the new is here!
2 CORINTHIANS 5:17

*O*ne morning I was watching a news program where a woman from the audience was chosen to receive a makeover. The producers of the show displayed a life-sized digital portrait of what the woman had looked like hours before, and then came the "big reveal." The previously disheveled-looking woman came out from behind the stage looking like a supermodel. Although I was excited for her, there was a part of me that wondered, *How long will she maintain this new image?* It's hard to imagine that a quick, two-hour change will last.

Superficial, overnight "change" without the working of the Holy Spirit usually doesn't last either. But when God is in charge, our personalities, outlooks, hopes, and dreams can change in an instant—because the change begins on the inside and works its way to the outside. I know a man who in a month's time went from being an abusive, alcoholic husband to being a loving, sober, supportive husband. And the change was lasting because his heart was surrendered to Christ.

When God sees our hearts are willing to change, He will come alongside us and empower us to do what we couldn't accomplish in our own strength. There is no end to what God will do when we extend our faith and trust Him to do the supernatural. Maybe you need a complete spiritual "makeover." Ask God for favor—and for the deep, transformative change that can start a new chapter in your life. Let Him lead you into something you've only dreamed of.

Holy Spirit, work within my heart. I surrender it
to You, and I am willing. Make me new.

Tracey Mitchell, Dallas, TX

Serve Like Jesus

He poured water into a basin and began to wash his disciples'
feet, drying them with the towel that was wrapped around him.

JOHN 13:5

In His wisdom, God makes us powerful and vulnerable at the same time. Honestly, my soul wishes that weren't the case. It doesn't mind becoming powerful, but the idea of vulnerability to others makes my heart long for isolation. If only we could keep one and discard the other. But that's not the way relationships work. Our culture has done us no greater injustice than forcing on us the counterfeit truth that fame and independence are keys to happiness. That kind of shallow thinking may make the world smile, but it makes God shudder.

Jesus modeled true power when He chose to wash His disciples' feet in an ultimate posture of humility and vulnerability. And when I retrace other game-changing moments in history, I find they often thread back to individuals who chose mutual contribution over individual acclaim. Think about revolutionaries like Luther, liberators like Mandela, humanitarians like Mother Teresa, and civil rights activists like Rosa Parks. Epic social shifts occurred when ordinary people decided serving humanity trumped serving self. Ordinary people became legends by becoming ambassadors for those without freedom and litigators for those who had no voice. They became legends the day they traded in What-about-me? attitudes to do what's best for someone else.

So don't be afraid of becoming vulnerable when you serve. In this way you echo Jesus' humility—and His strength.

....

Father, help me shape history by serving others.

Strength to Run

His hair began to grow again.
JUDGES 16:22 NCV

*T*he sound waves from the starting gun sent the focused runners into their race. The girl's pace was steady, and her strides were long. She gained ground with determination. This is what she had been training for!" her mother shouted as she rounded the final corner in first place. While the girl was breaking into her winning stride, the crowd gasped in shock as her body hit the ground and slid across the pavement. One by one the runners passed her as she rolled back and forth clutching her broken ankle in great pain.

Then, suddenly, the rolling stopped, and her delicate frame started to move. She pulled herself forward, elbow by elbow, dragging her injured body to the finish line. Determined, she shouted out, "I am going to finish my race!" One week later a reporter asked her how she managed to cross the finish line with such a serious injury. The young lady replied, "My perspective changed. It was no longer about the competitive win, but the desire to finish and to finish strong. I changed my perspective and regained my strength deep from within. In a split second I chose to embrace all that was within me, not the physical strength that had just failed me. Against all odds, I finished my race."

A change in perspective can refuel the fire needed to try again, to dream again, or become fully alive again. Regain your strength by giving yourself permission to see your life through a different lens. Allow the Holy Spirit to raise you up, to get back into your race, and "to grow again."

Holy Spirit, today I begin again. Light a fire inside me that would lead me right back into my race. I rely on You to renew my strength.

Tracy Strawberry, Orlando, FL

Stretch into Something New

"Nor do people put new wine into old wineskins; otherwise the
wineskins burst, and the wine pours out and the wineskins are ruined;
but they put new wine into fresh wineskins, and both are preserved."

MATTHEW 9:17 NASB

*I*magine it: you're in the airport check-in line, standing behind a woman who is furiously re-packing her suitcase. "I promise you it's going to fit. I know I can make it work. I have done this a million times. This old suitcase of mine has never failed me."

"But ma'am, the zippers are pulling apart at the seams," he responds. "I'm afraid it's not going to hold. Would you consider heading to the gift shop and picking up something that will hold everything?"

"Sir, I don't have time for that," she replies. "I'm sure if I just move some things around and shove my shopping into the side pocket it will be fine."

With a shrug the attendant relents, tossing the suitcase onto the conveyer belt. As it makes its landing, old faithful tears apart, scattering her belongings everywhere. Frantic, the attendant tries to rescue the costly new dresses that have gotten caught under the belt and ripped to shreds.

A new season in life requires a greater faith capacity—one that's capable of containing your increase. Maybe it's time for you to stretch, so you don't end up like the woman at the airport! And though you may feel you have missed His destination, remember that He is the God of multiple chances. Invite Him in to stretch your faith, bless you with innovative thinking, and step into something new.

Father, I pray for You to enlarge my capacity. Align my thinking
with Your divine destination and will for my life. Give me the
courage to leave the old behind and to embrace the new.

Accept God's Yes

"Make your tent bigger; stretch it out and make it wider. Do not hold back. Make the ropes longer and its stakes stronger, because you will spread out to the right and to the left. Your children will take over other nations, and they will again live in cities that once were destroyed."

ISAIAH 54:2–3 NCV

*F*ather, *in the name of Jesus, bless me and my husband, that we may increase our territory for You. Use us in greater ways, Lord, that You may be known to all the world.* This was my prayer, and it came from a stirring in my soul that would not settle. Then one day God answered: *Tracy, I want you and Darryl to let go of everything and move to Florida.*

I opened my eyes in disbelief and tried to escape the command that had just been given to me. I pushed back the thought and reminded God that my husband, Darryl, and I loved living near family in St. Louis. I thought we would live there forever.

I battled the conversation in my mind: *Tracy, you asked Me for increase. Are you willing to give up your all for My very best? In order to increase, you and Darryl must decrease once again. This time it will demand the surrender of your material possessions, the closeness of family, and every comfort that has been established here. Do you want My increase? Do you want My yes?*

What happens when enlarging your territory requires you to decrease and let go of what you have? Are you willing to give up your own dreams and desires for God? Darryl and I embraced His direction! He has enlarged our territory and let us reach the world for Him. The Lord will answer your prayer. Are you ready for His yes?

Good and gracious Father, I pray that You would increase and I would decrease. Give me the courage to move into Your yes!

Tracy Strawberry, Orlando, FL

Give Up Reasoning

A person's steps are directed by the LORD. How then
can anyone understand their own way?
PROVERBS 20:24

*H*ave you ever cried out, "Why, God, why?" In the face of another defeat, another illness, another setback, have you ever despaired, searching for a reason for the hardship in your life? I don't know the why, my dear sister, but I know God is faithful. At times like these I've been inspired by my sisters in Christ, how they respond and continue to remain faithful to the ways of the Lord. At times I have wanted to quit and have questioned God, but they've encouraged me to lean on Him. I stopped trying to figure out all the *whys* a long time ago.

So now I'm here as your sister in Christ—to remind you to trust Him as you always have and to remind you of the truth: you have been set apart for greatness. It's not an easy road, and I know it gets lonely at times, but count the cost before you make the decision to quit. Remember the sacrifices you've made, the hours of prayer, work, and seeking the face of God—and don't give up! Opposition comes with opportunity. The enemy is always trying to destroy what God is doing. So stand strong, my sister, and fight for your blessing!

Today cast down your voice of reason and embrace this season. Stop trying to figure it out. Dig a little deeper, stand a little taller, and walk a little stronger. The Lord your God is with you, guiding your every step.

Father, help me see my opportunities in the midst of opposition.
How great are You, O God. You are for me and never against
me. Your grace and mercy are new every morning.

Take a New Path

"I will say to the north, 'Give them up!' and to the south, 'Do not hold them back.' Bring my sons from afar and my daughters from the ends of the earth."
ISAIAH 43:6

What does *different* mean? It includes forward motion, new thinking, and God's way of doing things. As a new Christian I literally thought I could do *all* things through Christ who strengthened me. I took that to mean I could do anything and be anything *I* wanted to be, not knowing that following God's way was a prerequisite. I found myself floundering and wandering. The first order of business was not in the doing, but in the being. I had to become a committed woman of God.

Freedom is found in following. God will empower you to do all the things He has called you to do. If you are stuck, bound, or stagnant, I invite you to embrace God's path. He makes all things new. His leading is found within the pages of His Word, which are alive and speak to the hearts of those who earnestly seek Him. I encourage you to open your heart and mind to His grand possibilities and opportunities for your life by simply asking Him, "What do You have for me, Father? Where would You have me go? What would You have me do? How can I prepare?" When you abandon yourself completely to God, He will seal every part of His specific path for you with favor, protection, provision, and divine purpose. God Himself will push back the darkness for you. Your new path is paved with eternal purpose!

....

Father, I renew a steadfast commitment to Your will and Your ways in my life. Order my steps, and reveal the specific assignments You have for me along Your special path.

Tracy Strawberry, Orlando, FL

Fatherly Attention

He will not let you be defeated. He who guards you never sleeps.
PSALM 121:3 NCV

After my last meeting finished, I walked the bustling streets of New York City. I turned into Central Park, where the trees screen out the city blocks and the noise dissipates. I spotted a little girl lost in laughter with her father. He paid attention to her every move. In this moment I witnessed the great love of a father for his daughter. He was protecting her as she played and receiving her with open arms as she reached out to him.

As I closed my eyes, the verse in 1 Corinthians 13:11 came to my mind: "When I was a child, I talked like a child, I thought like a child, I reasoned like a child. When I became a man, I put the ways of childhood behind me." When I can't physically see, hear, or feel God at work in my life, I still know He is there with me and working on my behalf. I am no longer a child, but I *am* a daughter of the King, growing in His ways daily through His Word. I am confident in His nature, His character, and His promises. In the depths of His protection, I find my refuge, and in His Word I will find peace. His attention toward me is constant and everlasting.

I encourage you to throw off childish thoughts, words, and reasoning and walk as the woman of God that He has created you to be. Stand tall with confidence because you are royalty, the daughter of King Jesus, who leads you into triumph and upholds you with His mighty right hand.

Father, today I step into this world as a daughter of the King, desiring for You to be magnified and glorified. I turn my affections and attention to You, my God, and I thank You for Your fatherly attention.

Fight for Your Dreams

Do not depart quickly or leave in a panic. For the LORD goes
before you; the God of Israel is your rear guard.

ISAIAH 52:12 NET

*H*ave you ever felt worn down, knocked around, and used up? Perhaps you have felt like David asking, "How long, LORD? Will you forget me forever? How long will you hide your face from me? How long must I wrestle with my thoughts and day after day have sorrow in my heart? How long will my enemy triumph over me?" (Psalm 13:1–2).

Remember, Satan attacks those next in line for promotion. He's trying his best to wear you down. His goal is to convince you to give up. Your job is to outlast the devil!

When your dream is taking too long, don't give up. When circumstances aren't working out the way you thought they would, don't give up. When the breakthrough is not happening, don't give up. Determine that you will fight for your dream. When I say *dream*, I mean anything and everything you are believing God wants you to accomplish.

In this fight your opponent is the devil, not the people around you. So fight him with the words of your mouth. You give life to what you say, good or bad. Proverbs 18:21 says, "The tongue has the power of life and death." Become extremely disciplined in what you say.

Speak the Word of God over your dreams. Begin to declare your victory and Satan's defeat. And be encouraged that you are not alone. Isaiah 52:12 says, "The God of Israel is your rear guard." In other words, "He's got your back!" So with His help, you can fight until you win!

....

Lord, today I declare that I will not give up!
I will see Your victory in my life.

Terri Savelle Foy, Rockwall, TX

Find Your Focus

Keep your eyes focused on what is right, and
look straight ahead to what is good.

PROVERBS 4:25 NCV

*I*t is easy to get caught up in everything that needs to be done. If we aren't careful, years can go by without our making much progress toward the dreams God has placed in our hearts. The enemy, Satan, wants us distracted, busy, and overwhelmed, so we won't accomplish what God has for our lives.

Many people aren't laser-focused on what they want to achieve. Consequently December 31 comes around, and they are disappointed by another repeat of the previous year. They never design their destiny.

But if you focus, you can deliberately steer yourself in the direction you want to go. The Bible says, "A double minded man is unstable in all his ways" (James 1:8 KJV). Focus makes you single-minded and stable in all your ways.

How can you apply this practically? Rather than having five rooms in your house cluttered and messy, focus on organizing one room. Rather than having ideas for three different books to write, start writing one and finish. It's better to have one completed book affecting lives than three unfinished books helping no one.

I challenge you to focus on one skill that will help you the most in achieving your dreams. You may have to stop other things, but saying no to them is what will enable you to achieve your dreams. Success is about saying no to the good so you can say yes to the great!

....

Lord, help me get laser-focused to achieve the
dreams You have placed in my heart.

The Spiritual Force of Gratitude

One of [the lepers], when he saw that he was healed, turned back, glorifying and praising and honoring God with a loud voice; and he lay face downward at Jesus' feet, thanking Him [over and over].

LUKE 17:15–16 AMP

With one simple habit, you can shift your life in a new direction: develop a grateful heart. I'm not just talking about being a more pleasant person because you don't complain as much. A spiritual force is released when you give thanks and praise. First Thessalonians 5:18 tells us to give thanks in all circumstances. It doesn't say *for* every circumstance, but that we should give thanks *in* every circumstance.

I'm not suggesting that you ignore your hardships and struggles. Still, when something isn't going as planned or things are beyond your control, you can have an attitude of gratitude.

God responds differently to a grateful heart. When Jesus healed ten lepers, only one returned to say, "Thank You." The one who expressed gratitude was not only healed of the disease, he was made whole and restored.

Even if your circumstance feels hopeless now, I encourage you to say, "Thank You, Jesus" by faith for what you're believing Him to do.

Gratitude is powerful. Gratitude pushes out the negative thoughts that are trying to invade your mind. Gratitude opens doors that have been closed in your life.

If you want to achieve your God-given dreams, give up complaining about where you are and how bad it appears. Stay thankful and focused on where you're going, and you'll get there much sooner.

....

Thank You, Lord, for all You have done in my life and all You are going to do. Today I'll remember to thank You in all circumstances.

Give Yourself a Pep Talk

David was greatly distressed; for the people spake of stoning him, because the soul of all the people was grieved, every man for his sons and for his daughters: but David encouraged himself in the LORD his God.

1 SAMUEL 30:6 KJV

J'll never forget preparing to take the stage of the largest evangelical church in France. My daughter leaned over and asked me, "Mama, are you a little nervous?" I was about to minister to ten thousand people, but I answered, "I am confident to minister to thousands of people. I speak at the largest conferences in the world."

How could I reply courageously? I'd been using the principle that what you repeatedly hear, you eventually believe. You believe your own voice more than anyone else's.

There is nothing more powerful than speaking God's Word. His Word is His will. When you consistently align your mouth with what God's Word says, encouraging yourself with its promises instead of what you feel, you are activating the power of God to work in your life. Eventually your actions will align with your words.

You cannot talk failure and live in victory. If you feel stuck, start using your words to change your life instead of describing it.

God always places a dream in your heart before you can achieve it. Speaking your dreams into existence is part of the process in achieving them. In fact the Bible tells us God "calls into being that which does not exist" (Romans 4:17 AMP). So today encourage yourself in the Lord. Then take it a step further and start saying the right things.

Lord, I believe what You say about me and not just what I feel.
I declare Your Word over my life and my dreams today.

A New Way of Life

Without faith no one can please God. Anyone who comes to God must
believe that he is real and that he rewards those who truly want to find him.

HEBREWS 11:6 NCV

The habits you currently have are only good enough to get you what
you've currently got. If you don't change a habit, then you will go right
back to where you were. Fad diets prove this. To achieve greater things you
must create new habits—such as eating healthfully every day, rather than
trying something drastic for a week and seeing the pounds pile back on later.

Maybe you don't think you have time to add any new habits to your
schedule. Instead of looking at the time you don't have, try looking at the
time you *do* have and make the most of it. What could you accomplish
by eliminating only one hour every day from social media, television, or
unnecessary phone time?

I challenge you to start with one discipline of waking up twenty
minutes earlier to be alone with God. You'll soon gain stability, direction, vision, and intimacy with God.

Hebrews 11:6 says God "is a rewarder of them that diligently seek
him" (KJV). Make seeking God every day a part of your routine, like
brushing your teeth or washing your face. Soon you won't ask yourself if
you feel like it; you'll just do it.

Too many people think of growth as a period of life rather than a way
of life. Never cap off how much you can grow. Incorporate new growth
habits in your life that will lead you to the success God has for you. It's
not easy. But I can tell you from experience, it's worth it.

Lord, help me see where I can grow and change my
current habits so I can go higher with You.

Terri Savelle Foy, Rockwall, TX

Imagine If

*We fix our eyes not on what is seen, but on what is unseen, since
what is seen is temporary, but what is unseen is eternal.*

2 CORINTHIANS 4:18

A friend of mine vacationed on the beaches of Waikiki, where he spotted a magnificent mansion. He thought, *I couldn't imagine living in a house like that!* He heard the Lord quietly respond, *Don't worry about it; you never will.* That may sound harsh, but your imagination has a lot to do with what you will experience in life. If we cannot imagine it, it will never happen.

Imagining big isn't only for houses; it's a necessity for every dream your big God has for you. It isn't just playing pretend; your imagination is your ability to envision your future. Cultivating your imagination in faith is vital to shaping your life.

Many of us once had childlike faith as Jesus advocated in Matthew 18:3, but we've allowed the realities of life to limit our imagination and dreams. We cannot allow what's happening in the world around us to dictate what we imagine or what God can imagine for us.

Second Corinthians 4:18 tells us to fix our eyes on unseen things that God says are true: His promises, His plans, and His vision for us. We can't see the future, but we can have faith in the fact that God has great plans for us.

Allow yourself the freedom to imagine. Spend a few minutes visualizing the future you want. Rediscover the childlike faith to believe that if God can give you a dream, He can surely bring it to pass.

Heavenly Father, help me rediscover my imagination. Open
my eyes to the dreams and plans You have for me.

Taste God's Goodness

O taste and see that the LORD [our God] is good; how blessed [fortunate, prosperous, and favored by God] is the man who takes refuge in Him.

PSALM 34:8 AMP

*T*oday we rush through our days with so many activities that keep us busy, that there never seems enough time to spend with the Lord. There is a constant pulling for our attention and affection, and often we find ourselves overwhelmed in the mayhem. In those times, "taste and see" by taking refuge in God.

From the beginning of time it has been God's desire to visit with us—to refresh and renew our spirits. He longs for us to bask in His presence. *Taste* is a word that speaks to our desires, cravings, and longings, and too often our *taste* gets misdirected by things without eternal value. As we take a few moments to escape the hustle and bustle of life, we give our souls the opportunity to taste of God's goodness.

Amazing things happen when we redirect our attention toward rest in Him. God shows up in all His goodness, and we soon find ourselves longing for those quiet times with Him where we find delight and refuge. When we immerse ourselves in God's goodness, He turns our chaos into peace, our sorrow is traded for His joy, and our tired, weary souls find divine strength and courage. Prosperous is the woman who finds refuge in God. Favored is the woman who sits at His feet. Refreshed is the woman whose affection is set and remains on the Most High.

Lord, be the desire of my heart, and bring me rest in You.
Let my eyes be fixed on You, lover of my soul.

Brenda Steunenberg, Abbotsford, BC CANADA

See the World God's Way

Jesus wept. So the Jews were saying, "See how
He loved him [as a close friend]!"
JOHN 11:35–36 AMP

*O*ne morning God gave me a dream. In this dream I saw myself standing in the middle of a battlefield. I was dressed as a warrior princess, wielding a sword and shield, and sporting the strappiest leather sandals you ever did see! I stood face-to-face with the fiercest enemy I had ever encountered, and its name was *Fear*.

As I stood assessing this enemy, God walked on the scene and stood between me and my enemy. God was so big, I could no longer see the enemy. God, staring down my enemy, turned His head, looked at me, and said, "I've got this."

Talk about a perspective changer! True freedom and beautiful rest come when we are willing to lock eyes with the One who can see far beyond our perspective and who is never rattled by circumstances.

Are you facing a fierce enemy? Look at things from His perspective, and watch as He enters your battlefield and fights for you. God knows your life from beginning to end and all the pieces that make up the middle . . . and He's got this!

Thank You, God, for fighting my battles. I lay every burden
of my heart at Your feet and ask You to open my eyes to see
from Your perspective, not from my fears or inadequacies.
With You I walk in confidence and strength.

Encounter a Love That Does Not Fail

May your unfailing love be with us, LORD, even as we put our hope in you.

PSALM 33:22

Wouldn't it be perfect if life was made up of days filled with sunshine and roses, lattes and girlfriends, and there wasn't a care to be found? Maybe in our dreams! Reality is that life can come at us full force and often blindsides us with the unexpected, hurling debris of disappointment, fear, and pain, like a hurricane. What do we do in these seasons when answers to our questions seem impossible to find, when our dreams are shattered, and it seems like the very ground beneath us is shaking?

I recently walked through such a season, when all that could shake in my life, shook. I can tell you that I had two choices: worship and lean in close to the Father, or succumb to the pain and misery of my heart. Can I be honest? It was a choice. Spending time resting in the presence of the heavenly Father became my place of strength, and where my soul found rest. When I worshipped, His love came like a balm for my brokenness and soothed the ache in my heart. Unlike human love, which can leave us wanting, the faithful love of God meets us right where we are, heals every broken place, drives away fear, and leaves us forever changed.

Lord, find me at Your feet, worshipping You. Your love dissipates
my fears, soothes my broken heart, and overshadows my
disappointments. Thank You for Your faithful love.

Worship Without Reservation

David was dancing before the LORD with great enthusiasm.

2 SAMUEL 6:14 AMP

I want to tell you more about my place of rest, realignment, and resetting: the intimate place of worship. Worship is our extravagant expression of love, gratefulness, and adoration to God. Worship is all about Him—who He is and what He has done. And in this act of worship, we are changed! Whether we are soaring in a mountaintop season or find ourselves mourning in the deepest valley, worship is the catalyst that ushers us into the very presence of God. It is a place where God always meets us, sings over us, and where His grace is extended without reservation.

The woman who poured out her finest oil on the feet of Jesus found freedom in her act of worship (Luke 7). She gave her finest and most expensive sacrifice to Jesus. She worshipped Him without reservation, and in return He lifted her up out of the ashes and set her free. What a beautiful picture not only of her worship, but of Jesus meeting her right there in the strangest of places, freeing her from her heavy heart. As her tears mixed with the oil, as she dried them with her hair, Jesus lovingly gazed upon her, received her worship, and in return gave her the greatest gift of all—Himself.

Lord, I come to You without reservation and bring You my sacrifice of praise and my finest worship. Thank You, that in my worship, You lift me out of the ashes of my brokenness. You heal me, deliver me, and sing over me with joy.

Love Extravagantly

Standing behind Him at His feet, weeping, she began to wet His
feet with her tears, and kept wiping them with the hair of her head,
and kissing His feet and anointing them with the perfume.

LUKE 7:38 NASB

With tears streaming down my face, I looked at the tiny bundle lying in the crib and wondered, *What will I do if a year from now they decide to return her to her birth mom? What if I give all that I am to love her, only to have her ripped out of my arms?* Would I give my whole heart or hold back to protect it?

That day I decided that I would love with everything that was in me, no matter the cost. I am proud to say that this year our beautiful daughter will be graduating high school! And we will never stop giving all that we are in love for her.

Love is not cheap. I'm not talking about money but rather great vulnerability and sacrifice. This love we pour out is a wonderful love, but it pales in comparison to the love that God offers each one of us. His love raises us up out of the ashes of brokenness, floods us with His goodness, and positions us as daughters of the King. Just as our daughter, adopted by my husband and me, is an heir to our estate, you and I are heirs of God and all that His kingdom possesses. We stand boldly before our Abba Father, a full recipient of all His promises—and of His bottomless sacrificial love.

Thank You, God, for the extravagant love You displayed
in sending Jesus, Your Son, to take my place, to die on the
cross for my salvation. I walk as Your child, an heir to Your
throne, and a receiver of all Your promises for my life.

Brenda Steunenberg, Abbotsford, BC CANADA

Find Peace for an Overwhelmed Soul

Teach me Your way, O LORD, and lead me in a
smooth path, because of my enemies.

PSALM 27:11 NKJV

*L*ast year my husband and I experienced what no parent ever imagines will be part of their family story. We lost our beautiful twenty-two-year-old son to a drug overdose. To say my soul was overwhelmed was an understatement! I remember saying the words, "I don't know how to do this." I found myself in unchartered waters. What do we do when tragedy steps in and introduces itself? Can there be peace amid our grief?

One part of me wanted to curl up in a fetal position, pull the blankets over my head, and never come out again. But there was another part of me that knew there was One who heard my cries, One whose hands held the tears of my deepest sorrow, and One on whom I could firmly hold on to and find my footing. As tempting and justified as the fetal position was, I knew it could not be my choice.

There is a place of intimacy with God that moves us past the natural and ushers us into the supernatural. When we come before Him and lay down our burdens, heavy though they are, He is faithful to replace those burdens with the very essence of who He is. It is a beautiful exchange.

....

God, I am so thankful that as I draw near to You, You are
faithful to meet me. You exchange my rags for Your beauty
and my unrest for Your peace. Your joy is my strength!

Ask for Rest and Wisdom

God said to [Solomon] . . . "Behold, I have done as you asked. I have given you a wise and discerning heart (mind), so that no one before you was your equal, nor shall anyone equal to you arise after you."

1 KINGS 3:11–12 AMP

I am sure you have experienced seasons in life where you were uncertain how to take the next step or make the next move. I remember a dark time when I didn't know where to turn for help. During these restless days I prayed specifically for two things: wisdom and peaceful sleep. I knew the ability to rest well was linked to my ability to hear clearly from God. When I was fully rested, I was able to receive wisdom from God's Word. Without sleep, I was jittery, on edge, and emotional—unable to receive from anyone.

In addition to rest I've learned the secret to surviving difficult seasons is surrounding yourself with wise counsel, praying for wisdom, and seeking wisdom in the Word. As a young man, Solomon asked God for a wise, discerning heart. As king he would need prophetic insights on how to lead and judge the people within his kingdom. Maybe you too are in a situation where you need great wisdom. I encourage you to tap into the limitless supply of grace and wisdom God has made available to each of us.

When life seems overwhelming, ask for wisdom to point you in the right direction and rest to restore your soul. God will answer your prayer.

Lord, help me make healthy decisions. I ask for Your wisdom, knowledge, understanding, insight, good judgment, and restorative rest. I lean on You in taking my next step.

Be Memorable

Pharaoh said to Joseph, "Since God has made all this known
to you, there is no one so discerning and wise as you."

GENESIS 41:39

Joseph must have impressed the pharaoh, the king of Egypt. After all, the pharaoh relied on Joseph's counsel and leadership. I've often wondered what made Joseph so memorable. Was it charisma, confidence, or good looks? I think what impressed everyone about Joseph was his ability to credit God with his success.

When I traced the tale of Joseph I noticed that in every situation, good or bad, Joseph honored God by giving Him glory. He acknowledged God as the One who gave him incredible wisdom and discernment. He explained to Pharaoh that his gifts, economic strategies, and wisdom came from heaven.

Could Joseph have become arrogant? Absolutely. I cannot count the number of gifted leaders who have fallen by the wayside because they forgot to credit God with their success. Not Joseph. When placed in difficult situations, he relied on God for wisdom and guidance. No matter how dark the season, he trusted God for a favorable outcome.

Today God may be positioning you before influential people as he did with Joseph. As God promotes you, remember to give Him thanks. He is the source of your wisdom, talents, and prosperity.

....

Lord, help me be memorable in the minds of the people You've
put in my path, so I may be influential for You. Fill me with
courage and strengthen me to rely on Your Word. Today I choose
to stand in faith and honor You openly in every situation.

Close Doors Gently

A soft and gentle and thoughtful answer turns away wrath,
but harsh and painful and careless words stir up anger.
PROVERBS 15:1 AMP

*D*on't lock and throw away the keys to doors that you may need to reenter. It wasn't until I had grown up that I understood my grandmother's words. She wanted me to know that I could always leave a difficult situation gracefully. In her wisdom, she cautioned me not to burn down a bridge that I might need to cross again. This advice still holds true, especially in fractured relationships.

How many times have we let harsh words ruin or damage healthy relationships? I think most of us have slammed the door to our hearts when a matter could have been resolved through discussion. Think about it: when we are angry, we tend to shut out people who are irreplaceable in our lives. How often have we yelled or walked away when "a gentle and thoughtful answer" would have brought resolve?

I watched two women I admire admit they had been angry with each other for years. Standing before our small group weeping, they realized how much time had been lost because of harsh words. They publicly disclosed they could not remember the reason for their separation. Now they have reunited and are making an impact in business and enjoying a restored friendship. What have you lost with a parent, a child, a friend, or a colleague because of harsh words? Perhaps it's time to close a door gently or reopen a door you had previously slammed shut.

Dear Lord, please forgive me for responding in anger to a situation that could have been resolved peaceably. Today I commit my words to You. Let my conversation be gentle, loving, and peaceable.

Renee Fowler Hornbuckle, Arlington, TX

Work Passionately

She stretches out her hands to the distaff, and her hands hold
the spindle [as she spins wool into thread for clothing].

PROVERBS 31:19 AMP

I believe in hard work. My work experience has taught me that when we are passionate about something, we will work at it diligently. I define passion as a burning desire to gather all supplies, exhaust all resources, and test the limits of all possibilities. When passion is our driving force, we do not give way to difficulties, give up on our dreams, or give in to failure.

Passion helps develop our potential. It makes us more creative in discovering ways to fulfill our dreams. It also keeps us from falling away from our purpose. The truth is, that passion gives us the strength to rise up from bad situations and make difficult decisions. It gives us the ability to take our eyes off ourselves and make a positive impact in the world around us. A heart driven by passion isn't easily defeated. It takes hits, realizing detractors cannot stop it, because it has a purpose to fulfill.

God's Word tells us how passion and industriousness work for us. Proverbs talks about the virtues of an industrious woman. It describes her as being skilled, developed, focused, determined, and dedicated to designing an excellent product created out of her passionate work. Doesn't that sound like work from a passionate heart?

Be fueled by your passion in God's work, and you'll find yourself working diligently and effectively.

Lord, strengthen me to work passionately always. May I be
skilled, developed, focused, determined, and dedicated to
producing excellent results created from my passionate work.

Grow in Knowledge

This I pray, that your love may abound still more and
more in real knowledge and all discernment.

PHILIPPIANS 1:9 NASB

I recall a time when my six-year-old screamed at me, "Mommy, I'm a big kid now!" The only problem with this statement was she had just thrown a fit, acting like a two-year-old. The evidence of six-year-old maturity did not correspond to the way she had just acted. It was hard not to laugh at her claim of being mature.

Perhaps this is how we act when we have not yet grown and developed in the ways of God. We should exhibit traits and evidence of spiritual maturity. God's design is for believers to grow and mature. The book of Hebrews says, "Let us move beyond the elementary teachings about Christ and be taken forward to maturity" (6:1).

Growth is a natural part of all life. When we follow God's heart, we are given everything we need for spiritual growth. Time alone with God and in His Word allows us to grow in knowledge and discernment. Let's make it our goal to abound in knowledge by becoming disciplined in prayer, study, meditation, and listening to God.

As we grow in knowledge, we learn how to walk in obedience to God's will. We make choices to live according to God's viewpoint rather than our own, and we will know what it is like to be mature in discernment.

Lord, I know Christian growth takes time. I choose to deepen my
walk by growing in knowledge and abandoning all things that keep
my faith from maturing. Help me set aside quality time for You.

Renee Fowler Hornbuckle, Arlington, TX

Be a Loyal Friend

Boaz replied, "I've been told all about what you have done for your mother-in-law since the death of your husband— how you left your father and mother and your homeland and came to live with a people you did not know before."

RUTH 2:11

*L*oyalty is a desirable characteristic in a friend, a mate, or any relationship. Loyalty is the ability to stand by a person in good and bad times. It is the willingness to stick close by a friend when things don't go well or unexpected situations arise. I have learned loyalty is a virtue that is hard to recognize until times of testing come.

Ruth was loyal to her mother-in-law when their situation went south. After the loss of her father-in-law and husband, she could have returned home like her sister-in-law. She could have taken the easy way out. Instead she remained loyal to Naomi and followed her into a new life. The truth is that it is easy to walk with others when things are going well, but it takes a loyal heart to walk with someone when his or her future is unclear.

Perhaps you find yourself in a difficult season when people you never thought would leave you have walked away. Don't let the disappointment of their actions keep you from moving forward. Many people make the best choices they can when under pressure. And remember, not everyone is qualified to go with you into your next season. Ruth's loyalty to Naomi positioned her to receive the goodness of Boaz. Your loyalty is shown by what you do, how you respond, and your willingness to sacrifice your time for others.

Lord, help me be a loyal and trusted friend. Today
I choose to love and honor others.

Embrace Small Beginnings

"Who dares despise the day of small things?"
ZECHARIAH 4:10

y husband and I had struggled with infertility for years. On some days we were tempted to give up hope of ever becoming parents. We could imagine the picture of our family, but with the passing of time and no pregnancy, our anticipation had begun to give way to despair. Then something seemingly small turned the tide of our life.

When my husband and I saw our daughter on a sonogram for the first time, she was so small that my husband said she looked like a mosquito. For months he would call her *skeeter*. It was hard to believe that the tiny throbbing heart would one day develop into a beautiful six-pound, three-ounce baby girl.

Something similar was happening to the Jewish people in Zechariah 4. They had begun to believe that the temple of God would never be reestablished. As a result they were blind to the small signs of progress along the way. Just when they had almost given up hope, along came the prophet Zechariah with a reminder. He looked right into the face of small beginnings and declared that they would yet see the capstone of the temple set in perfect precision and order.

Are you holding on to a God-sized promise and seeing only a little bit of progress? Don't despise the small beginnings, but rather watch for them and embrace them. Remind yourself with every moment that God is overseeing His word and His promises. He has not forgotten you. Keep your eyes on the capstone of your faith, Jesus Christ.

....

Teach me to embrace and rejoice in small beginnings,
knowing that You will bring about great things.

Jan Greenwood, Lewisville, TX

Claim Your Inheritance

I pray also that you will have greater understanding in your heart so you will know the hope to which he has called us and that you will know how rich and glorious are the blessings God has promised his holy people.

EPHESIANS 1:18 NCV

When my sweet dad suddenly passed away in 2001, he left very little to our family in terms of possessions or wealth. But the longer he is gone, the more aware I am of the greatness of my spiritual legacy. It was my dad who sparked my interest in spiritual life. He also deposited within me some generational gifts, such as a love for people, a commitment to marriage and family, and a desire to honor Christ with my life. Over time I've come to understand, value, and claim the real legacy of my father's life.

In the opening of Ephesians 1, Paul spoke about the power and purpose of our divine gifts and callings. Then in verse 18 he turned his attention from teaching to prayer. Paul, in effect, prayed for a greater spiritual inheritance. He didn't ask for prosperity, influence, or position, but rather he prayed for enlightenment of the heart and the hope of our calling. He wanted us to lay hold of the blessings of God.

How many of us think of our heavenly inheritance according to the things we can see and measure, limiting our understanding of God's goodness toward us? What if there is a greater legacy yet to be seen for those who love the Lord?

I challenge you to pray boldly Paul's prayer over your own life. Ask the Lord for greater understanding of the blessings, promises, and plans that are hidden in His heart for you.

Help me, Holy Spirit, to have an enlightened heart that empowers me to claim the deepest blessings of my inheritance.

Gain a New Perspective

I remain confident of this: I will see the goodness
of the LORD in the land of the living.

PSALM 27:13

I am a two-time, stage four cancer survivor. Last year I went through an extended period I nicknamed *the death days*. From the moment I opened my eyes each morning until they closed again at night, I contended with a sense of impending doom. I was afraid, tired, and overwhelmed. My circumstances were desperate, and I constantly thought about my demise. Eventually I broke through the haze and remembered to choose life.

In Psalm 27, we find the future King David in a tough spot of his own. He was at war with enemies who were persistent in their desire to chase him down and kill him. David retreated into caves in order to survive. Yet David did not lose heart or despair, but rather he saw a vision of his future—one in which he would live.

We want our pain, discomfort, loss, or sorrow to be quickly overcome. We would rather believe in God's goodness after the fact than hold fast to our faith with patience during the trial as we wait upon the deliverance of the Lord. Yet in our waiting we gain a new perspective. In the secret places with God we remember His faithfulness, remind ourselves of His promises, and gain both strength and endurance to overcome even the most difficult trials. If you feel battered and hopeless, draw away from the violence to seek sanctuary with the Lord. Take heart and allow His love and truth to change your perspective.

....

Lord, You are a good God. Thank You for meeting me in my
most difficult moments with Your grace, mercy, and goodness.

Jan Greenwood, Lewisville, TX

Discern Open Doors

"I know what you do. I have put an open door before you, which no one can close. I know you have little strength, but you have obeyed my teaching and were not afraid to speak my name."

REVELATION 3:8 NCV

I sat at the table with my two new friends. The conversation between us was natural and flowing. In just a few moments we could sense something special beginning to happen. Then an "open door" to a dream began to form. As soon as the idea was birthed, opposition came. I heard us apologize for our weaknesses, express our doubts, and even vulnerably share our concerns about the risk and the cost. We had little strength, resources, or time. What if we tried and failed?

So many times we fail to discern an open door from the Lord because it comes at a moment of weakness or fear. We turn away from anointed friendships, conversations, or opportunities because we can't imagine God would entrust us with significant favor.

In Revelation 3, God spoke to the church of Philadelphia, known as the church that "kept the faith." They had endured great pressure to abdicate their newfound faith in Jesus. Just when they felt weak, the Lord chose to set an "open door" before the people. It wasn't their strength that gained them favor with God. Rather their obedience under pressure and their courage to speak His name were the catalysts to divine favor.

Just when you feel you have nothing left to give, watch out for an open door. Your weakness might just be a prerequisite for advancement. Speak up and obey. Christ will give you divine strength to keep the faith.

Thank You, Lord, for open doors. Fill me with divine strength to speak up and obey, and walk through them toward Your will.

Prepare for a New Season

The LORD your God is bringing you into a good land—a land with brooks, streams, and deep springs gushing out into the valleys and hills.

DEUTERONOMY 8:7

I had been employed in the same company and in the same department with essentially the same job for ten years. Then one day, almost out of the blue, I knew I was about to transition. The shift came with a flood of questions and emotions. First I felt free and excited. Simultaneously I felt sad and afraid. I'd lived in this position for so long that I had no idea what it would look like for me to move forward. I had grown comfortable in the familiar. It took courage and quite a bit of time to move out and obey and to start a new job.

In Deuteronomy 8, the Israelites were standing at the cusp of a long-awaited promise of God. Can you imagine going from decades of desert dwelling and suddenly being asked to embrace a future ripe with lush, rolling hills and water? Like a dream too good to be true, they must have been a little uncertain. Moses wisely used this moment to encourage the people by reminding them it was the Lord who was leading them.

If you are preparing for your own season shift, let go of what is familiar and comfortable and lift your eyes to look ahead. The vision set before you will be strong enough to draw you into the needed steps of obedience. If you feel fear or uncertainty, remember to rehearse the faithfulness of God. Remind yourself of His goodness and His love. Then have courage and begin to advance. You will see that the Lord is leading.

Thank You, Lord, for leading me into the promises of God. I embrace the season of transition before me. With trust in You I choose to obey.

Expand the Borders

"Enlarge the place of your tent, stretch your tent curtains wide, do not hold back; lengthen your cords, strengthen your stakes."

ISAIAH 54:2

ears ago my husband and I decided to add on to our existing home. Our home renovation project took about four months. Every single day a small crew of men showed up early at our house and began to bang, saw, and hammer. Those four months seemed endless to me, but to be honest, it was only a short season of discomfort. The reward was far greater than the cost. We enjoyed our sanctuary for years.

In Isaiah 54, we find God's people at a low moment. They had been reduced to a small remnant of God-followers. They had little strength, numbers, or resources. They hardly possessed any land at all. God wanted to expand the nation of Israel, but He was waiting on the people to position themselves to receive more of His favor.

So many times we want more of God and His promises, but we are unwilling to do the hard work of enlargement. We don't want to stretch, lengthen, or strengthen—it's too painful or too costly. So rather than obeying, we avoid the discomfort of expansion and settle for small and weak.

Is God asking you to enlarge your territory? Whether you are growing a business, expanding your home, or launching a God-sized dream, you will eventually have to cross over from vision to action. When you do, you may feel the stretch required to make room for more. Don't hold back. The reward will be worth the discomfort.

....

God, help me expand my territory. Teach me how to lengthen and strengthen my inner self. Turn my heart toward obedience.

Call Him Faithful

The one who calls you is faithful, and he will do it.

1 THESSALONIANS 5:24

I can't help but smile as I think back on my childhood days, dancing and lip-syncing to my favorite songs. Like most girls my age, I had big dreams. While carrying the lead in a school musical would have satisfied most of my friends, it didn't make a tiny dent in my desire to sing and travel the world.

As a teenager I began leading worship in our small family church and fell in love with the worship experience. Soon I began to pursue recording opportunities. In my mind the plans were all laid out. I would lead stadiums in worship. I would see nations worship God together. God must have smiled. Only He could see the twists and turns my story would take.

Time passed and I married my husband, Joe. We started a family and planted a church. My dream of recording music went unfulfilled. For years I led worship at our church, never realizing God would one day reawaken the dream I carried in my heart.

It was a long journey to recording my first album and singing before nations. Many times I thought my decisions and challenges in life would keep these dreams unfulfilled. But God's grace kept those dreams alive.

Maybe your story is like mine. It may not be a singing career that has been sidelined, but I feel confident there is a dream God longs to awaken within you. It doesn't matter how much time has gone by or the issues of life that you are working through. Believe God is faithful to His word and never give up on your dream. It's time to believe and dream again.

....

Father, I thank You for the desire to dream again. Wake it up in me.

Cathy Banks, Lake Charles, LA

Be Held in the Father's Hand

"Do not fear [anything], for I am with you; do not be afraid, for
I am your God. I will strengthen you, be assured I will help you;
I will certainly take hold of you with My righteous right hand
[a hand of justice, of power, of victory, of salvation]."

ISAIAH 41:10 AMP

*Y*ou will never have children." Those words almost shattered our faith. The thing my husband and I wanted most was a family.

It would be over a decade before Joe and I would hold our newborn in our arms. We will never forget that moment. As soon as the doctor said, "It's a boy," my husband took our son into his arms and held him as though he were handling the most precious thing he had ever seen. Like my husband's love for our son, God's love for us is endless and unconditional. Our Father promises to be there for His children.

Maybe you've never known the comfort of having an earthly father care for you. I assure you, your heavenly Father is attentive to your every movement. He sees the situations that make you fearful. He understands you won't always feel secure. There will be days your feet will slip. But through each season of life, He promises to protect and provide for your needs.

His love guarantees He will step in to protect us from things that would harm our hearts. His mercy comforts us even in our darkest hours. We are His children, and He longs for us to climb into His arms and rest.

Father, I have no need to fear because Your love is present to
comfort and protect me. I cast my anxieties at Your feet. You
are my source of peace, and I delight in being close to You.

Find Restoration

"I will repay you for the years the locusts have eaten—the great locust and the young locust, the other locusts and the locust swarm—my great army that I sent among you."

JOEL 2:25

J walked into church feeling overwhelmed by a situation I was going through. I tried to smile, but inside I felt my world was crumbling. The pressure of trying to hold everything together was beginning to affect my health. My body was exhausted from worrying about making business decisions. The truth was that I needed healing in more ways than I could imagine.

That Sunday I stepped onto the stage and greeted the audience. As I returned to my seat, I felt a sudden snap followed by a pop in my left knee. I screamed in pain and was immediately carried to a nearby medical center. After several X-rays the doctor confirmed that my meniscus was torn in two places. This meant surgery with six to eight weeks of recovery time.

As I was given the disheartening news, I questioned, *How could God let this happen to me?* My soul needed restoration, not more anxiety. To my surprise, during my time of healing I discovered a renewed strength in my faith. What I thought was a setback, God used as a season for me to recharge. Life became clearer, decisions were made easier, and I found grace in areas in which I had grown weary. Are you facing a setback, delay, or unexpected detour? Perhaps this is your opportunity to draw closer to God and recharge. Though it may seem that the "locusts have eaten" your plans, God will repay you in a currency that has eternal value.

Father, I trust You with every situation. You have a solution for every problem I face today.

Cathy Banks, Lake Charles, LA

Rise from Humble Beginnings

Your beginnings will seem humble, so prosperous will your future be.

JOB 8:7

We were excited God had called us to plant a church. Looking back I laugh at the memory of the first building we would purchase. Our faith and enthusiasm must have blinded us to what we were looking at. The small, red-brick building with plywood floors and ripped-up, red carpet seemed like a miracle. I remember the creaking sound the boards made every time someone took a step. On opening day there were only three people in attendance, but we acted as if there were thousands.

That was thirteen years ago, and we now have a beautiful building and the congregation has grown beyond our expectations. When others ask us, "What is the secret to seeing God do the miraculous?" I usually say, "We never despised small beginnings." When God begins something in your life, it is connected to an expected end. We cannot always see what the finish line looks like, but in faith we can catch a glimpse of what God longs to do through our lives.

Don't be disheartened if what God has called you to do seems small. Only He knows how big His dream is for your life. Start where He is calling you. Do all things with a spirit of excellence. The effort you put forth in the beginning is a good sign of how you will handle much larger things in the future.

Treat every small beginning as a doorway to greatness. Walk through it with great expectation. When you are totally invested in what God is doing, the result can be greater than what you could ever imagine.

Father, thank You for small beginnings. Give me the strength to do all things with a heart of excellence.

Soar

The people who trust the LORD will become strong again.
They will rise up as an eagle in the sky; they will run and
not need rest; they will walk and not become tired.

ISAIAH 40:31 NCV

I stepped onto the balcony of my hotel room in time to see an eagle take flight above the mountains. My thoughts drifted to things I had heard about eagles: their size, hunting habits, where they like to build their nests, and other interesting facts that make them different from other birds. I once heard someone share that when eagles encounter storms, rather than hide they use their wings to adjust to the storm. They use the wind to help them rise above the currents that could potentially destroy them.

It would take me many years to learn how to lean in and use the winds of adversity to my advantage. At first I resisted the stormy seasons in life. Now I run toward them. Like the eagle I've learned to adjust my spiritual wings and allow the currents to lift me above what threatens to dash me to the ground.

With great confidence I encourage you to rise up and face what you fear most. Maybe you are going through financial difficulties. Rise up. Perhaps you need healing in your body. Reach forward in faith. You may have a dream that seems lost. Look again.

Whenever you feel like crumbling in fear, fall into the arms of the Father. He will lift you up. You were created to soar above the storm.

Today I choose to rise above the winds of this world.
Help me rise high above my fears and doubts. I will
trust in Your Word and walk in calm assurance.

Cathy Banks, Lake Charles, LA

Move Forward

The LORD our God said to us at Horeb, "You have
stayed long enough at this mountain."

DEUTERONOMY 1:6

eturning from my mother's funeral I walked into a house full
of hydrangeas. The smell overwhelmed me and created a lasting
memory. I was still numb from the loss of my mother when six weeks
later my father passed away after suffering a heart attack. I was in shock.
Everything within me wanted to give up on life. I kept questioning,
"How do I gather up the pieces of my heart and move forward?"

I felt life had robbed me of what I loved most. As each day passed I
felt I was sinking deeper into a pit of depression. For ten years grief consumed me. I suffered in silence. I pretended to be happy on the outside
but was full of sorrow on the inside. It would take a decade of heartache
to admit that I'd allowed my life to stop with the passing of my parents.
The truth was that I had become a prisoner of grief.

Maybe your heart has been imprisoned by grief or pain. Or it could
be disappointment, loss of a dream, or failure that has locked you out of
life. There was a time when I had to make the decision to set myself free. I
used God's Word to break the shackles of complacency and bring myself
comfort. The Father will do the same for you. But you must be willing to
take off your clothes of grief and dress yourself for your destiny.

....

Father, I thank You that I am no longer stuck in the pit of
pain and heartache. Today is my day to walk away from
grief and into a place of victory. Fill me with Your joy.

Believe You Are Irreplaceable

I praise you, for I am fearfully and wonderfully made.
Wonderful are your works; my soul knows it very well.

PSALM 139:14 ESV

*A*s we allow God to work in us, a transformation begins to take place. Before long we see ourselves as irreplaceable in His sight. For God to complete His work in our lives, we must learn to trust Him completely. Sometimes that's not easy to do, because trust requires a great deal of vulnerability.

No matter how hard it is to put your confidence in others, I assure you, God can always be trusted. He will never hurt you, leave you, or betray you. By trusting in God, you open the door for Him to heal your brokenness. When you are healed from the inside out, you begin to trust and believe in yourself.

Some studies show that we have more than fifty thousand thoughts every day. That equates to as many as thirty-five thoughts per minute, many of which are negative. When our thoughts are negative, we tend to feel confused. If we are not careful, we will become double-minded and unstable in how we think, react, and make decisions. It's almost impossible to focus or think clearly when we are entertaining negative thoughts all day long.

Today I encourage you to evaluate your thoughts. Cast down wrong thinking and believe the best about yourself. You are amazing, unstoppable, victorious, and irreplaceable.

....

Dear Jesus, thank You for healing my brokenness and
enabling me to trust freely. Please anoint my eyes
so I may see myself the way You see me.

Beverly Gorman Bilbo, New Orleans, LA

Climb Out of the Pit of Discouragement

He lifted me out of the pit of destruction, out of the sticky mud.
He stood me on a rock and made my feet steady.

PSALM 40:2 NCV

*I*n 2005, the church my husband and I pastored in New Orleans was inundated with twelve and a half feet of water due to the wrath of Hurricane Katrina. For more than three weeks our building remained flooded. Overnight my husband and I became unemployed pastors, without a congregation, without income for the church or for our family, and displaced from our damaged home as we carried the weight of supporting the mortgage of a flooded church.

In the aftermath of this tragedy we found ourselves struggling with fear, confusion, and hurt, grieving the many losses of what we worked so hard to establish. We were in a deep pit. We struggled to comprehend how we would come through this situation and start life over again.

When King David faced impossibilities, he encouraged himself in the Lord. So that is what we began to do following Katrina. Amid devastating circumstances, we determined to praise God. We lifted our eyes from the pit and started the journey toward our recovery. Day by day our faith grew as we witnessed God's divine intervention. Even if you are facing the greatest disaster of your life, there is a way forward and a way out. Encourage yourself with the promises of God from the Word, and remember His actions on your behalf. He will set you on solid ground and make your feet steady once again.

....

Dear Lord, give me the faith to believe there are good things in my future. Replace discouragement with hope and heartache with joy.

Realize You Are Royalty

*Strength and dignity are her clothing and her position is strong and secure;
and she smiles at the future [knowing that she and her family are prepared].*
PROVERBS 31:25 AMP

Without permission, past failures have no power to determine what our future will look like. Being confident of who we are in Christ empowers us to boldly face difficult situations and courageously pursue our destiny.

Sometimes past mistakes make us feel disqualified to receive the promises of God. This makes me think of Bathsheba and what made her story memorable. What most people remember about her is the affair she had with King David, resulting in her pregnancy and the murder of her husband, Uriah.

While the timing and methodology was wrong, God's plan was fulfilled despite the sin. Bathsheba became a queen and the mother of King Solomon. In Proverbs 31, Solomon described the attributes of a virtuous woman. They were the instructions his mother gave him regarding the type of woman he should seek to marry. This passage defines the character of a godly woman and the benefits attained by allowing God's nature to be developed within.

When you feel plagued by past mistakes, remember Bathsheba and the legacy she left. She is in the genealogy of Christ. The mercy of God is endless. With His grace you too can "smile at the future."

> Heavenly Father, I come to You with a heart of gratitude
> that despite every past failure You have not only forgiven
> me as You did with Bathsheba, You have elevated me.

Stop Buying the Lie of Insignificance

*You were bought with a price [a precious price paid by
Christ]; do not become slaves to men [but to Christ].*

1 CORINTHIANS 7:23 AMP

How do you determine your value? The worth of something can often be defined by the monetary value assigned to it, typically determined by a professional appraisal. But your worth is so much more.

Christ paid an enormous price to redeem us from our sins. His death on the cross revealed how much He loves us and how valuable we are to the Father. Because of Christ's deep and unending love for us, the enemy tries his best to devalue our worth and make us feel insignificant. Far too often we buy into the lie that we are unworthy of God's love or favor.

Most of us ignore negative opinions of others, yet fall for the lies of our enemy. Why? After all, we know the enemy speaks lies to torment, taunt, or overwhelm our hearts. God's Word makes it clear that Satan disguises himself as an angel of light (2 Corinthians 11:14). In the Bible light and darkness are referred to as parallels for good and evil.

Today you may feel insignificant. If so, stop and consider whose voice you are listening to. Is it your voice, God's, or the enemy's? Remember, Jesus died for you because He loves you. You are valuable. With His Word and authority you can defeat and ignore the lies of the enemy and learn to know your true worth.

....

Dear Lord, deafen my spiritual ears to the lies of the
enemy. Help me see myself as valuable in Your sight.

Put Insecurities to Rest

God's grace has made me what I am, and his grace to me was not wasted.
1 CORINTHIANS 15:10 NCV

*F*rom past experiences I know that unforeseen stresses can bring out my most suppressed doubts and fears. Let me give you an example. Occasionally, when I was scheduled to sing or preach at a conference, upon taking my place on stage, insecurities surfaced, causing me to feel burdened with fear and intimidation. I knew in my heart it was simply the enemy's way of trying to silence me and prevent me from ministering effectively. Aware that God had prepared me for this, I would silently quote Scriptures, pray, and remind myself that God had equipped me for this calling.

Sometimes insecurities arise when we compare ourselves with others. God's Word tells us not to fall into this trap (Galatians 6:4–5). Comparison limits our development and inhibits our growth. It shifts our focus to others and away from what God has instructed us to do.

Today if you are struggling with feelings of insecurity, recognize the source of those negative feelings. Take authority over the lies of the enemy and with boldness stand your ground. Take your place and walk in victory. God has equipped you for great things.

....

Lord, enable us to identify who we are in You. Put to rest our insecurities, so they may never be resurrected again.

Beverly Gorman Bilbo, New Orleans, LA

Enjoy the Person You Are Becoming

God began doing a good work in you, and I am sure he will
continue it until it is finished when Jesus Christ comes again.

PHILIPPIANS 1:6 NCV

Since childhood I've dreamed about my future. Already my two-year-old grandson is dreaming about his as well. The other day someone asked him what he wants to be when he grows up. He replied, "A cuckoo clock." He acted out his answer giving full sound effects. Thankfully, he will eventually come up with more realistic life goals!

While we all have different dreams for our future, we face the same enemy, who desires to prevent us from achieving our goals. The enemy shoots arrows at our souls, bringing distractions and chaos. When this happens, it becomes easy to fall into discouragement, worry, and fear.

If circumstances in life have left you wondering if your dreams are attainable, I want to encourage you to repeat this idea: *"God did not create me to fail."*

The truth is that God destined each of us for greatness. Anytime we lose sight of our identity in Christ, we cloud the vision of our future. Growing up, I used to hear the words, "We are all a work in progress." Although it sounds like a cliché, the words are very true. Each of us is being transformed, developed, and made better by grace.

Many of us are too hard on ourselves. When things aren't coming together the way we anticipated, we reflect on our past, our hurts, rejections, and failures. It's time for us to let go of the past and embrace the season we are in. We must take time to rejoice in who we are becoming.

....

Dear Jesus, help me not to worry about who I am
becoming. Thank You for custom designing my future.

Trust God with Your Reputation

[God] rescued [Joseph] from all his troubles. He gave Joseph wisdom
and enabled him to gain the goodwill of Pharaoh king of Egypt.
So Pharaoh made him ruler over Egypt and all his palace.

ACTS 7:10

*D*id Joseph have an easy life? No, I would not say that. Yes, he was the favored child of his father, but certainly not the favorite of his ten older siblings. Can you imagine being in a family with that many older brothers and none of them are in your corner? Maybe the favoritism of their father or the special dreams given to him by his heavenly Father made his brothers jealous. Whatever the reason was, his brothers disliked him enough to sell him to a band of merchants.

Imagine being separated from your family and taken to a new country where no one knew you and you weren't familiar with their language or customs. Joseph had every opportunity to question God for all the difficult things that had happened to him. Yet he showed an inner confidence that seemed to defy the circumstances he faced. Perhaps that confidence was linked to divine wisdom. When you ask God for wisdom, there is peace and certainty about your future.

Maybe, like Joseph, you are facing tough situations. If so, remember that despite a rough beginning, when you trust in the Father, He will bring all the pieces of your life together. Joseph experienced rejection and betrayal. He was lied about and overlooked. Despite all these things, he acted with great wisdom and trusted God fully. And God rescued him and elevated him. Have hope that He will do the same for you.

Jesus, help me remember that even when things seem
chaotic and upside down, You are for me and with me.

Cheryl A. Davis, Conway, AR

Agree with God's Plan

There are many plans in a man's heart, nevertheless the LORD's counsel—that will stand.

PROVERBS 19:21 NKJV

Have you ever zoned out in thought? What were you thinking about? What were you dreaming of? What dreams were you planning to make a reality?

Do you remember as a child wanting something so much that you hesitated to ask your parents for it because you were afraid they would say no? The pain of missing out on the newest, latest, and greatest was just too much to process. Sometimes we do the same with our heavenly Father. We want something so much that we work toward that goal without taking it to the Lord in prayer.

In moments when our faith falters, remember God wants the best for you. His plans exceed anything you could hope for or imagine. Be willing to confide your desires to Him in prayer. With confidence, know that what He places in your heart, He will equip you to accomplish. In God's Word He reminds us that if we agree on earth concerning anything we ask, it will be done by our Father in heaven (Matthew 18:19). But the agreeing isn't just agreeing with each other, it is agreeing with God.

In your time with Him, listen for His voice, His plan. Dream, but always bring those dreams to your Father's throne. Ask for His favor, counsel, and wisdom. Let Him guide your plans.

Thank You, Lord, that You and Your plans are trustworthy. I know I can rest in Your counsel. Give me courage always to bring my plans to You along with discernment to hear Your voice.

Grow Strong Through Struggles

Jacob was left alone, and a man wrestled with him till daybreak.

GENESIS 32:24

*B*y the time Jacob reached the river Jabbok, he had experienced struggles, emotional stress, and family friction, and he had made a string of unhealthy decisions. But now, at a personal crossroads in his faith, Jacob reminded God of His promises. I believe that as he spoke about those promises, a passion reignited within him to see each promise come to pass.

Jacob was in a tough place emotionally. The last meeting with his brother did not end on the best of terms. In fact Esau had promised to kill Jacob.

In preparation Jacob sent his family, servants, and possessions on ahead. He was left alone with God—the only One who could really resolve his battle. He had stolen the blessing from his earthly father. He *needed* the blessing from his heavenly Father. That night Jacob wrestled with God, saying, "I will not let you go unless you bless me" (v. 26).

It is only in the surrender of our struggles that we find the strength to overcome them. Jacob brought his weaknesses before the Lord and wrestled with his issues until God redeemed them. That night he stayed awake and fought for victory. Because Jacob was unwilling to give up, he received God's blessing.

The next time you are at a crossroads, don't be afraid of wrestling with your issues. Get in God's presence, and cling to Him. Remember God's promises to you. Though you may wrestle through the night, His blessing will be on you in the morning.

Father, thank You that I can bring every struggle, problem, and circumstance to You. I will not let go of Your promises.

Cheryl A. Davis, Conway, AR

Overflow with Hope

May the God of hope fill you with all joy and peace as you trust in him,
so that you may overflow with hope by the power of the Holy Spirit.

ROMANS 15:13

*J*esus used stories to help His listeners understand spiritual concepts. He used seeds, soil, fig trees, barns, sheep, goats, fish, lost coins, and an endless list of other items. I wish He had thrown a chocolate fountain into the mix! Have you ever seen one? The smooth, sweet delight flows down in waves of unending chocolate. If you watch the fountain, you will see the chocolate overflow at the top, fall, and then be caught back up to overflow again.

Isn't this a sweet picture of hope? The Word says our lives can overflow with hope to those around us because we have the God of hope living in us. When we are connected to the source of hope, we can continually be filled with hope, and then be spilled and filled again.

I've learned that when we take time to linger in God's presence, we are filled with joy and peace. When we stay close to Him, we are naturally at peace. Everything seems to fall into place. But when we distance ourselves from His Spirit, we lose trust, and feelings of doubt overtake our hearts. The key is to keep our hearts near to our Father's. It's in His presence that we remain safe and secure.

Lord, I place my dreams, family, job, and finances into
Your care. Cover them with hope, peace, and joy. Let
me never forget that You are the God of hope.

Trust God to Settle the Score

The LORD caused the Egyptians to think well of them, and
the Egyptians gave the people everything they asked
for. So the Israelites took rich gifts from them.

EXODUS 12:36 NCV

While living under Egyptian rule, Israelites were treated as slaves. Burdened with the task of daily work, they had no rights or privileges. There were no blessings or abundance, but simply the drudgery of making it through each day.

Maybe you are going through a difficult situation or a season of injustice. It could be a spouse or friend has betrayed you, something was stolen from you, or you are being unreasonably burdened. Don't lose heart. God sees every action. He knows the hearts of those who have caused you pain. He understands what it is like to be betrayed by people or systems you trusted.

In those moments when we are bitterly betrayed, we tend to act more like slaves of sin than daughters of a King. The truth is you, my sister, are no longer a slave! You have been set free. Jesus, your Advocate, has confronted the enemy and won your case. You are redeemed and free to live without fear of judgment or captivity because Jesus took your place. If there is anyone who understands what you are going through, it is Jesus. He was lied about, mistreated, betrayed, and falsely accused. But because He submitted to the will of His Father, He came out victorious—and you will too.

....

I will trust You, Lord. I will walk in the protection of Your justice. I know
You will provide peace and safety during unfair circumstances.

Cheryl A. Davis, Conway, AR

Know Everything You Commit to God Is Secure

I will praise You, O Lord, with my whole heart; I
will tell of all Your marvelous works.

PSALM 9:1 NKJV

These days we can check online lists to help us find reliable professionals for maintenance, repairs, and special projects. Other people who have used their services have found them to be reliable and trustworthy, and they share their good experiences online. It's helpful to have a list of qualified people who will get the job done.

If we trust a company, we are likely to recommend their service to others. It's easy to pass along the names of those who do excellent work. In fact it is a pleasure to speak well of others. How about when it comes to sharing our faith? Are we quick to pass along our relationship with Christ? Can we honestly say that we share His name as much as we share other, less important things? When we enjoy something, we share it. When we find a good deal, we spread the news. What could be greater and more rewarding than sharing the freedom of God's grace?

Today I encourage you to make a list of ways you can share your faith. Write down the names of people you know who need to hear the message of God's redeeming love. Live your faith out loud. Meet privately, one on one with someone and share the Father's love. Speak of His goodness publicly. Share your faith story with friends, family, strangers, and those who need love.

Lord, I will tell of Your strength and mercy. I will be
quick to make known Your everlasting love.

Dry Your Tears

The LORD said to Samuel, "How long will you mourn for Saul,
since I have rejected him as king over Israel? Fill your horn
with oil and be on your way; I am sending you to Jesse of
Bethlehem. I have chosen one of his sons to be king."

1 SAMUEL 16:1

*F*ew things in life will stop us in our tracks. I felt as if my world stopped spinning the day I was diagnosed with breast cancer. This same feeling would overtake me when the doctor delivered more devastating news: my radiated skin would not tolerate the breast implant and it had to be removed. This last bit of news felt more devastating than the initial cancer diagnosis. It took a while to wrap my mind around the idea I would spend the rest of my life with no breasts.

For so long I looked for ways to recover from grief. I knew the process would not be easy; I would have to rely on the Holy Spirit for comfort and guidance.

If you are walking through a season of grief or separation, I encourage you to take time to recover. Your Father will walk beside you. Tears and grief will not last forever. Even though the situation you are in may be painful, it is not the end. Life may be unfair today, but there are greater days ahead. God is a master at turning our messy moments into beautiful miracles.

With great confidence, Lord, I set my eyes on the good
things that are in my future. I have assurance that I am
coming out of this situation stronger, happier, and healthier.
I know Your plans are to see my life prosper.

Let God Make You the Honored Guest

You prepare a table before me in the presence of my enemies. You have anointed and refreshed my head with oil; my cup overflows.

PSALM 23:5 AMP

*I*magine you are faced with making the hardest decision of your life. You should be uneasy, concerned, and anxious, but somehow you remain at peace. That is exactly what worship does for your soul. It takes you away from the battlefield and places you comfortably before the King.

Envision that you are invited to the King's palace. Let your thoughts drift to dining at His table, being renewed, resting in the peace of His goodness. In this special place you are safe from the darts of the enemy. You are no longer focused on the battlefield, but on the one who fights in your place. You feel captivated by His love, surrounded by hope. For a moment your thoughts linger on the One who holds your heart.

In the sacred space of worship, nothing negative affects your attitude. When the enemy tries to tear you away from the table and take you back to your troubles, you refuse. Your soul remains at rest.

I admit that surrendering in worship was not always easy for me. For many of us letting go isn't something that comes naturally. We are more comfortable trying to come up with solutions to our problems. But when we take on the weight of our worries, we push away from His presence.

It is time to pull up a chair and rest in His goodness. Drink from His cup of healing and sample the sweetness of surrendering to His will.

Today, Lord, I accept Your invitation to come and sit in Your presence.

Pause and Restore Your Soul

He lets me lie down in green pastures; He leads me beside the still and quiet waters. He refreshes and restores my soul (life); He leads me in the paths of righteousness for His name's sake.

PSALM 23:2–3 AMP

My fight with breast cancer affected my ability to rest. At night my mind raced ahead with unanswered questions, anxious thoughts, and feelings of uncertainty. My thoughts made my body restless. I went to bed tired and woke up exhausted. One thing that brought me comfort was the prayers of my husband. As he took me by the hand and spoke faith-filled words, my uncertainties washed away, and I drifted off to sleep.

I knew my body needed rest. The challenge was finding a way to train my mind to meditate on peaceful thoughts. Replacing anxious thoughts with positive promises from God's Word helped me recapture my peace. I discovered this simple action worked wonders. Anytime a negative thought entered my mind, I released it to the Holy Spirit. I thanked Him for taking care of me and invited Him to minister to me. Each time, I fell into a deep, restful sleep.

As you allow God to minister to you, His Spirit surrounds you with love and peace. Worry and stress are washed away as we anchor our trust in Him. Whatever situation you find yourself struggling through, remember to make room for His presence. Your Father is not blinded to your circumstances. He is aware of every step you make. His heart is to make you stronger than you've ever been before.

Thank You, Father, for sending help my way. Fill me with supernatural peace, quiet my heart, and give me rest.

Winona Steunenberg, Abbotsford, BC CANADA

Push Back the Darkness

Because the Sovereign LORD helps me, I will not be disgraced. Therefore
have I set my face like flint, and I know I will not be put to shame.

ISAIAH 50:7

This verse became a lifeline for me as I fought for my life. I knew the
battle to regain my health would push my faith to the limit. When
I first received my diagnosis, the Lord placed this verse on my heart. I
decided to have a necklace made from a flint arrowhead. It would remind
me that the Lord's strength is stronger than flint and His arrows would
safeguard my life.

I'm sure you have walked through storms of your own. Tragic
moments can happen without warning. If you are not careful you will
find yourself fighting longer and harder than you should. In times of
great heartache, I've learned to shift my gaze from my problems to Jesus.
Somehow just closing my eyes and envisioning His face brings a smile to
mine. Knowing He thinks about me brings hope and strength.

Remember, you don't have to know how God will work out difficult
things. The only thing you must do is trust. When my faith feels faint, I
make declarations. I speak phrases like, "I refuse to live in defeat," "I will
not live in fear but am full of faith," and "I walk in health and healing."
In doing so I experience renewed confidence and assurance. Try these
for yourself, and witness how the Lord helps you set your face toward a
new future.

....

Abba, I know You are with me through every storm and trial.
I receive Your strength. It makes me brave. Pour Your courage
into my heart. Drench me with Your love. Dissolve my fears.

Rediscover Your Rhythm

*You turned my wailing into dancing; you removed
my sackcloth and clothed me with joy.*

PSALM 30:11

I crossed the finish line. Eighteen months of breast cancer treatments were complete. My family was ecstatic, and joy filled our home. After months of fighting to live, I now felt lost. I had forgotten how to live *normally*. I needed to rediscover the rhythm of everyday living.

There is an undeniable rhythm to life. Our hearts beat in rhythmic synchronicity. Ocean waves collide in rhythmic fashion. Poetry is infused with rhythm. Dancers follow rhythmic beats. Everything around us pulses with a unique rhythm. Yet at times heartache can leave us following a far-out rhythm. We discover our lives are thrown off balance, the ease of living is gone, and everything feels harder than it should.

Maybe you have come through adversity that has knocked you out of your rhythm. You might be struggling to find your pace, or thinking, *Things will never get back to normal. I don't see how my life will ever be the same.* Instead of letting your mind linger on negative thoughts, try thinking good thoughts, such as *God can put me on a new course. Although things may not be what they once were, I believe the future holds something better.* Make the choice to press through trying times. Keep praying. Ask for divine direction. Keep a determined heart. Life has a way of surprising you with joy when you least expect it.

....

Father, thank You for bringing me through dark seasons. I am ready
to walk into a new spacious place where Your blessings can overtake
me. Help me maintain a positive attitude and a thankful heart.

Winona Steunenberg, Abbotsford, BC CANADA

Take Time to Rest and Recover

*Anyone who enters God's rest also rests from
their works, just as God did from his.*

HEBREWS 4:10

L ife has a way of pulling us down paths we never intended to take. Commitments, family, friends, and work make demands on our time and emotions. It is easy to become so busy caring for others we don't create time for ourselves.

One of the things I admire about my mom is how she enjoys her time with God. Sometimes her quiet time is a small, short break. She calls it her "two-minute vacation." She takes a deep breath and releases the stress of the day. It is a conscious, deliberate action that helps her refocus and regroup. I like this idea so much that I create mini-vacations in my day as well.

Consider adopting this practice of taking time off and enjoying God's creation. You could start by doing the small things that bring you joy. How about a walk down an unfamiliar path, getting up in time to watch the sun rise, biking along the shore, or resting by the pool? If you are to live healthily, you must take care of your body, mind, and emotions.

I encourage you to find a quiet place where God can whisper His words. Schedule time for rest. When you truly understand the power of resting in Him, you will arise with your soul refreshed.

Lord, today I will take time to rest. I will seek out a place
to hear Your voice. My body is a gift from You, and
I will treat it with grace and lovingkindness.

Change Course

The LORD said to Abram, "Look all around you—to the north
and south and east and west. All this land that you see I
will give to you and your descendants forever."

GENESIS 13:14–15 NCV

I prayed, saw my doctor, and participated in three months of therapy, but my shoulder was still frozen. The pain was ever present. I couldn't lift my arm. Nothing I tried brought healing. Then the Holy Spirit prompted me to attend a healing meeting five hours away. It seemed unreasonable. God could supernaturally heal me in the comfort of my own home. Yet the Father was shifting my thinking. He had more in mind than my healing; He was bringing me to a new level of faith.

As I entered the massive convention center, a cloud of worship settled over the people, creating a powerful atmosphere for God to work. In that place I tried ever so gently to raise my arm, but the healing didn't come that night. Surprisingly I was not disappointed. I knew in my spirit that God had heard me. Two days later, while drying my hair, I inadvertently lifted my arm above my head—with free movement and absolutely no pain! When I wasn't looking, Father God surprised me with my healing!

Carefully consider your conventional way of thinking today, and allow the Holy Spirit to change the course of your faith. With His gentle nudging and the Word of God to strengthen you, He will lead you on the right path to your healing, restoration, and wholeness.

Father, help me follow Your lead in my healing. I am willing to change
course to find the wide, open space in which You want me to rest.
Move upon my heart, and I will be made whole in Jesus' name.

Donna Schambach, Tyler, TX

Call the Great Physician

A woman was in the crowd who had been bleeding for twelve years, but no one was able to heal her.

LUKE 8:43 NCV

*C*an you see the woman's agonizing look of struggle? In her weakened, depleted condition, so close to death, this woman of determination and undaunted faith pressed through the throng, finding a way to touch Jesus. Certainly she didn't feel like a superhero of faith that day. She was at the very end of a twelve-year struggle. The doctors had given up on her; all hope was gone along with all her money. She stood alone in a pushy, noisy crowd. Despair threatened to overwhelm her, drowning her in a sea of great suffering and loss.

Yet her eyes had seen Him. Her ears had heard of the astounding miracles He performed. Something had filled her heart with wonder. She believed He was the Son of God, the greatest of all physicians, and she knew she must get to Him to live. With no options and a voice too weak to call Him, she used every ounce of her remaining energy to throw herself at His feet. And that one move stopped time. When her hand finally reached the hem of His robe, Jesus reeled. Healing virtue left His body and surged into her diseased frame. He pronounced her healed; her faith had made her well.

If you feel hopeless because of great suffering, I urge you to push past the pain, muster your voice of faith, and call out to Him with great expectation. He can heal you.

··

Jesus, my Great Physician, touch me with Your nail-
scarred hand. I desperately need Your healing power.
In You I know I will be made completely whole.

Rebuild

*"You will be known for repairing the broken places
and for rebuilding the roads and houses."*

ISAIAH 58:12 NCV

My father's evangelistic ministry was predominantly focused in the inner cities. I have watched the power of God reach alcoholics and addicts, freeing them from great bondage. I know a former AIDS victim whom God completely healed; today he and his wife are both pastors, and they have two children whom the doctors predicted they would never have. Over and over I've watched desperate people yield to God and put their faith in action. God heals families, restores health, and rebuilds every broken part of a yielded life!

He restores third-world nations too. Early in 1991 I accompanied Daisy and T. L. Osborn on their second Uganda campaign. They were thrilled to see God restore that war-torn nation from the devastation of Idi Amin with a better economy and growing infrastructure. I heard them preach to more than 250,000 people, leading them to national repentance. From that time on Uganda's spiritual climate also began to change. Godly leaders succeeded in turning the crisis around. A formerly hopeless, brutalized nation is being restored by the power of the gospel.

It doesn't matter where you live or what part of you is broken—call out to Jesus. He has a healing touch for you, and He will give you power to rebuild while He completes a spectacular, supernatural restoration in every aspect of your life.

Almighty God, You alone have the power to free me
of sin, heal me of brokenness, and transform my life
into something You can use for Your glory.

Donna Schambach, Tyler, TX

Follow a Prophetic Instruction

[Naaman] went down and plunged himself into the Jordan
seven times, just as the man of God had said; and his flesh
was restored like that of a little child and he was clean.

2 KINGS 5:14 AMP

No one knows exactly why Elisha told Naaman to go jump in the Jordan River, but we certainly have clues. Naaman was a proud, respected military man, used by God to help Israel. Elisha wanted more than a physical miracle; he wanted God to open the Syrian officer's eyes, so he would say, "Behold, I know that there is no God in all the earth, except in Israel" (v. 15 AMP). Elisha could have waved his hand and made the leprosy disappear—he had great power with God. But Elisha asked more of Naaman. By dipping seven times in the muddy Jordan, Naaman would demonstrate a submissive heart before God.

It's important to note that God can speak through trusted, prophetic voices in our lives—ones that have good track records. Parents, pastors, and teachers are all potential prophetic voices God uses to encourage us. They may also suggest we do something that stretches us. Often God urges us to act on our faith. He may say, *Stand up and walk!* when we feel like sitting or lying down. He may ask us to change an old habit. The Lord might challenge us to forgive, or ask forgiveness of a friend or family member. Obeying God may hurt our pride and coax us out of our comfort zones, but humility is often the catalyst for the miracles we need.

I hear You, Lord. Wash me; heal me; rid me of all
impurity. Whatever You ask me to do, I will obey.

Dethrone Your Secrets

*Everything that is hidden will be made clear and
every secret thing will be made known.*

MARK 4:22 NCV

One of my first kitchens was old and very small. The cabinets had many tiny compartments. One memorable day I noticed gnats flying around the sink. I saw no food left out. The kitchen window was closed. *Why so many gnats?* I thought. Over the next few days the ugly grey gnats increased in number along with my annoyance and growing curiosity. Finally I noticed the gnats swarming in one area in front of a small, low door—one I never used. I opened it, and a cloud of gnats escaped. Sitting in that secret cabinet was a bag of rotting potatoes. They were black; their smell was revolting. I had no idea I'd stashed potatoes there. Until that cabinet saw the light of day, I would have never known what was lurking in the dark.

The annoying gnats are much like symptoms of our illnesses. We might have headaches, upset stomachs, unexplained anxiety—any number of symptoms. But God must open every compartment of our hearts to reveal what is hidden and causing us to suffer. Secret fear, not brought to God, can cause anxiety and depression. Anger and resentment can cause tension and pain. Secret sin will eat us alive with guilt and condemnation. We must invite God to shed the light of His truth on our hiding places and dethrone all our secrets. When we are ready and willing for Him to perform a deep cleaning, our healing process can begin.

....

*Healing Father, I stand open and transparent before You. I
want everything within me exposed to Your light. If there is
any closed door to my heart, show me. I will open it.*

Donna Schambach, Tyler, TX

Receive Healing Through Praise

Heal me, O LORD, and I will be healed; save me
and I will be saved, for You are my praise.

JEREMIAH 17:14 NASB

O ne of the greatest miracles I've personally witnessed happened progressively with an outcome nothing short of supernatural. My dear friend, Pastor Debbie Lanier of Winston-Salem, North Carolina, was invited to speak at a neighboring church, but just before stepping to the microphone, she fell and slammed hard against the floor. Debbie said it felt as though something was pushing her down. The force with which she fell caused her femur to break and stab through her pelvic area. Every bone inside her pelvis was shattered. The prognosis was grim. She was not expected to walk for years. But she knew her God. At every appointment the doctors were in disbelief as she surpassed every goal early. In less than a month she was preaching again, and in less than three months she was running, jumping, and praising God while leading her church's Vacation Bible School program.

The emotional devastation was deep; her pain level was off the charts. Yet my amazing friend never quit. Minute by minute she offered praises to God. She worshipped with the Word and preached His healing power. Her faith was the victory that overcame. Today you would never know she had walked through the dark valley. She overcame with relentless praise. You can too. All you need is a Word to cling to and a bold declaration in your mouth.

You alone, God, forgive all my sins and heal all my diseases.

Go and Receive

Jesus said to the officer, "Go home. Your servant will be healed just as you believed he would." And his servant was healed that same hour.

MATTHEW 8:13 NCV

*O*ur lives forever changed when we caught the revelation that God not only *could* heal but *would* heal—that God had already taken care of sickness and disease when He died on the cross. This revelation came right on time; we had no idea our faith would soon be tested.

When our second son turned one, he suddenly became very sick and went into anaphylactic shock (a deadly allergic reaction) from drinking milk. We had just started the journey of learning that it's God's will for us to be healthy, so we had confidence to apply the Word of God like medicine over his life. Every day we spoke God's promises over his body. Our faith in healing began to grow. The journey to healing was not as quick or easy as I would have liked. But a year later our miracle came to pass. What had been diagnosed as a deadly allergic reaction to milk was completely gone. It was a documented medical miracle.

We learned that it was not a long, hard, exhaustive process to strive after healing. Instead we realized it was a simple, three-step journey. Whether you need physical or spiritual healing, you can find it by following these three easy steps: to *hear* God's Word about healing, to *believe* what Jesus said about healing is true, and to simply *receive* what Jesus already went to the cross to accomplish. Don't be afraid to believe for a miracle and know that God's plans for you are good.

Thank You, Father, that Jesus bought my healing, for my
spirit, soul, and body. Today I hear what Your Word says; I
believe it, and I receive healing for every part of me.

Joanne Hoehne, Bradenton, FL

Have the Heart of a Warrior

"Of course I will go with you," Deborah answered, "but you
will not get credit for the victory. The LORD will let a woman
defeat Sisera." So Deborah went with Barak to Kedesh.

JUDGES 4:9 NCV

I'm one of the more soft-spoken types. It took a long time for me
to realize God had placed a special calling inside me. That calling
had little to do with my personality but everything to do with my heart
to please God. I never imagined myself a speaker, and certainly never a
preacher. But despite all that, we launched a church in 2007.

My husband and I team preach weekly and co-pastor our church.
Let me tell you, I've taken a lot of hits and a lot of criticism for being a
woman pastor. There was a season when daily I received brutal, verbal
assaults for following the plan of God. As a person who is naturally a
people pleaser, this was a tough season. So why didn't I quit? Because I
knew I had clearly heard from God, and I was simply obeying Him.

Other people's opinions just don't mean as much considering God's
opinion. I know who I am in Christ, and I know what He's asked of me,
so I've learned to be a warrior. I will not let God's assignment go unfulfilled in my life.

Having a warrior's heart has nothing to do with being outwardly
aggressive, and everything to do with an inner tenacity to go wholeheartedly into spiritual battle as you see the promises of God manifested
and His perfect will fulfilled.

....

Father, thank You for giving each of us a unique assignment.
May You empower us to fight through every obstacle
and complete what You have entrusted to us.

Discover an Open Door

"Ask and keep on asking and it will be given to you; seek and keep on seeking and you will find; knock and keep on knocking and the door will be opened to you."

MATTHEW 7:7 AMP

Have you ever prayed for something for so long it feels more like a fantasy than a possibility? In 2004 my husband and I decided to finally start the search for the perfect home. After ten years of rejected offers and several contracts that had fallen apart, we were still without our dream home. During this time our dream felt like it was a million miles away.

One day out of frustration I decided to change some of the criteria in our home search, also lowering the price range. This new search found our dream home. I felt as if I were standing inside a dream. We ended up negotiating the sale for a fraction of what we had previously been willing to pay. But I had to look at the situation differently, through a perspective I hadn't looked at it through before.

Many times we keep looking to God for answers, but we are only willing to look at the situation from our viewpoint. What if Matthew 7 is not talking about begging God with unrelenting prayer requests, but about a passionate prayer that we see the answer through *His* heart and through *His* will? What if it's about how to truly seek Him in how to live, how to follow Him, and what our part is in the waiting period?

Let's stop asking God to bless *our* plans, and start realizing that God's plans are already blessed.

Lord, help me seek Your plan for my life. May I discover
the blessings of following in Your steps.

Joanne Hoehne, Bradenton, FL

Conceive Something New

By faith even Sarah, who was past childbearing age, was enabled to bear
children because she considered him faithful who had made the promise.

HEBREWS 11:11

In 2007 my husband and I planted a church. After two years and four different facilities, we felt God wanted to give our church a more permanent location. Then one day God whispered to my spirit, *The answer you're looking for is in the loaves and fish.* We had no idea what this meant. We went back over the story and began praying for direction. Before long God led us to take up a single offering, which totaled $11,000. The next challenge was to believe Him for a building without any further fundraising.

We didn't think it was humanly possible. We had never seen it happen before. Banks wouldn't talk to us. Friends and mentors tried to talk us out of it. But we were certain God wanted to do something new. It took a full year of crazy faith, but we ended up with a debt-free, multimillion-dollar facility.

God loves when His children are bold enough to follow Him into something new. We must get past birthing only things we are humanly capable of. Be brave enough to bring forth what God has put in your heart. It won't always be easy. It takes courage. But throughout the journey He will strengthen and guide you.

....

Today, Lord, give me eyes to see the things You want me
to conceive. Thank You for strength and power through
Your grace to see it accomplished for Your glory.

Be a Daughter of Courage

Jesus turned and saw her. "Take heart, daughter," he said, "your faith
has healed you." And the woman was healed at that moment.

MATTHEW 9:22

While many people think of faith in a laid-back way, I have learned faith is more active than passive. I believe faith is an *action* that backs up a *belief.* In the above verse we read about a woman who had a medical issue, causing her to hemorrhage. Culture kept women like her at arm's length. But there she was at the feet of Jesus. She believed Jesus was a healer and acted on her faith.

A few years ago my eighteen-year-old son went to the Dominican Republic on a mission trip. On the plane ride his glasses broke. He had worn glasses since he was very little and needed them to see.

When he called me, I asked him what he wanted to do. He said, "Mom, I believe God is healing my eyes. I'm going to use my faith and believe for a miracle." We prayed together and acted as if he were healed.

The next day his vision had not changed. He couldn't see much, but he acted as if he could. I asked him if he wanted me to bring a new pair of glasses. He replied, "No, Mom. I'm going to be healed, and I'm not settling for plan B." The next morning he woke up with his vision totally healed.

True faith takes courage to act on what has been promised. Faith is more than believing; it's being courageous enough to act on what you believe. I encourage you to step out in faith. Sometimes you won't see the miracle happen until you take the first step forward.

Thank You, Father, that when You call me to do something,
You never forsake me along the journey. Infuse me with
courage to step out and bravely believe Your promises.

Joanne Hoehne, Bradenton, FL

Be Securely Anchored

He must ask in faith without any doubting, for the one who doubts is like the surf of the sea, driven and tossed by the wind.

JAMES 1:6 NASB

I recently made some purchases through the convenience of online shopping. I ordered the exact items I wanted, paid by credit card, and excitedly awaited their arrival. As much as I was anxious and excited for their arrival, I knew that even if it took a few weeks to come, the delivery would indeed happen. Sure enough all the items eventually arrived. How crazy would it have been if two days into my waiting I got discouraged and went and reordered? "That's crazy!" you'd say. And you'd be right. There's no need to reorder and pay again. Instead the situation calls for patience and expectation.

Now think about what we are asking God for. Don't you think that when He promised us something in His Word, that He will be faithful to deliver it when we ask Him for it? So as you pray in faith for something, it's like ordering an item. The grace of Jesus has paid the price for the promise, and the delivery time is the time we get to wait expectantly for the promise and grow in our faith.

I always love overnight deliveries, but some of the greatest lessons of my life have been learned in the long-awaited delivery time. Instead of asking God for the same thing over and over, how about believing He's heard you, and spend the waiting time excitedly thanking Him and preparing for what is about to come?

....

Thank You, Lord, that You are faithful to hear and answer
our prayers. We can be securely anchored in the foundation
of Your Word and Your never-failing promises.

Speak to the Storm

Since we have the same spirit of faith, according to what is written, "I believed and therefore I spoke," we also believe and therefore speak.

2 CORINTHIANS 4:13 NKJV

*M*y mom worked extremely hard as a single mother of three. Over the years stress began taking its toll on her body, and she was diagnosed with cirrhosis of the liver. She eventually retired, and her health continued to decline to the point where she needed a liver transplant. She was placed at the bottom of a mile-long transplant list and advised by doctors to get her will in order. Our family began the process of being tested to see if any of us would be a match for a transplant, and two months before my wedding, I found out that I was. I knew what I needed to do, but if I did it, there would be a chance that I would not be able to have children of my own.

My now-husband and I prayed together and felt peace about our decision to start the process. A few weeks later we received a phone call from my mother's cousin telling us her husband had passed away in his sleep from an aneurysm, and she wanted to donate his liver to my mom. They rushed my mother to the hospital and began the surgery. She woke up with a perfect and healthy liver.

Through the weakest moment of my mother's life, she remained faith filled. She would fearlessly declare, "God didn't bring me this far for nothing. He has promised to finish the work He started." We stood on God's promise and proclaimed healing over her body—fully expecting a miracle—and that's exactly what we received.

God didn't bring you this far for nothing either. Stand on faith and God's Word, and believe He can free you from all that holds you back.

Father, give us strength to reach for miracles.

Sabrina Harrison, Dallas, TX

Pray Extravagant Prayers

When Jesus heard this, he was amazed. Turning to the
crowd that was following him, he said, "I tell you, this is the
greatest faith I have found anywhere, even in Israel."

LUKE 7:9 NCV

After my mom was diagnosed with cirrhosis of the liver and
received a miraculous, successful liver transplant, our family
began to walk through the stages of recovery. I was at work one morning
when my brother called to tell me my mom wouldn't wake up. We called
911, and she was rushed to the hospital. When she finally woke up fourteen hours later, she didn't recognize us at all. I cried out to God, begging
to have my mom back, and I tried my best to stay as calm and strong as
possible.

Within twenty-four hours my mom was back—fully awake—and
so was her memory. She had no recollection of what had happened, and
they decided to take her to a specialist to examine her in San Antonio.
The entire drive I cried out to God, begging Him for my mom's life and
thanking Him for giving her to us for this long. The song "Praise You
Through the Storm" by Casting Crowns came up on my playlist, and I
played it on repeat over and over until I arrived at the hospital.

When I arrived, my faith was different. I was stronger. I had peace.
I just knew my mom would live to share this story with so many who
struggle with disease and fear of death. I prayed she would be a living testimony, and today my mom lives and is healthier than she has ever been.
Never be too afraid or frightened to pray extravagant prayers, knowing
that whatever happens, you are in the hands of a loving God.

God, today I worship You with extravagant praise.

Submit Limited Faith to an Unlimited God

Faith is confidence in what we hope for and assurance about what we do not see.

HEBREWS 11:1

As a working mother of two, a wife, and a business owner, I have learned to wake up each day submitting my limited faith to an unlimited God. Faith is believing and knowing all things will work together for the good of those He has called according to His purpose (Romans 8:28). Faith is believing His will over yours.

At so many moments in my life, I have had to choose to trust His will over mine, even when it looked hopeless. And in those moments when I chose to have faith in Him, the outcome was better than anything I could have imagined for myself. I didn't understand why I was getting a business degree in college, but God knew I would be using it in my career. There was a time when I didn't think I would ever get married, but when I submitted my desire to God and began preparing myself to be a godly wife, I met the love of my life at just the right time. Faith is dependent upon our trust.

Do we really trust God enough to have the unlimited faith required to obey Him when it comes to our finances, our family, and a future career or spouse? Faith is knowing He will send the right people, open the right doors, and give us the right words when we need them. Faith is believing we are equipped to do all the things He has called us to do, even when we feel unqualified. Faith is the most powerful and greatest gift we could ever receive. Accept it today.

Lord, strengthen my faith as I follow You into the unknown.

Sabrina Harrison, Dallas, TX

Ask in Confidence

"Whatever things you ask in prayer, believing, you will receive."
MATTHEW 21:22 NKJV

I grew up going to church regularly with my family, and I attended a religious school when I was young. I learned Christian prayers, traditions, and rituals early on in life, but it wasn't until I started college that I began to feel a deeper longing to be connected to God in a more intimate way. A friend gave me a Bible, and as I began reading it, the hunger continued to grow. I started looking for a church of my own. I had always known who God was while growing up, but I never had a real relationship with Him until later in my life. I knew *about* Him, but the real pleasure came in knowing Him.

It's like the way you can know everything there is to know about your favorite celebrities—but you don't truly know them, and they certainly don't know you. It takes a deep connection and a significant amount of time spent with someone else to truly get to know him or her and form a healthy, authentic relationship. This is the kind of relationship God desires with each of us. And we can only get to know Him in this way by spending time with Him: by talking through prayer, honoring Him through worship, and understanding His character by reading His Word.

We can confidently approach His throne each day, just as we are, because of what Jesus has done for us on the cross. We can pray His Word over our lives, our families, our businesses, and our children. We can bring Him our joys, sorrows, and fears—because we have an intimate relationship with Him. This relationship gives us the confidence to ask for all we need and to live in the abundance of His love. Take the time today to know God; the privilege is already yours.

Father, help me know You in a deep, authentic way.

Fear Nothing

Even though I walk through the [sunless] valley of the shadow of death, I fear no evil, for You are with me; Your rod [to protect] and Your staff [to guide], they comfort and console me.

PSALM 23:4 AMP

*O*ften our first response when handling hurt, disappointment, and judgment from other people can be to shrink back in fear or resentment. But I have learned firsthand, we can never have victory over these situations until we learn to conquer the fear we are facing with God's truth. We don't always like the "dark valley" moments when we are passing through them, but we don't have to like them to appreciate the change they create. Those moments in the valley with God have helped me to understand it was never actually about me, but rather what God wanted to do through me.

Facing this fear led me to a deeper strength I never knew I could have. When we allow ourselves to be controlled by the fear, we choose fear over faith. Choosing to have faith over fear is a decision we all must make. I couldn't change the situation I was in, but I could make up my mind to let go of fear and eagerly expect the promises that God had in store for me.

In these moments we can learn to keep our eyes focused on God regardless of what is going on around us. God will often use the fear from life's circumstances to shake us out of our comfort zones and into His plan and purpose for us. I choose to trust God's promises, and fear will not stop me from giving God the glory! We can stand on those promises today, triumphing over fear.

Today, Lord, I lay my fears at Your feet.

Sabrina Harrison, Dallas, TX

Follow an Unconventional Instruction

She went away and did as Elijah had told her. So there was food every day for Elijah and for the woman and her family.

1 KINGS 17:15

I used to feel guilty because I had a "regular job" and could not give as much of my heart and devotion to serving at my church as I would have preferred. I spent six years in college majoring in business and education and felt confused by conflicting desires between serving people through work in ministry and the passion I had for business and developing others. I attempted to do both for a while and would work 50-hour weeks and then lead a children's ministry on the weekends. But I didn't feel as though I was making an impact in either, because I was working nonstop and wearing myself out. So I started to ask God to show me how to bridge my ministry and my career. I had no idea God was preparing me for what I would be doing today.

It seemed like it wouldn't have an effect at the time, but I continued to pray over my future and over the impact I desired to have in the lives of others. I continued to obey, to follow His leading, and to surrender my dreams. Today I'm seeing the fruit of those years of growth and preparation as my husband and I lead our company as a ministry to bridge the gap between the church and the marketplace. Our business has opened the doors to serve thousands, to give financial resources that are growing the kingdom, and to provide a platform that allows me to speak God's truth. My work is my worship, and I will continue to follow God's leading, one unconventional step at a time. I encourage you to keep praying, keep obeying, and watch Him grow your dreams.

Lord, give me wisdom and insight to follow You fully.

Govern Your Thoughts

The LORD will grant that the enemies who rise up against
you will be defeated before you. They will come at you
from one direction but flee from you in seven.

DEUTERONOMY 28:7

One of my close friends came to me and let me know that her family had decided to leave the church. I was devastated. Had I missed something? There was no explanation. It happened suddenly and without warning. What had we done wrong? Could we sit down and fix this? It took months for me to work through this situation. My mind and thoughts were mulling over what I could have, would have, and should have done. I would drive from my home to another location, playing scenarios in my mind of conversations with her and not even remember the drive when I got there. These conversations never happened, and I needed peace—the kind of peace that passes all understanding.

I prayed and asked the Lord how to have that kind of supernatural peace. First, I had to forgive. Second, He showed me that my mind was a filter for my thoughts. I couldn't stop thoughts from coming, but I could discipline what I did with those thoughts. God's Word says to think on things that are true, noble, right, pure, lovely, admirable, excellent, and of good report (Philippians 4:8). I had to discipline myself to filter everything through this verse. It wasn't easy. Eventually I gained peace. After many months, God restored my relationship with this friend. From this experience I learned to walk in forgiveness and govern my thoughts. Forgiveness and a disciplined mind are often followed by supernatural peace.

Father, help me forgive others as You have forgiven
me, and show me how to govern my thoughts.

Sandy Scheer, Tulsa, OK

Experience an Unexpected Harvest

"Still other seed fell on good soil. It came up, grew and produced a crop, some multiplying thirty, some sixty, some a hundred times."

MARK 4:8

Many years ago my husband and I moved to Oklahoma from California with our two small children under the age of three. We contracted with a reputable moving company. We were patiently waiting for our furniture to be delivered, but it didn't come. We called the moving company, and they confirmed that they had misplaced our furniture in storage in San Francisco. We had no idea how this happened. The moving company agreed they had made a mistake but wanted thousands of dollars, on top of what we had already paid, to release our furniture and bring it to Oklahoma. We were in our late twenties, in ministry, and we didn't have the finances to pay this unexpected amount.

We read the parable in Mark 4 and felt we had sowed faithfully over the years both spiritually and financially. We believed it fell on good ground and expected a harvest! This parable is commonly referred to as the parable of the sower, but I see it more as the parable of the soil. The soil of our hearts is what determines the harvest.

Christmas was a few weeks away, and times were tight because we had paid the moving company. This experience was powerful, because God didn't just take all our problems away. We had to believe and wait on our harvest. In a matter of weeks we had two unexpected sources send us money in the mail. The moving company delivered the furniture, and the unexpected money paid all the Christmas expenses and more than we could have imagined. Don't give up on your harvest!

Father, with expectation I look forward to receiving Your blessings.

Outlast the Drought

Elijah said to Ahab, "Go up, eat and drink, for there is
the sound of the roar of an abundance of rain."

1 KINGS 18:41 AMP

*H*ave you ever believed God for something and waited but didn't see it come to pass? I believe we all have. First Kings 18:41 tells us that Elijah's servant had to go up the mountain seven times before he saw any results. Why did it take seven times? Some receive their manifestation instantly, while others wait. God is faithful, and if we will be obedient by faith and stand believing, it will come to pass if it is God's will. I can give you example after example of how I believed God for something and it looked like nothing was happening. There were times I wanted to give up, but then the answer came. I shudder to think what I would have given up had I become weary or just apathetic.

At times well-meaning people would give me their opinion of why I wasn't seeing my prayers answered. It's scary to think of the times that I trusted people or their experiences over a promise that God already stated in His Word. We must outlast the drought, the silent months when it seems God is distant. He is not.

The Bible says He will never leave us nor forsake you (Hebrews 13:5). If anyone has moved or become distant, it's you. Dig deep and stand your ground. The Holy Spirit will guide you into all truth. It may be something simple. You may be a step away from your answer. Don't let time or the drought scare you or stop you. Your answer could be on the other side.

Holy Spirit, show me things I have overlooked. Give me
faith and endurance to outlast the droughts in my life.

Sandy Scheer, Tulsa, OK

Witness God's Protection

The LORD is my strength and my shield; my heart trusts in him, and he helps me. My heart leaps for joy, and with my song I praise him.

PSALM 28:7

*E*very child feels a need for a dad to protect and provide for him or her, and people usually view God the way they view their natural fathers. If our father was loving, it is easy to view God as loving. If our dad was a dictator, we might sometimes see God as a dictator. If we can get past any preconceived ideas that we've grown up with, we can come to trust God and know who our heavenly Father really is.

Psalm 28:7 is a great confession to use to overcome past disappointments along with present situations. Life can be brutal, and that's why God's promise is so clear that He wants to protect us and provide for us. He wants to give us a future and a hope. Jesus made it very clear when He said, "Let not your hearts be troubled. Believe in God; believe also in me" (John 14:1 ESV). He was telling us to trust Him. This is the key to realizing the dreams that are in our hearts.

We believe what God offers us is true life, knowing that our doubts are going to be persistent but not reliable. God's promises are always reliable. He will always prove He is trustworthy. God's protection is activated by your trust. God longs to protect you. He wants you to win in every area of your life. He wants that more than you want it. Choose to let Him bring it about. The Lord is your strength and your shield—the perfect heavenly Father. Trust Him!

Father, help me trust You in every situation. Thank You for being my perfect heavenly Father.

Envision a Solution

God opened her eyes and she saw a well of water. So she went
and filled the skin with water and gave the boy a drink.

GENESIS 21:19

*I*t's very common not to see the solution at the onset of a problem. In Genesis 21:19, God opened Hagar's eyes and showed her the solution. She saw a well and provided her crying, thirsty son with water. Many years ago, our son began to lose weight and lost thirty-three pounds in ten days. We admitted him in a local hospital where they gave us a bad diagnosis. The doctors and specialists couldn't find a cure and gave up hope. Then, out of the blue, my husband received a phone call from a ministry acquaintance he hadn't talked to in years. He said he had been praying for our son and told us it was a spiritual battle, but God was going to give us a plan for what to do.

The next phone call was from a missionary doctor in West Africa who had also heard about this ailment and asked if the doctors had prescribed a very common antibiotic that he believed would bring a cure. In time we convinced the hospital doctor to prescribe this antibiotic. Our son woke up the next morning healed.

All too often we hear of people going through similar trials, and the solution isn't visible to their natural eyes. The outcome is determined by the attitude of our hearts and the faith we have in God's promise. Romans 8:28 is a very reliable and sure word we can treasure: "And we know that in all things God works for the good of those who love him, who have been called according to his purpose."

Father, give me faith to believe You are working on
my behalf even when I can't see the answer.

Sandy Scheer, Tulsa, OK

Dinner with Jesus

When Jesus reached the place, He looked up and said to him,
"Zacchaeus, hurry and come down, for today I must stay at your house."

LUKE 19:5 AMP

*S*cripture states that Jesus visited and had a meal at Zacchaeus's house, which created a lot of heartburn among the people around him. They accused Zacchaeus of being a sinner. They judged Jesus for going to his house and having a meal. I love Jesus' response to the people. He said, "the Son of Man has come to seek and to save that which was lost" (v. 10 NASB).

The bottom line is this: God loves us. We love God because He first loved us. The Bible goes so far as to state simply God is love (1 John 4:8). No matter what shape our lives are in, God loves us. For the religious community of Jesus' day, that was too big a pill to swallow. They couldn't wrap their minds around Jesus being with someone they deemed unclean.

It's easy to see in God's Word what the posture of our hearts is to be: don't judge, don't condemn, forgive, and give. With a heart like this we trust that God gives back to us "good measure, pressed down, shaken together, and running over" (Luke 6:38). It sounds so simple, but it's a powerful formula that opens the world to us: be kind, invest in people, and trust that God is faithful to His Word.

Father, fill me with grace. Let me love others
unconditionally and without reservation.

Discern the Beauty of Your Uniqueness

*I praise you because I am fearfully and wonderfully made;
your works are wonderful, I know that full well.*

PSALM 139:14

I was channel surfing when I was captured by an angelic voice showcased on a television show. The vocals arrested me, but the interview is what intrigued me. A young woman shared her desire to become a recording artist. Her mesmerizing story included her journey of being a burn victim, which required multiple surgeries and a painful recovery. Standing before hundreds of people in the live audience and thousands of others through the network, she shared her love of music and call to be a recording artist.

In a beautiful, authentic way she shared that her talent did not die when she was burned. Embracing her disfigured body, she stood on the stage and told of how she saw herself as fearfully and wonderfully made, scars and all. She made it clear that long before her accident and her multiple surgeries, she knew she was created to sing.

As she focused on her God-given abilities, her confidence and enthusiasm spread into the audience. Her lack of self-pity left a lasting impression. Not once did she appear a victim of her circumstances. She embraced her uniqueness rather than running from it.

Maybe you are going through a difficult season in life. I encourage you to remember the source of your strength. Bring to mind what makes you beautiful and unique, and never lose hope.

Lord, we stand in awe of how You have created
each of us with different talents and gifts.

Debra D. Winans, Murfreesboro, TN

Feel Accepted in an Insecure World

You, LORD, hear the desire of the afflicted; you
encourage them, and you listen to their cry.

PSALM 10:17

I woke up at 4:30 one morning feeling anxious. I couldn't shake the feeling of not being fully prepared for the many tasks I had to accomplish that day. As I thought through the long list of overwhelming demands, I began to feel nervous, fearful, and uptight. To be honest I did not *feel* like a daughter of God. I questioned, *How can I produce anything of value with all these negative thoughts running through my head?* I also wondered why I had taken on all my projects knowing I could easily fall into self-doubt. I wanted to quit and walk away, but I knew I was too far into the projects to stop.

At that moment time did not feel like my friend, but an enemy. I was down to the wire, facing the uncomfortable truth: I was afraid of failing. Those defeating thoughts were dancing in my head before my feet ever hit the ground that morning. It wasn't until I was standing in my closet that I began to think more clearly.

I was so busy focusing on my faults, I failed to remember who God created me to be. As I took hold of my thoughts, I began to make a new confession. I began to declare, "I am a daughter of the King. I am accepted and loved by God." As I spoke these words, my faith strengthened and my mind recharged. I refused to allow negative thoughts to reduce my self-image to less than the way God saw me. My day went a different direction, and I was empowered to succeed.

Today, I can do all things through You, Christ Jesus,
who gives me the ability to succeed.

Let Go of Condemnation

At just the right time, when we were still powerless,
Christ died for the ungodly.

ROMANS 5:6

J am sure we can all agree that we have been guilty of making a few bad decisions along our journeys. Guilt can eat away at our confidence. The enemy of our destiny is constantly shooting arrows of blame and guilt at our souls. If we are not careful, those arrows will leave us feeling like victims when we are called to live victoriously. Even though we know the enemy is lying to our hearts, we still occasionally fall into the trap of believing those lies.

During those moment I often hear the Holy Spirit gently remind me, *You are mine. I love you. Let go of condemnation. You are forgiven. Be made free.* I love how the forgiveness of God means He has freed and released us from our transgressions. He lets us walk away free without any trace of condemnation or guilt.

Each day our Father offers us a limitless supply of mercy and grace. The lavish love of God helps us stay anchored to our purpose. His love gently disciplines us and draws us back to His heart. In seasons when we miss the mark, we are not alone. Jesus went before us and made a way for our sins to be cleansed. Knowing we are free of condemnation will give us peace to start and end our days in joy.

Father, Your strength is made perfect in our weaknesses.
Thank You for comforting us when we make mistakes. Fill
us with courage as we rise from our fallen places.

Debra D. Winans, Murfreesboro, TN

Stop Obsessing Over Your Flaws

You are altogether beautiful, my darling; there is no flaw in you.
SONG OF SOLOMON 4:7

I was trying on a garment from one of my favorite boutiques when a woman came out of the dressing room frustrated by her appearance. When I tried to compliment her on how she looked, she couldn't accept a single word of encouragement. Even another shopper joined in the conversation saying, "You must buy that dress. It looks fabulous! But I watched her reject every compliment and word of encouragement. I hoped she would at least entertain positive reinforcement and not stay hung up on what she considered her personal flaws. But don't we all feel this way sometimes?

The enemy of our confidence has a goal: to use our thoughts and concepts of self-worth against us. It is time we took captive our thoughts and remembered that our Father masterfully created each part of us. Through divine design He skillfully put us together. To speak against how He created us is to speak negatively of His creation.

There are more than seven billion people on the planet, and not one other person shares your DNA—not one. You and I are carefully handcrafted in the image of God. Everything He created is good, and that includes us. Are there areas we can work on and make better? Yes— but make sure the motivation for change reflects the image God wants you to have and doesn't come from being overly self-critical. If you are struggling to find a healthy self-image, get in His Word. There He reminds us of our loveliness. He lets us know we are His masterpiece.

....

Father, each time I look in the mirror, help me remember I am
fearfully and wonderfully made in Your perfect image.

Flourish

I am like an olive tree flourishing in the house of God. I
trust in God's unfailing love for ever and ever.

PSALM 52:8

*A*t the seasoned age of fifty-two, I decided to go back to college. Was it scary? You had better believe it! Taking classes both in the classroom and online challenged me in many ways. I admit it took a while for me to adjust to idiosyncrasies of the twenty-first-century collegiate experience. Over those early semesters I discovered how much had changed in the last few decades. Math seemed like a foreign language. Our assignments had to be submitted electronically with a host of other new online platforms.

To be honest I was overwhelmed. Everything seemed to be moving fast, and at first it was hard for me to catch up. Eventually I adjusted to my new world. I found myself not only surviving but thriving in my new arena. Isn't that like the goodness of God? He lovingly allows us to thrive during life's most challenging circumstances. He gives us grace for what seems impossible, hard, and weighty. Will we experience fear and apprehension? Probably, but God's grace propels us forward into the sweet place of victory.

In daunting endeavors we learn what we are created to accomplish. Although college has been one of my greatest challenges, I have almost reached the finish line. Of all the awards and honors I have achieved in my collegiate experience, my most-prized reward is learning to thrive despite difficulty. Our Father wants to see us flourish in every season of life.

Abba, You hold everything I need, lack, or desire. I place my trust in You.

Debra D. Winans, Murfreesboro, TN

Treat Every Ending Like a New Beginning

He who was seated on the throne said, "I am making everything new!"
REVELATION 21:5

Feeling derailed by life? Off-balance due to the actions of others? That is how I felt driving my children to school one morning. The daily routine was often filled with chaos and confusion. As soon as they climbed out of the car, tears raced down my cheeks. It was all I could do to hold it together emotionally. I was in the final stages of ending a broken marriage, and I was exhausted.

That day I felt overtaken by questions that had no immediate answers: *What's going to happen next? How do I start life over? How will it feel to be a single mom? Can I fill the role of both mother and father?* As I was processing these questions, my mind drifted to the words of an old song: "It is well with my soul." I felt a calming rush of peace. Yes, I am a single mother, *but it is well*. Yes, I am divorced, *but it is well*.

The ending of one chapter in my life took on a spectacular new beginning. Endings often involve pain, but the thrill of discovering good things in your future will give you the courage to follow your heart. Life has many chapters. One ending leads to a new beginning. Remember through it all that God walks beside you. He will never leave nor forsake you, and He makes all things new.

Father, my life is in Your hands. I trust You even when I cannot see You. Thank You for leading me down the path of righteousness.

Unfailing Love

I trust in your unfailing love; my heart rejoices in your salvation.

PSALM 13:5

God's unfailing love speaks of His favor, His friendship, and His promises. God's unfailing love is written all throughout His Word. Think about your salvation. Isn't it amazing to know that the Lord has placed you into a condition of safety? This means you can totally put your trust in Him no matter what your circumstance may look like. You may have just lost a loved one or spouse, or perhaps the doctor just gave you a not-so-good report. Maybe you went to work and found out when you arrived that you were no longer needed. These situations may seem impossible to face, and of course not anything to rejoice over; but when you put your trust in the Lord, you know He is not going to leave you nor forsake you (Deuteronomy 31:6).

He will bring a better job into your path. He can mend and restore a broken heart and relationship. He can bring healing to your sick body. But all this hinges on one thing: *Are you going to trust Him to work out the details, or are you going to try to fix them yourself?*

You live in a self-contained world. Everything you could ever want or need is at the tips of your fingers. But all of us will face situations in our lives that nothing in the world can fix. Only God can take you through them. His unfailing love will carry you there. And through His salvation, His deliverance, yes—you can rejoice!

Lord, thank You for Your unfailing love. Remind
me of my salvation, so I can rejoice in it.

Darlene McCarty, Cordova, TN

Be Provided For

Those who trust in their riches will fall, but the
righteous will thrive like a green leaf.
PROVERBS 11:28

Money can buy a car, a house, and a new dress to match those beautiful red shoes you just had to have. But there are things money cannot buy, such as the favor of God and His protection. If you are depending on the things of the world to bring you happiness, you will be greatly disappointed.

My mind goes back to a time when we had no money in the bank. My husband and I had only been married a few weeks. One Sunday night we were returning to Bible college when our car suddenly died on the interstate. What were we to do? We had no money, no cell phone, and we were stranded in the dark.

We had two options: put our trust in our circumstance or put our trust in the miracle worker. So we laid our hands on our dashboard and prayed a simple prayer. "Lord, You know our circumstance. We need to get back to college. We have no money. So we need You to heal our car."

It may sound crazy, but let me tell you what happened next. We turned the key, and the car started. We made it back to college, pulled in front of our apartment, and the car died. The story doesn't end there. The Lord sent a friend by to replace the fuel pump at no charge. We had prayed a prayer of faith and trusted in the Lord, and He brought favor.

Those who take root in the world will wither, but those that are grafted into Christ and are connected to His root will flourish.

Lord, I will trust You. Teach me to have faith in
You over anything else in this world.

Be Lifted Out of the Den of Destruction

The king was overjoyed and gave orders to lift Daniel out of the den. And when Daniel was lifted from the den, no wound was found on him, because he had trusted in his God.

DANIEL 6:23

*D*aniel's night of confinement in the lions' den ended in a morning of glory and deliverance. Can you imagine the excitement in the city as the news spread that Daniel had spent the night in the lions' den and had come out unhurt? God could have prevented Daniel from going into the lions' den, but by allowing him to go in and bringing him out unhurt, the Lord received greater honor.

No injury was found on him. How could this be? It's a clear and simple answer: he trusted in his God. Daniel had done no wrong. God recognized his innocence and sent an angel to shut the mouths of the lions.

You may have done no wrong, but you might feel captured in a den of lions. Don't defend yourself to your capturers. Let God do your defending for you. He's a professional.

If He can dry up a sea, remove a mountain, raise the dead, forgive sins, and purify a heart, He can protect you in times of trouble. Those who boldly and cheerfully trust in God to protect them will always find Him a present help.

....

Heavenly Father, we ask You to protect Your people. May they rise out of oppression like a shining star with no harm. We rejoice and trust in You.

Darlene McCarty, Cordova, TN

Perfect Peace

*You will keep in perfect peace those whose minds
are steadfast, because they trust in you.*

ISAIAH 26:3

The Hebrew word for "peace," *shalom*, means "undisturbed, perfect peace." Jesus can create undisturbed, perfect peace within your mind when storms are raging around you in every direction. Sleepless nights may overtake you. It may be hard to keep your mind focused on your job. Patience could be wearing thin with your family. You might have even told God, "I don't know how much more I can take."

When you have confidence in God, it doesn't matter what's going on around you, what you lack or need. It doesn't matter where you have come from or what has been done to you in the past. Your confidence in God cannot be shaken. You will choose to still trust in Him because you know He will deliver you. And because of this trust in Him, your mind can rest in perfect peace.

Judah had been subjected to reproaches and to scorn. The people had been stripped of their property and honor and had been reduced to the condition of prisoners and captives. Yet their confidence in God had not been shaken. They still believed that He would deliver them. They were kept in perfect peace.

When we feel shaken, we can look to all the persecuted and afflicted people of God, who amid the storms of persecution—even in prison and at the stake—have been kept in undisturbed, perfect peace. Their trust kept them steadfast, and it can keep our minds at peace as well.

Lord, I long for this peace. Cultivate trust in me, so
I can know You with a steadfast mind.

Trust and Do Good

Trust the LORD and do good. Live in the land and feed on truth.
PSALM 37:3 NCV

*F*aith and trust work together as we wait upon the Lord. A heart full of fear is not trustworthy.

This psalm was possibly written by David on the behalf of Mephibosheth, who had decided to leave a land where he had been treated so unfairly. David was convinced of his innocence and pleaded with him to dwell in the land with the reassurance of plenty and protection. David had confidence in God.

This verse says to "do good." Always treat evil with good. The best way to keep the mind from complaining and fretting is to be involved in "doing good." Have your mind occupied in something valuable and useful. Do something kind for someone else who may be having a hard day. If you do this, there will be no time to complain.

Joseph had plenty to complain about. His brothers betrayed him. He was lied about. He was placed into prison. But he continued to trust the Lord and "do good" for others. He interpreted a dream, and where did that take him? From a prison to the palace.

The last part of this verse is a command, not a suggestion. Where has God placed you? That's the land for you to abide in. Live calmly, securely, and with joy. Be thankful for what God has given you, bless others, and in return He will provide (feed) you the necessities of life.

. . . .

Lord, help me to be a blessing to those around me. Forgive me for complaining when I have so much to be thankful for. Help me today to give a hug, a smile, a compliment, and a handshake to someone who needs to see You through me.

Darlene McCarty, Cordova, TN

Shine Like the Dawn

Commit your way to the LORD; trust in him and he will do
this: He will make your righteous reward shine like the
dawn, your vindication like the noonday sun.

PSALM 37:5–6

I recently heard the story on my local news about a man named James, who had been falsely accused of a crime he did not commit. He spent thirty-two years of his life in prison because of the false accusation. Due to retesting of DNA found at the scene, his defense team was able to prove that the evidence collected did not belong to him. But this proof came only after thirty-two years of James' life had been taken from him forever.

This story doesn't sound fair, and you know what? It wasn't. But I've learned through life's circumstances that life is not always fair. How did James survive all these years? It was his confidence in the Lord that God would make righteous his reward and that he would once again shine like the dawn. And God did just that.

God can protect you, restore your character, and cause the darkness of clouds to disappear. He can cause the sun to shine without any clouds just as He did for James.

How? Commit your situation to God today, and He will protect your character and will cause the clouds to scatter. He will make your character perfectly clear and bright, like the noon sun. No clouds will remain on it.

Lord, I ask You from this day forward to be my Defender, my Protector, and my Advocate. In You I put my trust. Your vindication is all I need.

Make Peace with Your Past

Jesus said to the woman, "Your faith [in Me] has saved you; go in peace [free from the distress experienced because of sin]."

LUKE 7:50 AMP

*H*er reputation alone should have kept her away from the banquet Jesus was attending, but this sinful woman knew that Jesus was the only One who could forgive her, so she made an extravagant gesture of gratitude: pouring expensive perfume on His feet and wiping them with her hair and tears. The Pharisees were scandalized, but Jesus blessed her.

Have you ever felt that if people knew the real you, you would not be accepted because of what you have done? I know how difficult it is to feel broken because of rebellion and selfish choices, having so much regret and shame that you can't imagine ever feeling joy again.

After years of ignoring who I really was, I remember when I finally stopped to reflect on my life and the choices I'd made. I discovered there were four versions of me. The first was the one my family knew, second was the girl the public knew, third was the one I thought I was—and then there was the real me, the one God knew. That girl was a mess, artificial and empty.

As I wept with shame and regret, my heart ached because I could not go back and change a single thing. I knew I had chosen to do it my way. How then could God ever forgive me? Just as Jesus forgave the woman who had many sins, God forgave me and allowed me to forgive myself. He offers you the same healing—and it is miraculously freeing.

Father, I let go of my past so I can reach for my future.
Thank You for forgiving me and making me free.

Tressa Lemky, Winnipeg, Manitoba CANADA

Love Unconditionally

"Love your enemies, do good, and lend, hoping for nothing in return; and your reward will be great, and you will be sons of the Most High. For He is kind to the unthankful and evil."

LUKE 6:35 NKJV

One of my nieces was asked to write about a key person in her life for her fourth-grade class.

She chose a person who had encouraged, trusted, believed in, and supported her no matter what. One comment in her report stood out above the rest. It was a simple statement, yet it gave great insight into why she believed this person loved her: "She loves me just because I breathe."

Unconditional love is usually easy to muster with family and close friends, but what about our enemies? What about the people around us whom, for whatever reason, we don't seem to get along with or agree with? How is it possible to love them unconditionally when we don't even like them? Why would God expect us to do this? After all, doesn't He understand why they don't deserve it?

Today's verse doesn't say that He expects us to "feel" that love, but to act it out by doing good. In other words, what we say and do must be the same as if we loved them "just because they breathe."

I know it's difficult, but God's Word tells us we can. As we pray for these troublesome people, and as we are kind and giving, expecting nothing in return, we may never know the effect our unexpected kindness could have on their lives.

God, help us love unconditionally. Let others see You through our actions.

Transform Our Weaknesses

*He said to me, "My grace is sufficient for you, for
My strength is made perfect in weakness."*

2 CORINTHIANS 12:9 NKJV

God has given each one of us gifts and abilities. When we use those strengths, we are more likely to feel confident and secure. One of the gifts the Lord has given me is the ability to decorate and coordinate events. I have produced conferences, fundraisers, fashion shows, and weddings that have often been successful and well received. But despite that success, I can tell you that without the Lord and His assistance they all would have been disasters.

When I was thirty-five my doctor diagnosed me with a minor case of attention deficit disorder (ADD). I wasn't surprised, because when I was in school it had always been difficult to concentrate and stay focused. I was easily distracted, which made it difficult to complete assignments.

I asked the Lord to take my ADD away, but then I remembered: even though I had these tendencies, God had a way of making up for them. In whatever situation I found myself in, things always seemed to work out.

I actually felt closer to the Lord because I knew that whatever I achieved, we had done it together. I also loved sharing with other people what He had done to help me complete my tasks.

I encourage you to rest in the fact that Jesus will make your weakness perfect. It doesn't matter what you are facing today, because God has your victory.

Father, through my weaknesses, let me find a way to honor You.

Tressa Lemky, Winnipeg, Manitoba CANADA

Grow Deep Roots

The righteous shall flourish like a palm tree, he
shall grow like a cedar in Lebanon.

PSALM 92:12 NKJV

For a few weeks every winter my husband and I like to escape the cooler—okay, *freezing*—Canadian climate by heading south to Florida. In addition to the warmer temperatures, I love seeing the palm trees with their stately stature and unique leaves.

Whenever I look at them, I am reminded that "The righteous shall flourish like a palm tree." I must admit, I used to wonder why God chose to compare the righteous to this tree, but after taking a closer look at its characteristics I began to understand.

Despite being hard on the outside, the trunk's interior is supple enough to bend in extremely strong winds without breaking. Unlike other trees, the palm tree flourishes in the desert because its root system aggressively reaches as deep as necessary to find moisture, providing nourishment and a strong anchor for the towering tree.

This reminds me of my relationship with the Lord. When I choose to spend time with Him and study His Word, I gain a deeper understanding of what He wants for me. I not only feel closer to Him, but I gain a greater confidence and strength, which allows me to withstand the pressures of life.

My hope is that, like the fruit of the palm tree, which is known to become sweeter as the tree ages, we too can become sweeter and more attractive to those around us as we deepen our relationship with Him.

Father, help me flourish in every situation.

Speak Truth in Love

Speaking the truth in love [in all things—both our speech and our lives expressing His truth], let us grow up in all things into Him [following His example] who is the Head—Christ.

EPHESIANS 4:15 AMP

Facebook, Instagram, Twitter, and the endless ability to search anything and everything has made it even more difficult to know what is true and what is false. With the click of a button or tap of a finger, the world's opinions are ready and waiting to be heard.

It's no wonder then, that after researching any subject we can become more confused than when we began. Everyone seems to have his or her own opinion and ideas of what we should and shouldn't do.

As believers, how are we to discern what is truth and what is not? How are we to know what to do and what not do, what to say and not to say, and how to feel or not feel?

As we study Scripture, we will deepen our understanding and ultimately mature as followers of Christ. Then, when opinions and ideas come our way, we will be able to discern what is truth and what is a lie.

How then are we to share the gospel (which is really the most important truth there is) with those around us? Share in a gentle and loving spirit. Not everyone is going to believe what the Bible says right away, but at least we're letting them hear His Word—God's truth, not man's.

Our prime responsibility as Christ-followers is to share the gospel, whether by action or word. Let's follow His example by speaking and sharing the truth in love.

Lord, show me how to speak the truth in love today, answering the wisdom of man with the wisdom You bring in Your Word.

Come Out of the Wilderness

The child grew up and became strong in spirit. John lived in the desert until the time when he came out to preach to Israel.

LUKE 1:80 NCV

*I*magine for a moment how John the Baptist might have felt when he knew it was finally time for him to leave the wilderness and begin to preach to the Israelites—to proclaim that Jesus the Messiah had come and that they needed to repent.

I'm sure he expected that not all his words of hope and warnings would fall on willing ears, or that he might not be received with open arms. But because there was no doubt in his heart that this was his calling and purpose, he began his prophesied ministry with boldness.

Sometimes it's hard to believe that there is a "specific" call or purpose for our lives. We doubt that God can use us based on our past mistakes, lack of abilities, or resources. But if we do believe we all have a "God-calling" to fulfill, when He is prompting us to step out in faith, despite the circumstances, we will have the confidence and courage to move forward.

If you move forward, God will give you the vision, energy, direction, and provision to complete the work He has predestined you to do. Don't attempt to do it in your own strength, but instead draw close to Him.

You can leave your past behind, speak truth lovingly, and allow Christ to transform your weaknesses and love unconditionally as you come out of the wilderness to fulfill your God-call.

Lord, make me brave and strong in spirit as I step forward
into the destiny You have prepared for me.

Reassess Relationships

Paul insisted that they should not take with them the one who had departed
from them in Pamphylia, and had not gone with them to the work.
ACTS 15:38 NKJV

*G*rowing up I heard stories about "Father Time." In my mind this
fictional character was a bearded old man who walked with a cane
and possessed endless knowledge. Now I laugh at the thought of wisdom
being only associated with the elderly. As I travel, I meet with young
men and women who are full of wisdom, creativity, and energy. Looking
back, I wish I would have understood the value of pursuing wisdom at
an earlier age.

Some of our greatest learning moments will come through the experiences of other people. That means we must surround ourselves with
people who will have a positive influence on our lives.

In relationships it is necessary to exercise a good bit of insight. It is
a fact: people come and go in our lives, and they all play different roles.
But we still need to get serious about asking of those closest to us, *Is this
person's purpose to accompany me to my goals? Is that person here as a
God-given instrument to assist and maybe even guide me to my destiny?* In
today's Scripture verse Paul clearly understood that although many good
people surrounded him, not everyone would be beneficial in getting his
work completed. One of the hardest tasks in life is reassessing the people
who influence our lives most. True wisdom requires we answer the question, *Who is supposed to be in my inner circle?*

Lord Jesus, help me trust You with all my relationships. Give me
wisdom concerning the people I bring into my inner circle.

Shelia Isom, Danville, VA

Pursue Wise Counsel

Spend time with the wise and you will become wise.
PROVERBS 13:20 NCV

S ome of my most difficult lessons have been learned because I didn't listen to the right people. I can recall one such lesson when I was sixteen. My dad was dragging his feet in search of my first car, so I decided to venture out with my mom instead. The car I found turned out to be a real lemon, but I thought it was a dream. My father, being the wise counsel he was, tried his best to persuade me to look for another, but I wanted this one. I can recall those words. "Sis, if you want this car, then you can buy it." So I got the car, and an hour later I realized what a big mistake I had made, just because I wouldn't listen.

Often we find ourselves in situations we created simply because we refused to listen to wisdom. My dad knew that car was indeed a disaster, but he also knew it would be a lesson I would remember forever. Our heavenly Father operates in much the same way. He gently persuades us to sometimes wait and listen, but He never forces His wisdom upon us.

God's Word says that if we spend time with and listen to wise counsel, we, too, will become wise; but if we don't, there are consequences to our actions. We must be willing to weigh out each decision. Remember, waiting is not denial, but it can offer the best for us in the end.

Dear Lord, help me stop and listen to those who are truly wise.

Prepare for the Unexpected

"The wise ones, however, took oil in jars along with their lamps."
MATTHEW 25:4

*M*y hair is naturally curly, and getting it wet in rain certainly is not the ideal look for me. You would think looking outside and seeing massive clouds would have been a good indication that I should have taken along my umbrella, but no! I would have had to run back into the house to find one. *It will be okay, it's not going to rain*, I thought. When I'm wrong, my sleek, flat-ironed hair sports a sassy lioness look, which is exactly what happened!

No matter the present situation, it always pays to be prepared for sudden change.

One day everything can be going perfectly, and in an instant our lives are turned upside down. Are we prepared to move into the mode of immediate action? What good is a car without enough gas to get through unexpected traffic? We often have great intentions, but we lack the necessary ingredient that proves to give us success in whatever situation: preparation.

Today's verse gives us a clear picture of wisdom in action. The wise virgins knew that having lovely lamps would be useless if they had no oil to light them. Wisdom is a primary ingredient, but often we lack it in the simplest of situations. We have all been guilty at times of neglecting to think ahead to what might happen. We can walk in greater success if we just take a little time to prepare for the unexpected. After all, it could make our day so much better (and drier).

....

Lord, whatever the day brings, I'm ready.

Shelia Isom, Danville, VA

Grace and Wisdom

Give me wisdom and knowledge, that I may lead this people,
for who is able to govern this great people of yours?
2 CHRONICLES 1:10

$\mathcal{I}$ have met some amazing people along my journey of life, and knowing their stories often makes me wonder: *How in the world did this person survive what happened to him?* What keeps a mother strong when dealing with a handicapped child? How does a caregiver keep giving to a person with Alzheimer's? How does a missionary journey to a foreign country, live there, and help those he has never met? When life seems overwhelming, grace and wisdom give us the strength to go on.

Think about grace: it's almost inconceivable in a sense. Grace is a virtue; it is unmerited, divine assistance given to us by God. He truly loves and cares about our human decisions and dilemmas. Because of this amazing grace, we have access to a strength that sustains us whatever the circumstance. Now think about wisdom. God knew Solomon had the choice to ask Him for anything, but above all Solomon desired wisdom. He was aware that something greater than himself and all his skills would be needed to lead God's people.

As we travel this life, we will always have need of some great advice, simple truth, and God's grace to survive the hardships we must endure. Given time, a little wisdom can mean the difference between complete exhaustion or courage to finish. And a little grace can mean the difference between a broken heart or a healed one. Whether we're dealing with day-to-day life or leading people, God's grace and wisdom will prove to be our strength.

Lord, may grace follow me daily, and wisdom light my path.

Change the Environment

During the night the mystery was revealed to Daniel in a vision.
Then Daniel praised the God of heaven and said: "Praise be to the
name of God for ever and ever; wisdom and power are his."

DANIEL 2:19–20

Some years ago I worked in the emergency department as a registered nurse. I experienced the constant shift of the environment. Going from patients with a nose cold to a gunshot or stabbing wound sent my emotions reeling from high to low. But in each instance I had to remain sharp and focused.

When we face situations that bring panic or we find ourselves simply confused, it changes our environment. Our emotions play a vital role in the way we project ourselves to others. Sudden changes in our emotional environment can bring about a sense of anxiety and even frustration and can break our focus. So to maintain or change an environment for the better, we must find vision in God's power and wisdom.

In today's verse we read that Daniel was a man of dreams and visions, but unless God gave him understanding of these dreams, they would forever remain a mystery. This vision was the release that Daniel needed to change the environment around him. Daniel then praised God and sent a message of hope to those around him.

How often do we get the opportunity to shift the environment in which we live? Our attitude can reflect God's strength and wisdom and can change the aura of depression and hopelessness. We have a choice to be the conduit God can flow through to bring about change.

Lord, help me bring about positive change wherever
I go by having an attitude that reflects You.

Shelia Isom, Danville, VA

Be Still and Learn

Let the wise listen and add to their learning, and
let the discerning get guidance.

PROVERBS 1:5

*I*n a world of extreme busyness, being still is an anomaly. With long agendas and endless hours of exhausting work, we come to the end of the day and ask, "What did I really accomplish?" I often hear comments like, "I feel like I'm going in circles!" and, yes, many of us are. In times like these God has given us a predefined setting for productivity, and that is simply being still and learning.

Learning requires discipline, and discipline brings balance and wisdom. Proverbs is a wonderful reminder that if we can wait, be still, gather all the resources we've been given, and truly listen, we are defined as wise. Some of the saddest stories in life are of those who had great potential but were unwilling to learn.

We are given many opportunities to advance here on earth. Our heavenly Father also provides wonderful opportunities to advance spiritually. We must embrace those opportunities with a focused mind. Wisdom teaches us to be strong and courageous and to be who God has created us to be without reservation. It teaches us that "fear of the LORD is the beginning of wisdom" (Proverbs 9:10). In the end others will seek out those very wise people.

If you can truly be still, then listen, because there's a lesson waiting to be learned.

Dear Lord, help me to be still and learn.

Hold On to Your Dream

The LORD was with Joseph, and he was a prosperous man;
and he was in the house of his master the Egyptian.

GENESIS 39:2 KJV

One day when I have my own house, I'll live by my rules, or maybe no rules at all!" In our teen years most of us have voiced similar words, possibly while kicking the nearest object.

From the time we are children, the thought of complete independence seems like a perfect solution to our frustrations. Our impatient minds crave freedom without responsibility. Then in adulthood our thoughts imagine, *If only I could be my own boss.* If we are not careful, we will throw away the thing that brings us freedom: a submitted heart.

I've learned that lasting prosperity comes through submission to authority. In the Bible Joseph is described as a prosperous man. He was an Israelite, yet he advanced in the Egyptian kingdom. He was determined that his circumstances would not take away the dream God gave him.

Too often we blame our inability to pursue our dreams on our current situation, possibly even our jobs, leadership, or season of life. The enemy uses our reasoning, along with our fear of failure, against us. Take care not to believe the lies telling us, "Everyone is against you." Those lies will make us resentful and unable to move forward in faith.

Is there a dream that you've stopped reaching for? I encourage you to reclaim your dream. Maybe the unexpected season you're in is the perfect one for your dream to prosper.

Dear Lord, I am thankful You are with me! In this season, give me the courage to serve faithfully and trust Your plan for my life.

Rachelle Bilbo, Houma, LA

Speak Kindly to Yourself

*Pleasant words are like a honeycomb, sweet and
delightful to the soul and healing to the body.*

PROVERBS 16:24 AMP

We create worlds with our words. With each word we speak, we create a world of destruction or a world of promise.

Take a moment and remember some of the recent hurtful things you have said about yourself. Like many of our sisters, we may have thrown out frivolous insults like, "I'll never lose weight," or "I'm just not smart enough to apply for that job, go back to school, or start that business."

I know reliving our hurts sounds counterproductive, yet it's necessary to identify whether we've developed destructive habits of negative self-talk. Toxic talk is the number-one way the enemy shuts down our potential.

I want you to think of a lady in your life whom you adore. Repeat the negative words you spoke about yourself, but this time use her name instead. *Ouch*, right? You would never say these things to her, because they would be hurtful, discouraging, or even bullying. Yet we often poison our own potential with our words.

You were created in your Father's image, and you are His child, the one He adores. When you begin to speak only hope-filled words over yourself, you open the door for God to fulfill His purpose in your life. I invite you, precious daughter of the Most High King, to use your words to create a world of unending possibility.

....

*Dear Lord, I break the power of past hurtful words. Today
I speak of myself as Your valued and loved child.*

Be Part of a Tribe

*As soon as he had finished speaking to Saul, the soul of Jonathan was
knit to the soul of David, and Jonathan loved him as his own soul.*

1 SAMUEL 18:1 ESV

*I*n school I performed a simple science project using slices of bread.
I placed one slice in a plastic bag and left it in a dark closet for days.
The others I left in the bread bag in the light. The result was rapid growth
of mold on the darkened slice while the others remained fresh. I learned
mold breeds in darkness.

In the first book of Samuel, David found himself isolated in a cave,
afraid, and running from his enemy. He was quickly joined by other men
who were in trouble, in debt, or agitated by their circumstances.

The truth is we all experience dark seasons. Whom we welcome into
our cave and listen to during those moments will determine whether we
stay stuck in our situation or arise and face a new day with confidence.

The enemy would like to push us further into isolation. He knows
if we stay discouraged long enough we will fall in defeat. God, on the
other hand, wants us to conquer the things that try to destroy us. He uses
healthy relationships with other people to give us strength when we need
it most. Jonathan sought David out in the cave and encouraged him,
spoke truth to his fears, and prophesied life to his future.

I invite you, dear sister, to open your heart to brave hearted, godly
women who can draw you out of your present situation. Sin and shame
breed in darkness, but when you can be honest with someone who
understands the heart of God, you will experience freedom.

....

*Dear Lord, help me identify a tribe of women I
can confidently share my heart with.*

Rachelle Bilbo, Houma, LA

Embrace Divine Promotion

The LORD exalted Joshua in the sight of all Israel; and they stood in awe of him all the days of his life, just as they had stood in awe of Moses.

JOSHUA 4:14

*D*uring my husband's first college class, a loud-mouthed student raised his hand and asked the professor, "What qualifies you to teach this class?" Although the question was asked in a disrespectful way, it revealed a truth about our culture. Respect doesn't always accompany a title, but respect comes with proving yourself as a leader whom followers can trust.

When Joshua stepped forward to lead the nation of Israel, the people had great respect for him. This respect was not granted in a moment but rather through the momentum of his faithfulness. Joshua was a man who was faithful even when it was not his season, which made it easy to be respected when his time did arrive. Joshua had believed the good report of the Lord and fought for promises when others walked away, intimidated and fearful. That kind of rare faithfulness positions simple men to become significant leaders.

Maybe you feel your efforts to follow and serve others are going unnoticed or unappreciated. It's easy in this busy world to feel overlooked. The good news is God never overlooks a faithful heart.

I invite you, faithful daughter, to serve God with a relentless heart. Don't grow weary in well doing. Know that what you are doing is of great worth. There is no unimportant job in the kingdom of God.

Dear Lord, thank You for opening divine doors of opportunity.
I am grateful to serve You in any way needed. I love You.

Be a Compass

One who is righteous is a guide to his neighbor, but
the way of the wicked leads them astray.

PROVERBS 12:26 ESV

When I was six years old, I burned down our old Christmas tree. The only thing that saved me from my parents' wrath that day was that I was following in my older brother's footsteps. My response was finger pointing: "My brother made me do it!"

Our discarded Christmas tree leaned against our house, propped up next to the electrical outlet. My brother wanted to light a firecracker, and so he decided to use one of the branches to ignite it. After setting a branch on fire, he used it to ignite the firecracker. But not wanting it to explode in his hand, he quickly tossed it to the side, and he wisely put out the burning branch.

The mischievous plan worked . . . at least until I tried the same thing.

I lit a branch, lit a firecracker, threw the firecracker, . . . and watched our tree explode in flames. My lungs didn't have enough air to put out the flames.

While my brother didn't really *make* me do it, I thought I could, because, well, he could. The truth was that what was manageable for him was destructive for me.

There may be activities we feel strong enough to handle, but they could bring about destruction for someone who is less able to deal with the same situation. We need to make sure our actions inspire those around us without placing them in compromising situations.

Dear Lord, search my heart and show me any areas I need
to improve. Help me be a good and effective leader.

Rachelle Bilbo, Houma, LA

Possess a New Identity

Anyone who belongs to Christ has become a new person.
The old life is gone; a new life has begun!
2 CORINTHIANS 5:17 NLT

*N*aming my children was not an easy endeavor. My goal each time was to choose a name with significant meaning, but not one that would target my child for bullying. I wanted something uncommon but not weird, and one my husband and I would agree on.

Throughout the Bible we see how important names are to God. It was not uncommon for Him to change the name of an individual to make it better reflect his or her identity. In the book of Genesis, we see God change Sarai's name to Sarah, which means "mother of nations." The interesting part is that Sarah was barren at the time of this name change. God changed her name to reflect her future. The plans God had for her defied her current circumstances. Rather than address her problems, He spoke about His promises. He relabeled her crisis. He didn't see a barren womb but instead a womb carrying the nations.

When we place our faith in our Father, He redefines our future. Maybe you feel as if you are unable to live up to the expectations of what God is asking you to do. Maybe you feel shame and guilt over your past and you doubt you can change. Maybe the enemy has blinded you from who God is calling you to become. Don't let negative thoughts separate you from God's plan. Learn to see yourself as God sees you. He continues to call you clean, beloved, and anointed.

Dear Lord, I cast off any hurtful words or labels that would redefine my worth. I reach forward and accept Your promises.

Be Adopted

"I will not leave you as orphans; I will come to you."
JOHN 14:18

As a kid growing up in the sixties, I'll never forget this sight—a framed certificate centered and prominently positioned on the wall of Sally's bedroom, which read *Certificate of Adoption.*

Adoption was signed, sealed, and guarded as a shameful secret in the 1960s, yet Sally's parents publicly proclaimed and affirmed her adoption for all to see. Why? My sweet friend's parents specifically sought out Sally for adoption. She was wanted, chosen, asked for, included, and loved—so well loved.

Like a heart beating, love pulsated in Sally's home. Shame was exchanged for adoption into her new family as her new name was positively proclaimed for all to see. Sally was grafted into the family, her new heritage established, and her new bloodline openly and honestly acknowledged.

This is how Jesus adopts us. Have you read His promise? *I will not leave you as orphans; I will come to you.* Jesus announces that He will come to each one of us. There is no stone He will leave unturned to come to you. Are you ready to receive Him and all He has for you? The invitation is open. Be adopted by Jesus today.

Here's the deal: You, dear friend, are wanted, chosen, asked for, included, and loved—so well loved. You too are adopted into a new family when Christ comes to you and you come to Him. Your name is proudly proclaimed as a daughter of the King of kings and Lord of lords forevermore!

....

Father, help me know I am forever Your child.

Susan B. Mead, Homer, LA

Be Guarded

The Lord is faithful and will give you strength and
will protect you from the Evil One.

2 THESSALONIANS 3:3 NCV

*H*ow often do we find ourselves in over our heads, seeing no way out of our mess? We feel weary, vulnerable, and exposed; we are worn down by trials and trouble; we are defeated, dejected, and depressed. We need hope to shine, yet all we see is rusty, dusty, and dim. We wonder how in the world we can work our way out of our own messes.

And there it is—hope shining brightly for us to see the promise God extends to each of us when we turn to His Word and His way. And we realize what happened.

The evil one, the enemy of our souls, loves to dish up distress. We simply failed to turn our troubles over to God, trusting Him with them. Instead we turned toward our own wills and ways. We experienced frustration, anger, and felt overwhelmed, which morphed into fretting and forgetting God's promises.

Yet our Father God is faithful in all His ways. He invites us to return to Him. He is *El Shaddai*, our all-powerful and all-sufficient Sustainer, who gives us strength and protection. May we find rest as we lay our heavy loads that defeat us at the foot of the cross, trusting God with the details that otherwise derail us.

Here in this place where God guards us, we find strength and protection from all the woes and worries that have distracted us. God invites us to come closer as He guards our hearts and our homes.

Father, help me release everything to You. You
are faithful to strengthen and protect me.

Be Delivered from Danger

He shall give His angels charge over you, to keep you in all your ways.
PSALM 91:11 NKJV

*B*oom! Flames flashed over five stories tall. Nails impaled flesh—arms and legs—and injured so many lives. The impact in that moment was incredible, and eight seconds later the second bomb blasted two blocks away. The unforgettable day of the 2013 Boston Marathon turned from serene to surreal, from magnificent to mayhem in a moment.

The grandstand seat I had previously enjoyed put me in the midst of people scrambling for their lives. My prayers were simple: *He orders His angels to protect you wherever you go.* I call this my 911 prayer. The words that followed were simply, *Jesus, Jesus, Jesus* as I prayed the name above all names. He delivered me and many others from danger that day.

I read in Psalm 34:19 that "the righteous person may have many troubles, but the LORD delivers him from them all." I am not righteous, yet Christ in me is. The same is true for you. You can turn to Jesus. He invites you to call on His glorious name in your times of trouble. He delivers His people.

How often do you remember to turn to Jesus in your daily living? Why does it take a catastrophe to cause you to call on the Lord? Do you find that true in your life? How I wish I did not need catastrophe, yet it is in the times of trouble I remember to call on my Lord Jesus. In the day-to-day living I want to call more often on my sweet Deliverer. The promise God makes is this: He delivers you from all your troubles.

God invites you and me to trust Him, to call on His sweet name. His is faithful to deliver us from dangers, big or small.

Thank You, Lord, for protecting us in every situation.

Susan B. Mead, Homer, LA

Receive Shelter

"Call upon Me in the day of trouble; I will deliver
you, and you shall glorify Me."
PSALM 50:15 NKJV

God's whispered invitation may sound the loudest when you are at your lowest.

September 11, 2001. When you hear 9/11, your thoughts immediately turn to the moment you saw first one fiery tower fall, followed by the second. Terror reigned across the land that day.

A jet was propelled into a wing of the mighty Pentagon and another into an open field in Pennsylvania after a brave soul rallied a group to overcome the assailants.

Firefighters climbed up steps that were destined to fall, yet their mission to remove people from harm's way ruled the day.

So many lives were lost, yet so many others were spared. We do not know why some survive and some do not in any given situation, yet we know that God's ways are higher than our ways, and He has a plan.

Have you found yourself in a situation that appeared bleak, when the world was falling down around you and you needed shelter immediately?

God invites you to turn to His Word, call on His mighty name, and receive His shelter in your times of trouble. Do you hear Him?

Your heavenly Father God invites you to come closer. As you lean in and lean on your mighty Lord and Savior, your troubles tumble away and turn to thankful praise. You find that during God's Word you accept His open invitation and feel His shelter.

....

Lord, help us wrap our heads and our hearts
around Your will and Your way today.

A Fortified Place

The name of the LORD is a fortified tower; the righteous run to it and are safe.

PROVERBS 18:10

As a little girl, I called the name of my daddy and flew into his open arms like a kitten running for cover when a threat arose. His safe embrace was a place I felt protected from harm.

The need for protection grew as situations arose that required different resources. On the playground, a stick became a mighty sword, a towel (and diaper pin) became a cloak or cape. A piece of cardboard strapped with duct tape was brandished as an impenetrable shield. I held my weapons high, confident, powerful, and protected. Things were so simple back then.

The playground became the world as we grew, and the enemy tramped around, arrogantly drawing near. God whispered and drew us into His arms; yes, our Daddy's arms still embraced us.

Some of us, however, were distracted, diverted, and divided from the strength of our Lord by the prowess of the enemy's tricks and tactics, perhaps by the flaws of our own daddy. Yet we have a promise where we triumph. "Resist the devil and he will flee" (James 4:7); nonetheless there is one thing we must do to command the enemy to stand down. We must pick up the Word of God and wield it well.

May I invite you to wrap yourselves in the powerful name of the Father, your protector and fortified tower? Thank God, He was, is, and will be our strong tower forever. What an amazing place to depend on when the enemy growls and prowls around.

....

Thank You, Father God, that You alone are my eternally safe place.

Susan B. Mead, Homer, LA

Safe Refuge

The LORD also will be a stronghold for the oppressed,
a stronghold in times of trouble.

PSALM 9:9 NASB

*F*rantic fists pounded the front door. A frightened wail followed, "O God, let me in, please let me in."

The opened door revealed our beautiful neighbor battered, beaten, and bloodied by the man pledged to love and honor her, yet evidence showed otherwise. Our arms opened wide as we pulled her into a safe place and a loving embrace. How much more does our heavenly Father long to pull us into His mighty arms? He alone is truly our safe haven.

Trauma, grief, and unbelief can set in. We ask, *How, Lord, can this tragedy happen among Your sons and daughters?* We proclaim our love for each other, yet our actions reveal so much pain, torment, and hatred.

Abuse or oppression always follows when the purpose of an object is not valued. Our purpose is to love each other as Jesus cherishes us, yet a gap develops, causing a breach in the relationship with the Lord and each other.

Let's run back to Him, our stronghold in times of trouble. He has a strong hold on us, His beloved children. Let the words of the psalmist wash over us with an open invitation to step into His shelter and refuge.

Turn to Him now, for He will hold us in His mighty arms as He provides safe refuge from our troubles. Lean in, for we are always welcome there, regardless of what has been done to us or by us.

Lord, with confidence we know You are our
safe refuge in times of trouble.

Restore the Wounded

Confess your sins to each other and pray for each other so that you may be healed. The prayer of a righteous person is powerful and effective.

JAMES 5:16

*R*ecently, as a friend and I counseled another woman, comparison crept in. As she addressed one wound after another in this person, I found myself mesmerized by her gift. It was beautiful. However, envy slowly choked life out of my own confidence and replaced it with offense. Thoughts like, *Do you care what I have to say?* and *What do I have to offer?* began to fester. I was ineffective in partnering with both the Lord and my friend in restoring this woman.

Satan, initially gifted by God with perfection, wisdom, and beauty, fell from heaven. Instead of partnering with God, he chose envy, comparison, and offense and abandoned the partnership. Now hatred drives his opposition to God and us. He knows a house divided cannot stand, so his goal is to lure our eyes from our own giftings, promote comparison and offense, and leave us wounded, ineffective, and unrestored.

When these resentful feelings torment you, beware: Satan is whispering lies. This thief is afraid of *you* partnering with God. Taking these thoughts captive and confessing them to one another and the Lord is a sign of humility and maturity.

Choose to celebrate the talents, gifts, and callings of others. It will restore your partnerships. This shield of honor also protects both you and the beauty of God's gifts in others and the effectiveness of your prayers.

Lord, forgive my comparisons. It hinders both
my partnerships and my prayers.

Deana Morgan, Grapevine, TX

Make Your Mistakes Right

If you hide your sins, you will not succeed. If you confess
and reject them, you will receive mercy.

PROVERBS 28:13 NCV

*H*ave you ever awoken after a good night's rest and instead of enjoying those first few moments of peace, a lack of peace tells you something is wrong? You begin a quick mental search looking for your source of emotional pain. The moment you find it, you think, *Oh, yeah . . . there it is.* In a nanosecond anxiety takes over every cell in your body, consuming every glimmer of joy, peace, or rest in its path. You begin to think, *It'll never change. This is too much. It's all up to me. I failed again* sets in, and suddenly you feel physically exhausted. Wanting to numb the feelings, you close your eyes and justify another thirty minutes of sleep. Your hope is held hostage. With no light ahead, no way out, the beliefs behind your burdens steal your rest.

We've all experienced this moment. Life can stress us with challenges, causing us to question if somebody, anybody, or even God really cares. This can leave us feeling isolated and alone.

Studies show sickness and pain in the body is caused by inflammation, and inflammation is caused by stress and anxiety. Stress and anxiety are the result of fear, and fear is the result of unbelief.

If this resonates with you, I encourage you to confess. Confession is when you take your eyes off the problem, put them on Jesus, and acknowledge you need Him. His mercy, by design, will give you wisdom, heal your unbelief, and give you rest.

. . . .

Lord, I confess the unbelief stealing my rest today. I invite You into
my challenges and acknowledge only You bring sustaining peace.

A Taste of Hope

*Know also that wisdom is like honey for you: if you find it, there
is a future hope for you, and your hope will not be cut off.*

PROVERBS 24:14

In Jewish history children learned a foundational lesson their first day of school. Capturing their attention, the teacher would place drops of honey on each child's fingertips, then instruct them not to eat it. Imagine their desire to taste this rare gift glistening from their fingertips, yet having to wait. Keeping them in suspense, the teacher would place his hand over each child's head and speak this blessing: "May the Word of God be delicious on your lips and in your body, like sweet honey in your mouth." This truth landed in their spirits, they were finally released to savor each honey-laden finger. This was their first taste of the Word of God.

As honey became a student's connection to the Wod of God, the cross became a symbol, marking a place in history where salvation was made possible.

For me the cross is a symbolic reminder of my birthright and authority, paid for by Jesus. He opened doors to a heavenly eternal future and gifted me with His Word and the Holy Spirit, both of which provide a daily taste of hope. And this hope will not be cut off.

Like honey and the cross, the Word of God provides a daily taste of hope. Like the teacher's outstretched hand over a child's head, imagine God's hand of blessing over you today. May these next words be like honey.

....

Lord, Your Word is a taste of hope. It nourishes me,
again and again, that You are for me. I love You.

Deana Morgan, Grapevine, TX

Build Bridges

*Brothers and sisters, if someone is caught in a sin, you
who live by the Spirit should restore that person gently. But
watch yourselves, or you also may be tempted.*

GALATIANS 6:1

I once read a tale of an older gentleman restoring a broken bridge across a valley in the middle of nowhere. He was asked, "Why would you waste money on such a large undertaking?" The old man replied, "I'm not investing in the bridge; I'm investing in the individual who may need this bridge if they ever have to cross this difficult valley." What a demonstration of generosity, empathy, and grace!

When someone is caught in sin, I have found this is a good question to ask: "Which character am I: a bridge builder or a judging skeptic?" Am I one who uses her time, talents, and treasures for the restoration of others or one who selfishly judges others?

Every choice to sin is born from a burden, a longing to be filled out of a deep broken place within us. Jesus' death and resurrection built a bridge across a valley of sin and separation––and it leads to the Father.

I have learned why He warns us not to judge others: it opens us up to be judged. Instead, God invites us to partner with Him in restoring others, with gentleness and mercy, regardless of their valley. Mercy triumphs over judgment.

God is inviting us today to reflect the heart of His Son, Jesus. If He came to heal the brokenhearted and rebuild broken bridges, we can too.

Lord, show me those broken or new bridges that will
provide solutions for the tender needs of others. They
are worth building or rebuilding. I am Yours.

Repair the Broken

The disciples picked up twelve basketfuls of broken pieces of bread and fish.

MARK 6:43

Twelve hungry, tired disciples sought to avoid responsibility by asking Jesus to send five thousand people away to find their own food, only to hear Jesus say, "*You* feed them." One agitated disciple informed Jesus of the cost of feeding so many. Still Jesus asked the disciples to bring Him what little food they found. He held it up for God's blessing, it multiplied, and then they distributed it. Even after feed the multitudes, each disciple discovered an abundance of food awaited them.

One evening, while attending a women's event, I personally needed prayer and direction after entering a soul-searching season of asking, "Who am I?" Instead of the answers I desired, I heard Jesus say, "Deana, love on these women who came with you." I stood quietly with growing agitation. As I watched others receive needed prayer, I was left feeling excluded and unloved. I replied with, "No. I serve all the time. I need answers."

But He countered, "I know what you need. Trust Me. Partner with Me."

Yielding, I gave Him the little I had left in me to serve. In turn He magnified my offering, empowering me to pour out. Later that evening out of His overflow, He began answering my question, "Who am I?" Those revelations still lead me today.

Unaware of who we are and who He is, we might focus on the little we have. But when we partner with God, He multiplies our offerings, leaving us with His abundance.

....

Lord, help me look past the little I feel I must offer. Your ways release abundance, revelation, and breakthrough.

Deana Morgan, Grapevine, TX

A Brave New Heart

"I told you these things so that you can have peace in me. In this world
you will have trouble, but be brave! I have defeated the world."

JOHN 16:33 NCV

What do phrases like, "Stop feeling that way," "Calm down," or "You're too emotional" stir in you? Do you feel voiceless, unimportant, or shamed? Do you even find yourself conforming?

Once after hearing "Calm down," I felt condemned. My desire to be heard was squashed. Overwhelmed I closed my eyes only to hear my inner voice screaming. My trapped emotions had unleashed a cacophony of mental and physical pain pounding my temples and tightening my chest. Shut down, I faced my familiar options—give the silent treatment or comply.

Have you been there? Guess what? You're not crazy. Yet many generations continue to believe the only way to deal with unruly emotions is behavior modification, such as "Stop it!" These people can't handle your emotions, so they reject, stifle, and condemn yours until you comply.

If we are made in the image of God, an emotional being, emotions must have a purpose. They inform us. But where is peace when we are living in emotional pain?

Facing your pain will require you to have a brave heart. Think of a recent moment when you experienced emotional pain. Like the bride whose eyes are fixed on her groom, close your eyes and picture Jesus. He *is* peace. Run to Him; let Him hold you. Breathe deeply and say,

....

Jesus, I lay this painful event in Your hands in exchange for
Your peace. I want to tell You how I felt when . . .

Have Coffee with an Encourager

Jonathan, Saul's son, arose and went [into the woods] to
David at Horesh, and encouraged him in God.

1 SAMUEL 23:16 AMP

As women we are all unique and none of us is replaceable. God has given each of us our own set of talents and gifts. Some of those may be used in the corporate world to develop careers or to engage in humanitarian efforts or to build families. They are all important, but especially when we use them together. An amazing power occurs when women come together. We can be uplifted and healed because of the strength received from spending time with one another.

The strength we draw from mutual support can bring healing, both emotionally and physically. I know of women who have been healed of physical issues once they received emotional comfort and support from other women. Over the years I've learned it's also healthy to have a variety of friends. None of us needs friends who agree with us all the time. We need those who will challenge us to think differently about situations, those who have a different life view. Others may be practical and down to earth, creative, or inspiring. And we always need one with whom we can just be comfortable hanging out and doing nothing.

During times of trouble, in a place of doubt, disappointment, or despair, seek out an encourager. If you need someone like this in your life, don't hesitate to ask God, who delights in giving you every good thing. You will catch a glimmer of hope in your sister, even in the time it takes to drink a cup of coffee.

Father, thank You for the gift of sisterhood. Help me build
and nourish friendships that bring us mutual strength.

Julie Nolan, Marion, IL

Think Before You Leap

In an abundance of [wise] counselors there is victory and safety.
PROVERBS 24:6 AMP

I thought God had brought him into my life." I should have listened to their advice, but it was given by people who had recently deeply hurt and betrayed me—people I had trusted to have my best interest at heart. If only I had stopped in my tracks when my heart was sounding the alarm, I would have been saved from deep regret, embarrassment, guilt, and shame. In hindsight going down a different path would have been preferable.

Praying and waiting for God to answer can be difficult when the answer is delayed. But it is worth the wait, and we need to take time to get confirmation. We can get in our own way, causing much harm by assuming He is saying yes to something just because we want it to be so.

Having godly mentors who give sound advice can be life-changing. We are not meant to travel this life path alone, floundering to survive with no help. A counselor, mentor, or coach can guide us in making decisions based on reality, not how we want things to be.

First Timothy 3 and Titus 1 provide an excellent list of those we should seek advice from and trust. Their character traits include being blameless, faithful, not overbearing, not quick-tempered, not violent or given to dishonest gain, sincere, respectable, hospitable, loving what is good, and exercising self-control.

As you learn and grow, you will feel content knowing you made good and right choices. And you will develop a multitude of counselors to keep you on a safe path.

Father, thank You for wise counselors who will safeguard my heart.

Build Your Faith

He gives strength to the weary and increases the power of the weak.
ISAIAH 40:29

*F*aith doesn't just happen. It's not a fleeting thought. Faith is a powerful concept. It dictates how we live. It determines what we think and how we speak. We should be aware of faith every day. We need to build, nourish, and practice it. Total lack of faith leads to hopelessness, and the consequences of it can bring devastation.

For more than thirty years Walter worked for two well-known ministries. He was brilliant. He was full of life. He knew the Word. He was surrounded by people with strong faith. Every week he heard inspiring messages. But it wasn't enough. He didn't maintain his own faith. Tragically he lost all hope and committed suicide.

We live in a fallen world. Life isn't perfect. We all have moments of doubt and despair. But we don't have to get stuck there. It's a conscious choice. Reading and reciting Scripture is the key. Put verses that inspire you on notes around the house, in your purse, car, closet, or drawer. Remember, God says to cast all your cares on Him (1 Peter 5:7). Know that He supplies all your needs. Trust Him.

When Jesus' disciples were discouraged, He invited them to release their burdens onto Him. In fact He not only gave them the opportunity to let go of the things weighing them down, but He also promised they would find peace for their souls.

> Father, help me rely on Your words to encourage my heart.
> When I am tempted to look at the circumstances around me,
> help me look to the heavens, where I will find peace.

Julie Nolan, Marion, IL

Break Free from Discouragement

Why are you in despair, O my soul? Why have you become restless
and disquieted within me? Hope in God and wait expectantly for Him,
for I shall yet praise Him, the help of my countenance and my God.

PSALM 42:11 AMP

I often wonder why women can be so critical and hard on themselves.
We compare ourselves to others. We wish we had what they have
and think their talents, looks, or intelligence are better. We remember
and replay any faults or bad decisions that led us to a bad outcome.

We hope and dream and have expectations of how things should be.
But then life happens. We lose a loved one, people disappoint us, sick-
ness attacks, or someone else gets what we have worked for and deserve.
Things out of our control can change our lives in an instant.

When we are struggling, it can be difficult to look forward and see
that good will come. We can hear a story like ours that has an ending
full of blessings, healing, and transformation. We get inspired—there is
hope for us! Then we turn around and listen to that voice inside that says
we aren't worthy or good enough.

Discouragement is a loss of confidence or enthusiasm. It can be soul
crushing. We all experience it, but there is hope of overcoming it. It may
not happen overnight, but life will get better. A friend of mine has a
tattoo that says, "This too shall pass." It reminds her that life is part of a
balance. Even though bad happens, good always comes too. So use your
words to break free. There is power in speaking positive statements. It
can change the atmosphere and your thinking.

Father, when I am tempted to compare my life with others', remind me
that You have a purpose and plan for me, and You made me to fulfill it.

Retrace Forgotten Promises

*"Do you have eyes but fail to see, and ears but
fail to hear? And don't you remember?"*
MARK 8:18

*G*od is our source. He has the answer for all that concerns us. We may not understand why our prayers aren't answered the way we want or think they should be. But in time we will always see God work things out for us. We will never be disappointed when we trust Him.

Even the disciples had doubts and didn't understand the magnitude of what they were experiencing. They were traveling when they realized they had only brought one loaf of bread (Mark 8:14). Jesus had to remind them of two miracles they had witnessed personally when five thousand and four thousand people were fed with only a few loaves of bread and fish.

One day, upon reflection, I was reminded of how faithful God has been in my life. I had gone through a time of isolation after an injury, and my children and I had to live with relatives. I was in pain every day, so having a social life was difficult. But eventually I started healing. During that time I found a house that felt like home as soon as my children and I saw it. God also brought some amazing friends into my life. Further retrospection led to acknowledging how grateful I was that God had walked my children through the difficult teen years, and that they now had good jobs and wonderful spouses. What a journey. God is so good, even when we don't always see it at first.

Take a moment to relive your journey, looking for the ways God has blessed you. Let the memories lead to praise of your caring Father.

Father, let me see Your hand at work in every situation.

Julie Nolan, Marion, IL

Look for the Rain

*"I will send you rain in its season, and the ground
will yield its crops and the trees their fruit."*

LEVITICUS 26:4

*H*ave you ever sat by the window and watched rain fall from the sky? Dark, wet, and gloomy, the gray clouds seem to envelop everything. The dreariness of the day doesn't just make things dark on the outside, but it can overshadow our joy and emotions on the inside.

I've often wondered why our emotions seem to be negatively affected by something as ordinary as a change in weather. We know rain is good and necessary to life. Common sense reminds us that if every day were bright and sunny, all life would eventually wither away.

Today's Scripture verse reminds us that rain is an essential part of preparing the soil to receive and germinate the seed. Unless the soil receives adequate moisture, the harvest will fail.

In the same way the soil needs rain, so our souls need to be watered by the Word of God. When we read His Word, our souls soak up truth and the hard places of our hearts become soft. We must make time to sit and soak in God's presence—to let worship water the dusty places of our souls. Then dormant areas of our lives are nourished and revived.

So look for the rain. Look for the cleansing and freshness that come after the rain. Seek Him during the storm, and see the blooms of new growth spring up in your life.

Father, send the refreshing rain of Your Word into my life.

Hear a Divine Whisper

*After the earthquake came a fire, but the LORD was not in
the fire. And after the fire came a gentle whisper.*

1 KINGS 19:12

On a cold December day, my boss called me into her office and said, "I'm sorry, but we're not renewing your contract." It felt like I had been punched in the stomach. My career at CBS News was over, and I was out of a job. I never imagined myself unemployed. The career I had invested two decades building seemed to collapse before my eyes.

One minute I was living my dream; the next, it all seemed to vanish. When I arrived home that night, I hit my knees and began to pray. Even though it was a shock to my heart, I knew this news did not catch God by surprise. In my prayer time I heard Him quietly whisper, *Trust Me.* In the days to follow He began to lead me in the direction I was to go. His words brought me comfort, and daily I waited to see where the journey would lead next.

That quiet whisper provided the strength to get up and a reminder that those who know their God will not be moved. Before my last day at CBS, I had an offer for a new job with a substantial pay increase and a settlement check worth two months' salary.

When the earthquakes and fires of life have disrupted your plans, let God's gentle whisper always provide a voice of direction in the dark. Even if your worst fears are confirmed, He is near and intimately working on your behalf.

Father, help me trust You with everything I don't understand. In
my struggle I see Your true character, and You craft mine.

Diana Lynn Smalley, Dallas, TX

Be Held in the Hands of God

*"Don't worry, because I am with you. Don't be afraid, because
I am your God. I will make you strong and will help you; I
will support you with my right hand that saves you."*

ISAIAH 41:10 NCV

When the storm rages and when trouble is on the horizon, our tendency is to fret. When facing a cancer diagnosis, a divorce, or a betrayal, it can be easy to slide into the pit of discouragement. But God doesn't want us living in fear. In fact He commands us to *fear not!*

He promises to strengthen us, help us, and support us. We must make our first response one that defies all senses, and trust the Lord.

When we see the enormity of our God, our problems look small. But it starts with a decision to listen to His voice and look to the heavens. Our God sees our trouble. Our God hears our cry. Our God knows our circumstance. He has given us the grace for today. We are in the palm of the hand of the One who crafted the universe and yet still called us by name. There is nothing so little it slips by His sight. All things are under His command. When we put our trust in the Lord, He upholds us in His mighty hand. There is no situation or circumstance too difficult for His reach.

Father, I will choose not to worry or be afraid. Program me to first look to the heavens, for my strength and help come in the name of the Lord.

Learn the Love Language of God

"God so [greatly] loved and dearly prized the world, that He [even] gave His [One and] only begotten Son, so that whoever believes and trusts in Him [as Savior] shall not perish, but have eternal life."

JOHN 3:16 AMP

*A*s a journalist for many years, I've covered thousands of stories filled with heartache. I've seen countless parents bury their children after accidents, after acts of violence, or under military honors as soldiers killed in action. There are few things more painful. How many of them would have traded places and given their child the chance to live?

Our Father knows that pain. He loved us so much He sacrificed His most-prized possession, His Son. Jesus took our place. The shed blood of Christ then became the one and only way to the Father's heart. Beloved, know Jesus, and know the heart of God. When we draw near to Jesus we will experience the Father's love. God sent us a part of Himself, undeserving of punishment to bear the weight of the world in our place. That is how our Father loves. The God who created everything, gave us, who are sinful, all He had.

God is a giver. He desires to know us as His own. In our mother's womb He crafted our personality traits, gifts, and talents. As coheirs with Christ we are not to wallow in our iniquity but to walk in our kingship as worthy children of an anointed King.

....

Father, thank You for the gift of Jesus. Let me see Jesus and know Your heart that all would see You in my gifting and talents. Make my life a reflection of Your sacrificial love for me.

Diana Lynn Smalley, Dallas, TX

Weep like Jesus

Jesus wept.
JOHN 11:35

Several years ago, I went home for a weekend visit. My mother met me at the door. She was crying. "I have cancer," she said. "It's aggressive and growing fast. I feel like the Lord is calling me home." She was fifty-nine. The doctors gave her a 10 percent chance of survival. Hopeless over the news, she sank into a debilitating depression. We sent out prayer chains, but I was unable to pray. Alone in my quiet place there were no words, just tears.

One morning after her emergency surgery, the Holy Spirit woke me. I was still asleep, but I could hear the Spirit interceding on my behalf for my mother. It was the most beautiful, fervent, and powerful prayer. Then I saw a vision. My mother was seated and oil was pouring over her from head to toe. It felt warm, loving, and thick. Moments later I awoke to a call. The tumor was removed and the cancer cells were dying. She was healed!

Have you ever been so broken you couldn't pray? Jesus was. When Lazarus died, He wept. In the garden He was greatly distressed to the point of death. It is human to despair. God is close to the brokenhearted. He bottles our tears. In those despondent moments His Spirit intercedes before the throne on our behalf. The broken moments pave the way for the miraculous. In our weakness He is strong.

....

Father, when the battle has taken my words, You see every tear.
Holy Spirit, thank You for continually interceding before the
throne on my behalf. Replace my brokenness with praise.

Put Away Your Mask

Create in me a pure heart, O God, and renew a steadfast spirit within me.
PSALM 51:10

*I*t happens every morning on network news: politicians scare the public with doomsday scenarios over new legislation, there's a scandal over a nude selfie, and accusers come forward to blame a prominent TV newsman of sexual misconduct.

Our culture is becoming more self-centered and shallow by the minute. The evidence is all over the media and reality shows. Famous "housewives" hurl insults at each other as they travel the globe with hair and makeup teams. They own the nicest cars and biggest homes. But if you ask the average person who these so-called celebrities are tomorrow, she won't remember, and it won't matter.

The work of the Lord stands forever. God works through our character. He prioritizes the inner spirit over the external, always molding and growing us, calling us deeper into Him. Transparency is our difference. Often difficulty refines us. We start to see ourselves as Christ does, trivializing the phony narrative of a "perfect life." Authenticity allows us to be fully used by Him. If we aren't real about our struggles, the character of Christ will never shine through us.

It's okay to have nice things, but years from now, no one will remember the car we drive. They will remember our strength in the storm, our kind word or helping hand, the refusal to gossip with the rest of them. When we put away the mask of this world, our reflection will look like Him.

Father, make my character my most beautiful possession.

Diana Lynn Smalley, Dallas, TX

Know the Will of God

"If you remain silent at this time, liberation and rescue will arise for the Jews
from another place, and you and your father's house will perish [since you
did not help when you had the chance]. And who knows whether you
have attained royalty for such a time as this [and for this very purpose]?"

ESTHER 4:14 AMP

*N*ew England, where I grew up, is known for harsh winters, so naturally most get through those frigid dark months knowing the change of season is inevitable. Spring is coming. Trees and flowers that have been buried under snow and ice all winter will start budding and blooming. Animals will make their way out of hibernation.

All that has been dormant during the winter will emerge from darkness to reveal itself. Much like the flower bulb rooted in a dark place beneath the soil for a time, we also have an inevitable moment of revealing. Our callings are formed in the secret place, in our prayer rooms, through our trials. And our Father takes ownership over every intimate moment that crafted His plan for us. What lies in secret belongs to Him.

However, when it is time to bloom, God shares His mighty work. Nothing pleases Him more than to watch His children rise to the destiny He ordained. When that moment comes, it is up to us to claim our rightful place. Much like the roaring ocean and the sunrise and sunset, God's will marches on. He will see His plans accomplished and His purpose fulfilled. It's our privilege to answer His calling and take our place in those plans.

....

Father, show me Your divine will and give me the boldness to
stand and be counted when my moment of revealing comes.

Forgo Fear

"Who of you by being worried can add a single hour to his life?"
MATTHEW 6:27 NASB

*L*iving fearful is like running in place, exerting a lot of time and energy, but never going anywhere. Because of fear, most of us struggle with worry and anxiety. For years I fell into the trap of worrying about things that would never come to pass. When I realized how much time I was wasting by living in fear, I began to change my negative way of thinking. The truth is, if we don't watch over our thoughts and words carefully, we will find ourselves trapped in the vicious cycle of fear.

The enemy of our souls has an agenda to redirect our focus away from our dreams by exhausting us, hindering our productivity, and stealing our time. One of the greatest strategies he uses to derail our faith is to arrange situations that would tempt us to let go of our faith and pick up fear.

In the second book of Timothy, Paul wrote about fear. He made it clear that God does not give His children a spirit of fear, but power over every demonic assignment that the enemy tries to attach to our lives. When we surrender our faith and choose to live anxiously, we overreact to ordinary situations. Fear clouds our judgment and blocks the blessings of walking in faith.

Remember, God has not wired you to live in fear. He created you to experience the supernatural rewards of faith. Embrace the power, love, and discipline that He has given you in place of the spirit of fear.

Dear Jesus, thank You for giving me the power to overcome fear. Strengthen my faith and give me peace.

Bethany Bilbo Rasmussen, New Orleans, LA

Extend Grace

"Don't judge others, and you will not be judged. Don't
accuse others of being guilty, and you will not be accused
of being guilty. Forgive, and you will be forgiven."

LUKE 6:37 NCV

*M*any times it is easier to hold others to a higher standard than we do ourselves. We cannot expect perfection from imperfect people, while giving ourselves a "grace pass" for our mistakes. It is easier to judge others when we have no idea of the private situations they may be walking through.

Leaders are often criticized more harshly because they are out in front. They become a quick target for verbal attacks, yet leaders need grace also.

I love the approach Jesus took when finding others in the middle of messy mistakes. To the adulterous woman, He became living water. To denying Peter, He gave words of life. To doubting Thomas, He showed His healing hands.

If there is someone in your life who needs grace, be like Christ and give grace in excess. Grace isn't in short supply. I've learned that when you sow grace, you reap it. There may be a time in your future when you need grace extended toward you, so it is important to always extend grace.

Dear Jesus, teach me how to extend grace toward others,
even in circumstances where I am hurt and confused. Help me
forgive quickly and be slow in my judgment of others.

Protect Your Thoughts

*Be continually renewed in the spirit of your mind [having
a fresh, untarnished mental and spiritual attitude].*

EPHESIANS 4:23 AMP

*E*very war is first won or lost in the mind. Anytime we leave our thoughts unprotected, we become an easy target for attack. If the mind has power to control the entire body, then it is important for us to pay careful attention to where our thoughts are leading us. Our thought life will eventually spill over into our actions.

It is impossible to surround ourselves with people who constantly speak negative words without being adversely affected. Those who are the most influential in our lives will possibly help to determine the way we think and the direction we take in life.

To guard our future we must evaluate our relationships. There will be seasons when we need to step back and separate ourselves from relationships that have grown unhealthy. The apostle Paul shared that one of the best ways to protect our thoughts is to withdraw our attention from unnecessary arguments, keeping ourselves out of contentious conversation. Second Timothy 2:23 states, "Don't have anything to do with foolish and stupid arguments."

If you are to have healthy thinking, you must take every thought captive. When you protect your thoughts, you protect your future. Today promise yourself that you will weigh out each word you speak and keep your thoughts in line with God's Word.

....

*Dear Jesus, purify my mind and thoughts that I may please You.
Teach me how to protect my mind from negative thoughts.*

Bethany Bilbo Rasmussen, New Orleans, LA

Live Free from Condemnation

Those who are in Christ Jesus are not judged guilty. Through
Christ Jesus the law of the Spirit that brings life made
you free from the law that brings sin and death.

ROMANS 8:1–2 NCV

*H*ave you ever done or said something that caused you to immediately feel a tinge of guilt? Is there something you wish you would have left unspoken?

Perhaps we've said things that have left us feeling guilty or condemned. There is a difference between conviction and condemnation. Conviction is when the Holy Spirit deals with our hearts, urging us to repent of our wrongdoings, so our relationship with God remains intact. Condemnation, on the other hand, is not from God but from the enemy. He wants us to feel bound by our words and actions, preventing us from experiencing freedom in Christ.

When we accept Jesus into our hearts, His Spirit brings us life, setting us free from the condemnation of sin and death. At that moment condemnation is broken from our lives. We are set free from the enemy's lies and schemes. If, however, we make the decision to embrace feelings of condemnation, we accept the lie that grace is not enough to cover our sins, and we return to spiritual captivity.

Remember, Satan is the author of lies and the accuser of God's children. Daily he seeks opportunities to accuse you and bring you into agreement with his lies. Refuse them. Guard your heart from anything that would keep you away from the love and grace of the Father.

Thank You, Lord, for paying the price for my freedom so
I no longer carry the burden of condemnation.

Let Grace Make Sense of Your Mistakes

"Come now, let us settle the matter," says the LORD. "Though your sins are like scarlet, they shall be as white as snow; though they are red as crimson, they shall be like wool."

ISAIAH 1:18

What a relief it is to know Jesus has settled the matter, and yes—it's official—we are forgiven. To fully accept His forgiveness, we need to also forgive ourselves. When we do not embrace freedom from guilt and shame, the enemy of our souls tries to bind us up with condemnation. It is only when we make the decision to let ourselves off the "shame hook" that healing can begin in our lives.

There is no greater feeling of security than knowing Christ has washed away our past and made our hearts new. We have all made mistakes, and I am confident each of us will slip up and do something foolish again. The good news is that our mistakes do not define our future. The previous chapters of our lives do not decide how our story will end. In fact a few bad chapters are simply the introduction to the story of grace.

Behind every scar is a story of healing. Though the marks of an injury may remain, the pain is removed. The scar is a memory of healing that has taken place. It is a beautiful thing to remember what God has brought us from. I encourage you to share your healing story, and let it bring hope to someone who needs restoration.

....

Dear Jesus, thank You for washing away my
past. Today I accept Your forgiveness.

Bethany Bilbo Rasmussen, New Orleans, LA

Walk Away from Your Chains

Suddenly an angel of the Lord appeared and a light shone in the cell. He struck Peter on the side and woke him up. "Quick, get up!" he said, and the chains fell off Peter's wrists.

ACTS 12:7

As a new mom, my emotions were all over the place while I watched my son experience his firsts. I will never forget the cry he made when he received his first immunizations. Once the nurse finished bandaging the injection spot, I immediately scooped him into my arms. It was heart-wrenching to watch my son endure a moment of pain. The only thing comforting my heart was knowing that what brought him pain now would keep him healthy later.

It's never easy to watch a loved one go through pain, especially when we are unable to prevent it. I've discovered it's just as hard to watch others go through a difficult season as it is to go through one ourselves. Our deep love for others will draw us into their heartache, tragedy, or pain. If we are not careful, we can take on the pain of others, forgetting that we are there to help set them free.

Just as God set Peter free from his chains, His desire is to set you free from whatever prevents you from moving forward. What are the chains in your life? Are they past mistakes, a fractured relationship, addiction, or fear? It's time to let go of whatever has held you captive. The love of Christ can set you free. Embrace His love. Let Him unlock the areas that have kept you bound.

Jesus, I thank You for paying the price for my freedom. I declare, I am no longer enslaved by the enemy, but I am free in You today.

Be Present

As God's own chosen people, who are holy [set apart, sanctified for His purpose] and well-beloved [by God Himself], put on a heart of compassion, kindness, humility, gentleness, and patience [which has the power to endure whatever injustice or unpleasantness comes, with good temper].

COLOSSIANS 3:12 AMP

*H*ave you ever tried to have a deep conversation with someone who is constantly looking at her phone? Or perhaps she is shifting her gaze all around the room? Maybe she seems to be disconnected from the conversation. I don't know about you, but it makes me want to just stop talking. If I have to fight for her attention, she probably doesn't want to be there at all.

I am so glad that when I talk with Papa God He is always present. He hears my every word and every cry. Even when I don't have words for feelings deep in my soul, the Holy Spirit will take my groans and tell Papa, "What she meant by that groan is . . ." And Papa hears and understands. While we are not perfect like Papa, we can be present. Because He forgave me, loved me, healed me, and saved me, the one thing I can do is be present for those around me the same way He was present for me. But I cannot do it on my own.

So before you rush into your busy day, take some time with Papa and ask Him to help you put on a heart of compassion, kindness, humility, gentleness, and patience, so you can be present with those around you—forgiving and loving in the same way He forgave and loved us.

Abba, thank You for grace to love others the way You love them.

Enjoy Solitude

My people will live in peaceful dwelling places, in
secure homes, in undisturbed places of rest.

ISAIAH 32:18

Solitude can be daunting when you do not have peace. I was a single mom barely in my thirties, going after my dreams and trying to find myself. I had been with the same company for seven years when they suddenly merged with another company. I had to choose between losing my job or moving myself and my two small boys to Chicago.

Uncertain of what to do, I spent a considerable amount of time crying out to God. I had been a Christian long enough to know I had to hear from God if I was to make the right decision. The deadline came, and I told my superiors I would not be making the move.

The next weekend I attended a Bible conference where I came to a booth advertising a local Bible college. With faith but no finances I did the unexpected and enrolled. Suddenly I found myself in class—and all alone. No job. No coworkers. To my delight I had the greatest contentment and peace I had ever known. Shortly thereafter, my director informed me the company was experiencing a hiring freeze, and she asked me to stay on with the company and service my clients. I could even work from home. This was such a gift from God. Not only was I able to provide for my children, but God had answered my secret prayer to go back to school.

When everything around you seems unstable, don't be afraid to fall right into the Father's arms. He has a plan for you that's even better than what you could come up with on your own.

Father, I place every hard decision in Your hands. Give
me faith and bravery to jump into Your arms.

Lean on God

Commit your way to the LORD; trust in Him also and He will do it.
PSALM 37:5 AMP

*A*lmost everyone knows the popular lyrics to "Lean on Me." Sometimes when my friends are going through tough times, I echo those words, letting them know they can trust and depend on me for whatever they need.

The problem with trust is that once trust is broken, it is hard to get back. My biological father was absent until I was about four years old. The man who became "daddy" to me, sexually abused me until I was twelve. This shattered my trust in men. As the years went by I lived a self-destructive lifestyle. I used men to make me feel valuable. My soul longed for peace and purity, but I didn't know how to find it.

Some years later I met the ultimate Father. It was hard to imagine He could be real. Slowly and gently the love of the Father broke down every wall, stone by abusive stone, until there I stood, blameless and unafraid. He tenderly clothed me in righteousness with a garment of salvation, cleansed me of my past and fears. Years later I could walk into the hospital room where the man who had broken my trust lay dying. Now leaning on the arm of the One who restored my trust, I could lead the one who broke my trust to my heavenly Father. It was a miraculous moment.

You may have had experiences that taught you it was not safe to lean on the ones who should be holding you up. But you can know that the Father will always be there for you. Trust Him. Lean on Him. He'll help you carry on—and become someone others can lean on too.

Father, thank You for being someone I can lean on with no fear.

Kimberly Oliver, Weatherford, TX

Let God Lead

Teach me to do Your will [so that I may please You], for You are
my God; let Your good Spirit lead me on level ground.

PSALM 143:10 AMP

I can remember crying out to God, asking Him to take away the pain
of loneliness. Recently divorced, I was now a single mom, and life
was difficult. I craved a deeper relationship with Him. I heard others
refer to God as Father, but having an absent father as a child made it
difficult for me to think of God as being a Father.

Around that time a good friend, Wendy, came into my life. Wendy's
father was a pastor, and they seemed to have the picture-perfect life. I
went to their home for a Christmas gathering and remember feeling
peace and enjoying the virtues of true family values. That weekend I
read verses in my Bible that said I could ask anything of the Father, and
He would do it for those who love and trust Him. It may sound simple,
but because I didn't have an earthly father I had no concept of how to be
a daughter. I asked Him to show me how to be a daughter.

Everywhere I looked there seemed to be portraits of fathers spending time with their daughters. I noticed fathers nurturing, encouraging,
comforting, and blessing their daughters. Before long I began to understand my role as a daughter. Most importantly I had a clear picture of the
love of my heavenly Father.

If you are learning to be a daughter to your Father God today,
remember to let God lead you. Ask Him to open your eyes and give you
insight into how He loves and cares for you. He may surprise you.

Father, take my hand and lead Your daughter today. In every
situation I know Your comforting arms are there to shield me.

Slow Down

My dear brothers and sisters, always be willing to listen
and slow to speak. Do not become angry easily.
JAMES 1:19 NCV

I often think about what it would be like to live in a less chaotic world. While I am grateful for technology and the advances we have made in how we connect, I often feel we've missed the mark in truly connecting. E-mail, social media, cell phones, Internet, tablets—everything seems to be a way to connect without experiencing real connection.

Lately I have noticed I'm always on the go, running fast, checking things off lists, and not making time for the things that matter most. When I find myself moving too fast, I tend to get my feelings hurt over trivial things. Or I find myself suddenly snapping over something insignificant. When we rush through life, it is easy to get offended or hurt, because we are not investing enough time in God's Word or relationships that matter most.

We not only have to make time for God, we need to make time for one another. I encourage you to make time today to truly connect with someone in a way that makes the other person know how special he or she is to you. Instead of texting, give him or her a call. Rather than email, write a handwritten note. A simple smile, touch, or laugh can make each of our lives better. I am convinced being intentional about slowing down will bring us peace and joy.

Father, give me wisdom to manage my time and energy.
Today help me place my priorities in the right order.

Kimberly Oliver, Weatherford, TX

Think the Thoughts of God

As he thinks in his heart, so is he.
PROVERBS 23:7 NKJV

What you think about will eventually tumble out of your mouth. Conversely, what you speak about often enough will become an action. I know I am guilty of having negative thoughts. When I have an upcoming business prospect or lead on a sale, I can get hung up on thoughts like, *What if something goes wrong? What if the buyer changes his mind? What if the loan falls through?* The truth is, those what-ifs seldom come true. I just put myself under unnecessary stress and anxiety over things that never come to pass.

I am relieved to know that God doesn't think like we do. His thoughts are higher, wiser, and greater than what we imagine. But that doesn't mean we cannot think His thoughts. He gave us His Word so we wouldn't get stuck in our way of thinking. When my thoughts become negative or faithless, my life mirrors those thoughts. When I align my thoughts with His thoughts and speak His promises over my life, my life shifts in a positive direction.

Though each day may not start out perfectly, I've discovered making positive confessions like, "This is the day You have made; I will rejoice and be glad in it," and "Father, I embrace the good plans You have for my life" steers my day in the right direction. I encourage you to begin each day with a positive thought, followed by positive verbal confessions from God's Word. Then what's in your heart will spill out positively in your life.

Father, place Your words in my mouth. May I
think Your thoughts and do Your will.

Serve with Love

*Honor her for all that her hands have done, and let
her works bring her praise at the city gate.*

PROVERBS 31:31

Her hands dice onions, and we choke back tears. When heartbreak comes unannounced, the family rushes toward one another. The women gravitate to the kitchen. We speak in under-the-breath whispers. A baby has died in our family. Who can know why? There are crushed hearts and wails and hunched shoulders and an empty room with a crib. The air is thick with grief. Eyes swell. How did Nana know we needed someone to cook soup? She simmers the onions in broth on the stove, stirring slowly. The sweet steam rises, challenging the bitter air.

What will come now? Will we sink into this death and heartache, or will we rise? This family will never be the same. Grandmothers, nieces, nephews, aunts, uncles, cousins, grandfathers—everyone carries this young couple's loss. Only grace can fill the cavernous void of a baby whose life slipped from her mother's grasp.

These hands will go back to this kitchen again. We will come with love. As Nana shreds the chicken, her aged, veined hands tell stories of heartaches and miracles, a life of prayer. Her hands tell us the secret of real beauty. She serves her family. Her life is private. And it is in private that she sows seeds of faith. Everything we do in the quiet moments of grief reflects everything we are.

It is in the dicing of the onions, the stirring of soup, the service—in private the moments few see—that we find our greatest call. A public light never shines so bright as one who lights her family as a lamp.

Dear God, help me be a light to my loved ones today.

Jennifer Strickland, Colleyville, TX

Receive Good Gifts

The LORD God is a sun and shield; the LORD bestows favor and honor;
no good thing does he withhold from those whose walk is blameless.

PSALM 84:11

As a child, my blue eyes longed to see the sun. One time, lying on the prickly green grass of my backyard, I tried to look straight at it. Today I am nearsighted. Maybe it was my little girl longing to encapsulate the range of the bluest sky, the rich golden rays, the whole landscape that did it.

One day God will be our Lamp. "Now God's presence is with people, and he will live with them. . . . He will wipe away every tear from their eyes, and there will be no more death, sadness, crying, or pain" (Revelation 21:3–4 NCV).

Whatever has been lost will be gained. Everything that has died will be raised to life. Everything that has torn open the soul will no longer bear the mark of loss. Love will fill every void like a crystal fountain in full force.

So just as I did as a child, we must open our eyes. Though we should never try to look at the sun, every day we must search for the Son in all His glory. The more we seek, the more we will find. Whatever you are facing right now, look intently for the Son to shine through those storm clouds. Let go. Know that He is good, and He will give you more than you can imagine. He will withhold from you no good thing. Everything will be redeemed.

Dear God, today I give You my losses, disappointments,
and heartaches. I ask that You take them into Your
able hands and transform them into blessing.

Using Resources Wisely

Remember, O God, that my life is but a breath.

JOB 7:7

When a worn and worried woman walked into the bank and pleaded for overdraft fees to be removed from her account, the teller called Jane, the manager. In her precise way Jane approached the woman the way Jane did everything, with sleek, professional style.

Jane began reviewing the account, thinking it would prove how irresponsible this woman was. Her brow furrowed as she saw that the woman's money went to missionaries and hungry children. Jane's stern demeanor cracked. "When you first told me about this, I thought I would see something very different. But even if I reverse the charges, you will still only have $67.89. Is this the only account you have?"

"Yes," the woman said, explaining her husband had left her with three children. "But I haven't given up my missionaries," she said, smiling. "You just watch! One day I'm going to walk in here and make a big deposit. My God is faithful. If He can trust me with a little, He will entrust me with a lot."

Jane's stern face softened and flushed. Tears spilled down her cheeks. "I am a widow and have been alone most my life. I have worked in this bank for thirty-seven years, and never has anyone affected me the way you have." Jane reversed the charges and taught the woman how to keep a careful ledger of her check register. Whenever Jane wonders if God will care for her, she remembers the woman who walked into the bank and declared His faithfulness.

Dear God, help me be trustworthy with my
finances, and to trust that You will provide.

Jennifer Strickland, Colleyville, TX

Receive More Humility

God opposes the proud but shows favor to the humble.

JAMES 4:6

eth Moore said, "Humbling ourselves is far less painful than inviting God to humble us."[1] For this reason she gets on her knees in front of her audience before she speaks—and so do I.

Who wants to be humbled by God? We all face seasons when circumstances become so painful we wish we could fast-forward or rewind. But we can only face every moment head-on. We can only walk *through* the valley of shadows to reach the pasture.

As a speaker I've always believed God reigns over my schedule. Yet in the most difficult times, He has not released me from speaking. When life deals me a hard hand, I always seem to look down and find a microphone in front of my mouth. He must do this because He knows He can work through us best when we are broken. How else can we touch broken people?

In the breaking of bread He fed thousands—twice. Both times it appeared He had so little to give. But in the end there were baskets full of leftovers. So it is with us. We feel inadequate to fill the great hunger. Yet if we rise to the call to be an offering to a broken and hurting people, He turns our inadequacy into sufficiency; our little becomes a lot.

Our own deep awareness of the pain of the human story makes us great messengers of light during others' darkness. He blesses us, breaks us, and gives us as an offering. Miraculously, we feed the broken.

God, please multiply my little into a lot.

Follow God Fully

God said to Balaam, "You shall not go with them; you
shall not curse the people, for they are blessed."

NUMBERS 22:12 NKJV

The Bible tells a story about a man who searched for God's answer in everything he did. When a powerful king told Balaam to curse the Israelites, Balaam didn't bow down to the king's command. Instead, He told the king's messengers, "Spend the night here . . . and I will report back to you with the answer the LORD gives me" (Numbers 22:8).

When Balaam met with God, God told him no. He slept on it, then replied to the king's princes, "Go back to your own country, for the LORD has refused to let me go with you" (v. 13). The king then sent more influential people, offering a larger reward. Balaam's answer is one we should all memorize: "Even if [the king] gave me all the silver and gold in his palace, I could not do anything great or small to go beyond the command of the LORD my God" (vv. 18–19). He told them to spend the night, while he found out what else the Lord would tell him.

The Lord relented, telling Balaam to go with the men, but to "do only what I tell you" (v. 20). "Do only what I tell you." If there is one way we should live, this is it. When people ask us to do something important, let's go to God first before bowing down to their request.

....

Dear God, I promise to come to You first and hear
what You must say. And then, I promise to obey.

Jennifer Strickland, Colleyville, TX

Receive Divine Protection

He saw the troubles of the people of Israel, and
he was concerned about them.

EXODUS 2:25 NCV

*L*aura's daddy told her never to talk to strangers. But when the man approached her in the park, asking if she had seen his lost puppy, the seven-year-old followed right after him. "See how many times you can go down the slide!" the man called out to Laura's brother, as he grabbed her behind the wall of bushes and pinned her down under the giant oak tree. Laura's helpless body was frozen with fear.

Just then a car crash and the wailing lights of an ambulance made the man run away, leaving Laura tear-stained, her dress dirty and disheveled. Decades later at sixty-six years old, Laura still froze with fear whenever her husband touched her. Some intercessors asked her in a moment of prayer, "Where do you think Jesus was when it happened?"

"Oh, He was right there in the intersection," she said positively. "He was the policeman." Tears streamed from her eyes as they squeezed shut. In her imagination her little-girl body ran toward Jesus.

"Look at Him. What does He say to you?" her prayer partners asked. In her vision Jesus told her it wasn't her fault, that all children disobey their parents sometimes, that He loved her and she was very special to Him. He held and comforted her, telling her she was never alone, that He was always right there with her. The countenance of Laura's face changed that day. Finally she knew she was safe to be touched by her husband who loved her, for the Lord had set her free.

......

Jesus, please show me how You see me. May Your words
spoken during my confusion be the truth that sets me free.

Accept Sudden Promotion

The angel said to him, "Behold, I grant you this request also;
I will not destroy this town of which you have spoken."

GENESIS 19:21 AMP

After college, Courtney returned to the same grocery store job she'd had while in high school. With a child to support she could not risk losing income and was unsure of how to reenter the job market. She felt overwhelmed, as if her dreams were dying. *How does someone discover a way to start life over?*

One day Courtney's pastor asked her a series of thought-provoking questions: "What is your ideal dream job? What would you attempt to do if you weren't afraid of failing?"

Together they brainstormed and came up with possibilities for her future. Then, in faith, they prayed for God's favor and grace. Several months later Courtney became a child welfare specialist. She entered the workplace with the opportunity to change the lives of others.

God knows who to send into our lives to give us that needed push. God's favor and grace are such sweet blessings. They show up, reminding us to trust God because only He knows what is best for our lives. I encourage you to let God lead you into a new season. Sometimes the reason our lives do not see positive change is that we do not ask Him for big things. We are content to believe for small things but stop short of believing for the miraculous. Your dreams may look as if they will never come true. Reach for them anyway. When you surrender your life to God's plan, He will take you further than you can imagine.

Heavenly Father, thank You for favor and for all the
blessings that You have in store for me.

Sandra Pate, Baton Rouge, LA

Walk Away with a Divine Promise

She said, "May your servant find favor in your eyes." Then she went her way and ate something, and her face was no longer downcast.

1 SAMUEL 1:18

*A*t some point we must let go of our desperation and know that God has heard our prayers. What do we do when we've cried, lost sleep, and exhausted our minds looking for solutions? Sometimes the only way to move past a problem is to rely on the promises of God, to take Him at His word and believe He will never tell us something that isn't true.

That's what I had to remind myself as I watched my friend wrestle with mental illness. The depression never seemed to lift, self-medication was a problem, and emotional disconnection with those who loved her was painful to watch. But through it all, we learned to depend on God's supernatural peace.

The Bible speaks of peace that passes all understanding. With our own strength, it's hard to find peace in overwhelming situations. During those times we must rely on Him to bring us safely through our darkest seasons.

I am thankful my friend is no longer controlled by depression and irrational violent outbursts. Today she is self-sufficient, loving, and patient. Because of God's faithfulness her darkest days are behind her.

Can you look past the problems you are facing today and see a hope-filled future? I invite you to ask God to take control of the things that concern you most. He is faithful. His love is unending.

Father in heaven, I trust You to bring me out of where I am to a better place. Strengthen me and give me perfect peace. I do not rely on my wisdom but look to You for answers and solutions.

Build Something Memorable

The one who is wise saves lives.

PROVERBS 11:30

$\mathcal{M}$omma Annie lived to be 115 years old.[2] One day I asked her to explain the secrets of a long, healthy life. In her broken drawl she replied, "Be sure and tell them about the three Fs. Faith is number one. You've got to believe beyond any doubt. Family is second because those are the people God chose for you. Remember, you can have friends and foes right there in the family. So stay close to the ones God gave you. And number three is . . . eat less candy and more fruit."

In her unique way Momma Annie let her children know that the simple things—faith, family, and fruit—needed to be a daily part of life. These were the secrets to her fulfilling journey. Her age wasn't the only thing that made her remarkable. Momma Annie taught her family to keep God at the center of all they did. She believed in building something that would outlast her time on the earth. That's why she taught her family to share their faith, and over many meals she made sure everyone knew the value of salvation.

The Word of God says that the one "who wins souls is wise." What wisdom this sweet little lady born to sharecroppers imparted to us all. She taught us that legacy is measured by the souls we lead to the Lord, not the things we accumulate.

Father, show me how to unify my family. Help me understand that to build a legacy I must teach others about Your love and grace.

Sandra Pate, Baton Rouge, LA

Rise and Accept Divine Opportunity

The angel said to her, "Do not be afraid, Mary,
for you have found favor with God."

LUKE 1:30 ESV

Who starts a modeling career at twenty-eight years old with no prior experience? When you look at me, it's obvious my nose is scarred, my teeth are crooked, and I have a pigeon-toed gait. Yet as I paced the floor waiting to take the first flight to Manhattan, I remember praying, *If this is not You, Lord, please stop me. I need to know that this is Your will for my life.* Although I didn't expect a dramatic sign, I received one. The Holy Spirit directed my attention to a stack of photo albums. I chose the one with toddler pictures in it. And there it was—a photo of me at four years old on the stage during the church Easter parade. I felt that was the confirmation I needed to move forward.

A lady approached me in a restaurant and asked me if I was willing to model. I said yes, and she wrote down a phone number that connected me with an opportunity to model for Oscar de la Renta on the fourth day of my arrival in New York City. I went on to work independently in Milan, London, New Zealand, and other places around the world.

Are you willing to say yes when God presents you with divine opportunities? Do you believe faith can be a fantastic adventure? I hope you will embrace the things God sends your way. There are assignments only you can fulfill. Trust His plan to lead you somewhere new.

Father God, You are the only one who knows my story from beginning to end. You know how to position me where I need to be. I look forward to great things in my future.

Get Comfortable in a New Place

*God granted Daniel favor and compassion in the
sight of the commander of the officials.*

DANIEL 1:9 AMP

*T*he riot consumed the city, and the National Guard was called in as things escalated. While violence raged around the Stevens family, a nine-year-old child wondered, *When will the violence stop?*

On her knees she asked God to move her family to another place. She trusted God to take her family far away from the darkness of the city. The answer came when her father announced he had received an unexpected job transfer. While other family members were unsure if moving far away was a good idea, the child knew that God had given them favor and would prosper their journey.

Adults aren't the only ones who hear from heaven. God fills children with His wisdom, knowledge, and understanding. During tough times it is important to listen to their voices as well. In fact Jesus showed great wisdom in His early childhood. He went to the temple to learn and share the mysteries of God.

In whatever situation you find yourself, you must trust that God has placed someone there to affirm your faith, make your way easier, and help you along the journey. Don't rule out someone's wisdom because of age, gender, or social background. God will use someone you least expect to send the answer you are looking for.

Heavenly Father, Your comfort and peace wherever I go.
Help me be more sensitive to those around me. Give me eyes
to see You in them and ears to hear You through them.

Sandra Pate, Baton Rouge, LA

Receive Unexpected Recognition

"Even the Son of Man did not come to be served, but to serve, and to give his life as a ransom for many."

MARK 10:45

For thirty-one years Mary was the first one to arrive and the last one to leave the church. With her servant's heart and good attitude, she was willing to take on any task. Whenever others needed help, she was there ready to assist. Imagine how surprised Mary was when the entire church gave her a surprise party, celebrating her years of service. Her face glowed as she was presented with gifts, a banquet, and cards filled with gratitude.

Those who have a servant's heart make themselves available to meet the needs of others. Their focus isn't turned inward but outward; they don't look for others to meet their needs but look to meet the needs of others. They understand by serving others with a spirit of excellence they are honoring the Lord. It is rare to find someone who is so unselfish in how they serve others.

Jesus defined a servant's heart this way: "Even the Son of Man did not come to be served, but to serve, and to give his life as a ransom for many." It is incredible to imagine the Son of God came to the earth to serve humanity. He could have taken on the form of a king, but He chose the role of a servant. It is important that we serve others with a pure heart, not for praise or recognition but because we love God and share His heart in wanting to meet the needs of others.

Father, help me love You more by serving Your people with Your heart.

Wrap Yourself in Love

Beyond all these things put on and wrap yourselves in [unselfish] love, which is the perfect bond of unity [for everything is bound together in agreement when each one seeks the best for others].

COLOSSIANS 3:14 AMP

*I*n the woods of East Texas, temperatures don't usually dip below freezing, and they rarely stay cold long enough to sustain snowfall. Last year when my family visited New York City, it didn't take us long to discover we hadn't packed enough cold-weather clothes. Instantly we knew we would have to buy hats, gloves, and scarves to wrap ourselves up so we didn't freeze to death.

I wish I could wrap myself in love this easily. The icy chill of selfishness always sneaks into my thoughts, convincing me to look out only for myself. It's when I step into the love of God that I begin to place the needs of others before my own. His love cloaks me like a warm blanket on the coldest day in winter. His love thaws out my hardened heart, and I am free to love authentically. For that moment I can feel the perfection of God's love: pure, sincere, and beautiful.

God's Word challenges us to *put on* love and *wrap ourselves in* love. Wrapping ourselves in love means we immerse ourselves in God's love until it fully envelops us. Without this wrapping action we live cold and frigid lives, and remain detached from others. But with it we find unity, agreement, and generosity.

Father, Your love is perfect and unselfish. Wrap me in Your love and help me seek the best for others. Help me to love like You do.

Shana Strange, Longview, TX

Rescue the Captive

> When Abram learned that Lot had been captured, he called out
> his 318 trained men who had been born in his camp. He led the
> men and chased the enemy all the way to the town of Dan.
>
> GENESIS 14:14 NCV

*F*our powerful kings ransacked Lot's hometown and took his family captive. Wasting no time, Abram gathered his men together and set out to rescue his nephew, Lot.

Have you ever felt captured by a hidden addiction, toxic relationship, or dark situation? I have. When I had a food addiction, a friend loved me enough to step in and intervene. My addiction had plundered my soul, and I felt helpless to change. Most days I felt miserable, and I internally ridiculed myself for not being stronger. But the truth is, sometimes Christians just need the help of others. Thankfully, between the love of my friend and God's strength, I overcame the darkness. She rescued me from an unhealthy lifestyle that would have destroyed my life.

God's Word reveals that "where the Spirit of the Lord is, there is freedom" (2 Corinthians 3:17). The heart of the Father is to see you free from everything that would hold you back in this life. Freedom is available to anyone who desires to be made whole. The beautiful part is that once you are free from the thing that binds us, you can rescue others.

If you have struggled and overcome in an area, go and share that freedom with others. Be like Abram running to the rescue of his nephew. Run after them. Rescue them. Give back to others in the area you have received.

Father, help me run after the lost and broken like You do. Show me how to love without limits, and never let fear hold me back from reaching out.

Cast Off Fear

There is no fear in love. But perfect love drives out fear, because fear has to do with punishment. The one who fears is not made perfect in love.

1 JOHN 4:18

When our business failed, I wept for days. My tear-streaked face revealed what my makeup could not conceal: fear. In that moment I felt as if someone had squeezed the life out of me. My emotions were a wreck; I even wondered if God was punishing us. I kept questioning, *Did we miss God's will?* Nothing made sense.

After years of owning a business, the economy forced us to liquidate our inventory and close our doors. Our lives were turned upside down in a matter of weeks. The hardest part was, we didn't have a safety net of savings stashed away. All we had left was our faith.

Even though this was a dark season in our lives, I learned a lot about the constant love of God. In fact I discovered His love overcomes our greatest fears. Even when we deserve punishment for our mistakes, His love overshadows our failures.

During this season my true thoughts about the love of God were revealed. On paper I said the right things about God's love. I could describe His faithfulness to others but could not embrace it for myself. When our lives came unraveled, I realized I didn't fully believe those things. I still believed the lie I needed to deserve His love or, worse, He would punish me for wrong choices.

But that's the thing about this great love; it can't be earned, bartered, or sold. It's constantly reaching, even during the darkest times.

Father, open my eyes to Your extravagant love. Teach me to immerse myself in it when I'm tempted to clothe myself in fear.

Shana Strange, Longview, TX

Carve a Path

Also you shall purposely pull out for her some stalks [of grain] from the sheaves and leave them so that she may collect them, and do not rebuke her.
RUTH 2:16 AMP

I felt the tentacles of hopelessness latch on to my heart. My feet had sunk deep into the muck of my life and I found myself in the middle of a mess. My husband and I felt the weight of despair crashing down on us like a ton of bricks. Being newlyweds at the ages of eighteen and twenty seemed like a good idea until the bills began to stack up and my husband lost his job. Then I lost my college scholarship and couldn't find employment.

But God provided for us through the generosity of my parents. My dad took my husband under his wing and helped him start a business. Those early years were difficult, but God helped us overcome our financial struggles. Over the years we started five different businesses—all because someone carved a path for us.

Living in a self-absorbed culture, it is easy to focus only on our needs and desires. But carving a path for someone else echoes the heart of God. From my parents' generosity, we not only started businesses but ministries as well. My parents probably didn't know that carving a path for us helped build the kingdom too. In the same way you never know where your generosity will lead.

Father, I want to love deeply like You. Teach me to live openhanded. Help me be intentional in leaving behind resources for others. I want to create a path for others to follow.

Reach for Others

She opens and extends her hand to the poor, and she reaches out her filled hands to the needy.

PROVERBS 31:20 AMP

I went to lunch late one day feeling *beyond* hungry. *Beyond* hungry is different from just plain old hungry. It's a state of hunger where one feels agitated stomach pains and experiences emotional outbursts. I ordered my food online, hoping it would be ready when I arrived. I stood at the counter smelling the delicious barbecue sauce, grilled chicken, and potato wedges. I couldn't wait to shovel the food in my mouth and silence the hunger monster.

But on my way out the door, I saw him sitting there. Disheveled. Dirty. Sad. I wondered how many days had passed since he last showered or enjoyed a meal. I knew I needed to hand him my food. I hesitated. My growling stomach made we want to protest the nudge to give up my lunch. Then I thought about how easy it would be for me to grab something else on the way back to work. I handed him my bag, and he graciously accepted it.

It felt good. For those brief moments I felt incredibly blessed. Instead of a clenched fist, I opened my hand and reached out to someone who was hurting.

We live in a culture that casts the unwanted away, but God tells us to reach for them. Clothe them. Feed them. For heaven's sake, help them. If as believers we won't help the hurting, broken, and lonely, who will?

Father, daily remind me to reach for others, just like You do for me. Teach me to live selflessly.

Shana Strange, Longview, TX

Covenant Friendship

Jonathan made an agreement with David, because
he loved David as much as himself.

1 SAMUEL   ADD: 18:3 NCV

My mom made my sister fix my hair and drive me to school. I'm sure most days I stepped on her last nerve, especially when her busy high school life of cheerleading and boys needed attention. I suppose most big sisters get annoyed by needy younger siblings.

But my sister's life changed when at seventeen she found herself in an abusive marriage with a baby on the way. Life shifted quickly, and she morphed into a grown-up overnight. Over the next few years, we became the best of friends.

Before long we were doing everything together: raising our children, serving in ministry, and taking vacations together. During the darkest times in life she was my safe place. I've shared things with her no one else will ever know. Along the journey we have laughed, cried, and grieved our losses.

As I look back over my life, I realize my sister and I fit the biblical definition of being in a *covenant relationship*. The only thing that can separate us is death, and even then, I feel we will be best friends in heaven and our houses will be close to each other.

Covenant relationships are rare and beautiful. Never take the gift of friendship for granted. How about you? Do you have someone in your life you consider the best kind of friend? What can you do to express your gratitude to him or her and be a better friend to that person in return?

Father, thank You for reminding me of the value of a covenant friendship.

Pick Up the Fragments

When they had all had enough to eat, he said to his disciples,
"Gather the pieces that are left over. Let nothing be wasted."
JOHN 6:12

*T*he crowds were large and growing by the day as Jesus went about teaching and healing.

Even as He tried to remove Himself from the pressing crowds, He felt compassion for them. They had followed Him for days, and everyone was hungry. Unwilling to leave them weak and wandering about the desert, He performed a miracle and fed the masses following Him.

Just when everyone was full of fish and bread, He gave His disciples a simple instruction: *pick up the fragments.* Jesus was paying attention to the details of their lives. He didn't want anyone or anything to go overlooked.

The same is true in our lives. In a culture where some people are written off as insignificant, Jesus stops and pays attention to their needs. Those the world would discard, the ones who have made mistakes, abused their bodies, or wasted their lives are the ones Jesus takes time with.

By instructing His disciples to pick up the fragments, He made it clear that nothing or no one goes unnoticed. He paid attention to everyone: prostitutes, thieves, traitors, and tax collectors. The same should be true in our lives; we should be intentional about reaching out to everyone. In fact, why not take time to create a list of those we know who may need an extra word of encouragement, an opportunity, or simply a friend to confide in?

....

Father, help me pay attention to the small
details I would otherwise overlook.

Nora Ross, High Ridge, MO

Cultivate Good Speech

Let your conversation be always full of grace, seasoned with salt, so that you may know how to answer everyone.

COLOSSIANS 4:6

I am always concerned my words will become a part of someone's list of *things to never say*. There are so many blogs and articles advising us on what we should or shouldn't say. There is one titled "Ten Things You Should Never Say to Someone Who Is Grieving." Another tells us "What Not to Say to Someone Having a Panic Attack." Another one warns us "What Not to Say on a First Date," and, my favorite, "Things You Should Never Say in Front of Your Pet."

With all the political correctness and warnings of what we shouldn't say, I've often wondered if there is anything we *can* say without getting into trouble? Not long ago, I found myself wondering if I should quote a verse to someone who was having a bad day.

Maybe we feel uncertain about whether what we are saying lines up with God's definition of *good speech*. Or we even wonder if what we are asking God for lines up with His will for our lives. We want the most beautiful or handsome spouse, even though they may not be the person God has for us. We want to be well and live forever, when God has a plan for our eternity. God's definition of *good* may be different from what we call good.

When our thoughts and words are in line with our Father's, we can ask anything of Him and have assurance that He hears and answers our prayers.

....

Father, place Your words within my mouth. Let
me respond with wisdom and love.

Embrace Godly Regret

Sadness as intended by God produces a repentance that leads to
salvation, leaving no regret, but worldly sadness brings about death.

2 CORINTHIANS 7:10 NET

Say you're sorry" is a phrase we often teach our children to say right
after they've pushed another child down or taken something that
isn't theirs. We also tell them to quote this phrase when they say unkind
or disrespectful things. I've often wondered, *Are we really helping them by
forcing them to say something they may not feel or mean?*

I've learned that sometimes a child will say these words to avoid
discipline. I've even watched a child say sorry as he was pushing his sister
to the ground! As funny as this may sound, I am not sure God would
ever ask us to say we're sorry unless we mean it. Sorry isn't a quick route
to repentance. It should be a heartfelt feeling of remorse or regret. God
desires us to feel regret for sins. The regret should keep us from commit-
ting the same sin again.

Society tells us today to apologize even if we are not remorse-
ful. Although this sounds good, this version of sorrow only lasts for
a moment. It has no power to create lasting change. By contrast, God
desires for us to have a heart that longs to please rather than disappoint
Him. God's version of sorrow will lead to lasting hope. As we experience
true sorrow for our sins, we experience victory and peace.

....

Father, today I let go of all excuses, and I choose to live victoriously.
Cleanse my heart, and give me a heart that longs to please You.

Outgrow Your Surroundings

The LORD is my shepherd; I shall not want. He makes me to lie down
in green pastures; He leads me beside the still waters. He restores my
soul; He leads me in the paths of righteousness for His name's sake.

PSALM 23:1–3 NKJV

*F*or many years the church my husband and I pastored needed additional property. Our congregation was outgrowing the building we were currently using, and there was no room to build or add on rooms. Knowing we had to move, we began looking for a larger facility.

My husband, Dan, and I spent many days praying and looking at properties. A while into the search, we found a Christian camp in our community. We became friends with the owners and shared our vision of what we would like to do with the property. One day in late spring, Jack, the owner, told Dan how much the property was worth and told him he felt God wanted us to have it. Dan was excited Jack was willing to sell, but the truth was, we didn't have 10 percent of what the property was worth. To our surprise Jack said he would sell the site to us for a quarter of its value.

It was hard for us to wrap our minds around the size of what we were considering buying. The property had more than seventy-seven acres and contained two football fields. It wasn't long before God helped us move into the miracle property. Along with the move came peace and assurance that this was the place we were supposed to be.

Maybe you are in a season where you have outgrown your surroundings. I encourage you to have faith and believe that God will position you exactly where you need to be next.

....

Father, order my steps with Your words. Show
me where and when I am to expand.

Stop Recording Your Failures

You will again have compassion on us; you will tread our sins underfoot and hurl all our iniquities into the depths of the sea.

MICAH 7:19

I accepted Jesus into my heart when I was in the second grade. Looking back now, I find it humorous to think of *how* and *why* I accepted Christ. I had a dear aunt who talked to me about things that were to happen as detailed in the book of Revelation. She described the rapture of the church and the time of tribulation that is to come. She told me if I didn't accept Christ, I would not go to heaven. And worse, if I was left on the earth and didn't take the mark of the beast, they would cut off my hands and head. This seems like a very frightening way to make a seven-year-old accept Christ . . . but it worked!

As a young girl I was afraid I was going to slip up and sin and miss Jesus' return to the earth. It took many years before I understood God's goodness and grace. I was in constant fear of doing something that would displease the Lord. I often recorded my sins so I could make sure to ask forgiveness for all of them. It was a huge relief to realize God was not keeping track of all my sins. The truth was, the sins I kept repenting over had already been washed away by grace. If I had remained in bondage, keeping track of my sins, I wouldn't have experienced freedom to overcome them.

One of the things I love most about God is His amazing goodness. He shows us our need for forgiveness, and then grants it.

Father, thank You for unending grace and for wiping all our sins away.

Nora Ross, High Ridge, MO

Know God's Healing

Jesus turned and saw her. "Take heart, daughter," he said, "your faith
has healed you." And the woman was healed at that moment.

MATTHEW 9:22

My sister-in-law was fifty-six years old when she died very suddenly. We did not even have a chance to tell her goodbye. We had prayed for her to be healed. I even stayed after everyone had left. I did not want her to be alone when God healed her and she woke up. Our family still struggles with her loss. I read verses such as the one in Matthew and think, *Why was this woman healed and not my sister-in-law?*

God has taught me many things through the tragic loss of my sister-in-law. First, God is with us no matter what happens. He celebrates our physical healing, and He walks with us when we experience the death of a loved one. Second, God still heals. There is no disease too complicated or issue too small for Him to heal. He is interested in everything that happens in our lives, whether big or small. Third, God's timing transcends ours. He does not view death as we do. He sees it as a transition into His presence. After my sister-in-law took her last breath, I saw the words "And the woman was healed at that moment" in a new way. At that moment my sister-in-law was made whole in heaven.

Does every prayer for healing end in healing? Yes, when our definition of healing lines up with God's viewpoint. In every situation let us remember God is our Healer.

··

Father, thank You for healing my body Your way. Today I lean
on You to restore my mind, soul, and energy. Even when I face
uncertainty and tragedy, I place my confidence in You.

Number Your Days

Teach us to number our days, that we may cultivate
and bring to You a heart of wisdom.
PSALM 90:12 AMP

Have you ever wondered what the phrase "number your days" means? It's not the ability to count how many days we have lived or to predict how many days we have remaining. It's a gentle reminder that we only have so many days on this earth to live out our purpose. It is meant to encourage us to seize the day by living each day to the fullest.

Recognizing we only have so much time is a gentle nudge to make sure we are spending our time wisely. It will also encourage us to grow in wisdom. We are accountable for how we spend the time God gives us. We need to make sure we are doing the things He wants us to do and not just the things we enjoy doing. If we honor God with our time, we will work toward filling our days with things that will bring Him glory.

There are 8,760 hours in our year. What will we do with the time we are given? How will this year be better than the year before?

Remember to keep every dream, hope, relationship, and challenge in the proper perspective. If you feel time is slipping away, ask God to redeem your days in the earth. He will restore what feels like wasted time. He will redeem every season in your life.

....

Gracious Lord, I treasure each day You give me. Thank You for the opportunity to live each day with great purpose in mind. Teach me to number my days, that I may grow in wisdom and truth.

LisaKay Kaye Gurney, Frisco, TX

Write the Vision

Then the LORD answered me and said: "Write the vision and make it
plain on tablets, that he may run who reads it. For the vision is yet for an
appointed time; but at the end it will speak, and it will not lie. Though
it tarries, wait for it; because it will surely come, it will not tarry."

HABAKKUK 2:2–3 NKJV

*L*ife has a way of bringing us to a place where we need to make
a fresh start. Sometimes we arrive at that place because of our
actions, but sometimes God brings us to a place of newness because He
has something beautiful in store for our lives.

You may be starting over right now. Maybe you're working toward
breaking a bad habit, or you feel you have drifted away from a dream or
calling. It could be you need to get your finances in order. Whatever it is,
follow God and let Him give you a fresh start. I encourage you to leave
bad decisions in your past and focus on the new things God is placing
before you. The journey may not be easy. Yes, it may take a while to get
on track, but patiently wait. His promises will come to pass. Just because
something is delayed doesn't mean it can't or won't come to pass. Have
faith in His plan.

Father, regardless of what has happened in the past, help me look
up from where I am now. Thank You for setting a new beginning
before me. I will wait patiently on Your plan. When You tell me,
I will bravely step forward and walk out Your calling for me.

Ask Difficult Questions

When the queen of Sheba heard about the fame of Solomon and his relationship to the LORD, she came to test Solomon with hard questions.

1 KINGS 10:1

*A*s a founder of a nonprofit organization, I spend time with amazing life coaches and ministry and business leaders. Whenever we are together, I try to ask as many questions as possible. I've learned that asking difficult questions provides powerful insights and solutions. I am mindful not only to ask questions but to be quiet, listen, and take notes on the wisdom others are sharing.

Do you need wisdom in this season of life? Is God asking you to do something hard or something outside of your comfort zone? I encourage you to embrace the opportunity to seek out wisdom. View the new challenge as a way to grow in the strength and character of Christ. Trust that He knows what is best for you. He wants to help you. He also wants to reveal things to you that will help others draw close to the heart of the Father.

Our words have more impact on others than we imagine. Words, when planted in the mind and heart, produce fruit. It is important to watch over our words, speaking only those things that are good, pleasing, and full of wisdom. Let's use our words to form good questions, so we can gain wisdom.

....

Lord God, I want to be a lifelong learner. I have a long way to go, but I desire to learn from You and those You have planted in my life. Give me a teachable spirit. May my words please Your heart.

LisaKay Kaye Gurney, Frisco, TX

Give Lavishly

When they had come into the house, they saw the young Child with Mary His mother, and fell down and worshiped Him. And when they had opened their treasures, they presented gifts to Him: gold, frankincense, and myrrh.

MATTHEW 2:11 NKJV

How often we think we have nothing to give, yet compared to much of the world, we have a lot to offer. We have so many worldly comforts, and often, rather than helping others, we want more.

To be honest, I am sometimes tempted to ignore the needs of others because I simply don't know how to help them. When I am at a loss for how to help, I run to my Father in prayer, asking Him to show me how I can bless others. Sometimes the greatest blessing is to point others to the heart of God, the One who holds the keys and all the answers.

Giving isn't always about monetary exchange. A great way to bless others is to give away clothes you or your children no longer wear. We can share food from our surplus or go without some of what we have and give to food pantries. Above all, we can give love. A hug, smile, or kind word can go a long way with people who need to know others care for them. My motto is, "No matter how little you have, you can always find something to give."

Life is like an echo: In the measure we give to others, God will give to us. What we send out will come back. What we sow, in time, we will reap.

Dear Jesus, forgive me for the times I've ignored the needs of those You have placed in my path. Use me to bring hope to the hopeless and Your peace to those in pain.

Invest in the Word

She considers a field and buys it; from her profits she plants a vineyard.
PROVERBS 31:16 NKJV

The above verse reminds me of my precious grandmother, whom I called Nanny. She was a woman of strength, love, and faith. And, most importantly, she loved God deeply.

I loved staying with Nanny on the weekends. I'd wake up early on Sunday mornings to the smell of coffee brewing. I knew if I was quiet, I could peek out my bedroom door and see her sitting in her favorite chair. Her Bible would be lying open in her lap and her coffee cup would be right beside her.

As I walk back through my childhood memories, I am thankful for a wonderful grandmother who placed in me qualities I would carry through life. It was her influence that led me to fear God, work hard, help others, and have concern for those less fortunate.

Nanny has been with the Lord now for more than thirty years, and I miss her dearly. And still, when I wake up, my thoughts drift to her and I find myself doing the things she once loved: making my favorite coffee, sitting in my favorite chair studying the Bible, and talking with my Lord. In His goodness God places us around other people who can help grow our gifts and develop our talents. The greatest thing we can do is pour our time and love into each other.

Father, may I have a heart of humility. Give me the strength
to serve rather than be served, and teach me to invest in
others wisely. I want to be used by You as You see fit.

LisaKay Kaye Gurney, Frisco, TX

Lead Others Gently

But the wisdom that comes from heaven is first of all pure; then peace-loving, considerate, submissive, full of mercy and good fruit, impartial and sincere.

JAMES 3:17

I believe most of us admire strength. It's something we tend to respect in others, desire for others, and desire for ourselves. Strength is the ability to do things that need a lot of physical or mental effort. It's the choice to continue through the pain even when it feels unbearably hard.

As we journey through life, we will have to make many decisions. If we choose to let our emotions get ahead of godly wisdom or good counsel, we will find ourselves in trouble. God wants us to make wise decisions. Walking in wisdom is choosing to do now what we will be happy with later.

We must walk in God's wisdom realizing the choices we make today will affect us down the road. Our actions are based on our choices in this moment. Our actions are based on what we've decided to make of ourselves, not on what life has dealt us.

Gentleness breeds peace, calm, and consistency of character. The gentle person attracts the trust of others because of this strength.

Make the choice that will ultimately benefit you and everyone else in your world. No matter how unfair or unjust or disappointing life may be, choose to look ahead, act ahead, live ahead and get ahead.

Heavenly Father, help me to follow You on good days and bad days. Set my pace so it complements and does not compete with Your purpose. When my concerns begin to consume me, Your love will perfect each one with unfailing grace. In Jesus' name, amen.

Give Faith a Voice

The prayer of faith will restore the one who is
sick, and the Lord will raise him up.

JAMES 5:15 AMP

*M*any years ago I tried sharing my faith with a neighbor. As I talked, she politely listened but quickly changed the subject. One day her dog, Max, was hit by a passing car, which injured his legs. Madeline's husband wasn't home, her baby was crying, and she was upset. My daughter, who was seven years old, ran over to find out what was going on. Seeing what happened, she said to Madeline, "You should call my mom so she can pray for Max."

In desperation, she called and shared what happened, nervously asking me to come over to pray for him. I'm not sure she envisioned me laying hands on her dog and praying specifically for his back, hip, and legs to be healed. But as I prayed, calmness came upon Madeline and peace filled the room. Before my daughter and I had time to get home, Madeline called. Excited, crying, and laughing, she explained that Max had gotten up, walked around, and had begun acting like his normal self.

Faith is believing God is true to His word. When something goes wrong in our lives or with those we love, our first reaction should be to pray in faith believing God will hear and answer our request.

Our faith is built by speaking God's Word out loud. Today, whatever challenge you are facing, take this opportunity to pray bold, confident prayers in faith. And watch the Father do what He said He would do.

Lord, when I face challenging situations, help me call out to You in faith. I trust You will uphold Your word and fulfill all Your promises.

Karen Brown, Branson, MO

Speak Healing Words

For God did not give us a spirit of timidity or cowardice or fear, but [He has given us a spirit] of power and of love and of sound judgment and personal discipline [abilities that result in a calm, well-balanced mind and self-control].

2 TIMOTHY 1:7 AMP

*F*ear is not from God. When we walk in a spirit of fear, it is impossible for us to live out our faith. Fear not only stops us in our tracks but it produces stress, panic attacks, anxiety, and depression. God didn't create us to feel overwhelmed by life, but He promised His Spirit would give us peace, love, and a healthy, balanced mind.

The enemy is good at whispering words of defeat. The truth is, his lies are the exact opposite of what the Holy Spirit longs to do through and for you. The Holy Spirit, who resides in you, is ready to speak words of life, hope, and healing over you. He longs for you to embrace the good things God has already reserved for you.

Remember, within you is supernatural strength and power to face your fears. When you recognize fearful thinking, you can replace negative thoughts with positive words. Instead of agreeing with the lies of your enemy, you can counteract those thoughts by confessing and saying aloud, "God did not give me a spirit of fear, but of power and love and a sound mind." Sing it, say it out loud, and keep it anchored in the center of your thoughts. Keep before you the truth: you are blessed and loved by your heavenly Father.

....

Father, help me recognize my fears before the enemy tries to use them against me. Help me embrace the healthy mind You've given me.

Do Something New

A man who had been unable to walk from birth was being carried along, whom they used to set down every day at that gate of the temple which is called Beautiful, so that he could beg alms from those entering the temple.

ACTS 3:2 AMP

*T*he book of Acts shares the story of a lame man who spent his life relying on the compassion of other people. Every day his friends arrived early to carry him to the spot where he would sit and beg for money. Late in the evening his friends would return and carry him back to his house. He spent years of his life waiting for others to meet his needs.

One day Peter and John, Jesus' disciples, passed by the man and asked if he would like to receive healing. Excited, the man said yes. He embraced the opportunity and received his miracle. Arising from his mat, he began to stand, walk, then leap. Excited, he ran into the temple and praised God for his miracle. The simple action of saying yes to the healing power of God transformed his life forever.

One of the greatest miracles we can receive is the transforming power of God. When we invite Jesus into our hearts, we give Him the opportunity to transform our lives from the inside out. For some, this means healing in our bodies, receiving wholeness in areas where we've been broken. For others, this means the restoration of fractured relationships.

We don't always receive what we ask for in the way we think it should come packaged. Sometimes God gives us something better than what we feel we deserve. Today embrace the goodness of God. Receive His invitation to receive something good—something new.

Lord, I stand ready to receive unexpected gifts,
healings, miracles, and increase.

Karen Brown, Branson, MO

Reach Again

She thought to herself, "If I can just touch his robe, I will be healed."

MARK 5:28 NLT

*A*s Christians, we believe divine healing is an essential part of the gospel. Through His death and resurrection, Christ made a way for us to receive healing from anything that harms our minds, emotions, or bodies. Many times I have been asked, "Do you believe in faith healing or divine healing?" I believe they are linked together. Healing is divine because we have no power to receive healing apart from Him. It is also *faith* healing, because faith ignites or sets into motion our healing.

I've often wondered, *If God can and does heal people, then why do some experience healing while others do not? Is it all up to God or is there something we can do?* Our faith is the key to our victory. Through faith and patience we can tap into the healing power God has made available to each of us. If you are praying for healing, keep praying until you see it happen.

Stand on the healing promises contained in God's Word. Most important, expect to receive the miracle God has laid up for you.

In the book of Mark we read the story of a woman who had an issue of blood. She spent all her money relying on the opinions of doctors only to find her condition was growing worse. It wasn't until she came to Jesus that she received her healing. When she reached out to Him, Jesus said, "Your faith has made you well" (5:34 NKJV). Today if you need healing or know someone who does, reach out to Jesus. He longs to make you 100-percent whole.

....

Father, thank You for divine healing. I have faith to believe
that with one touch, one word, You can make me whole.

Be Made Whole

[He] pardons all your iniquities, [and] heals all your diseases.
PSALM 103:3 NASB

God is faithful and full of compassion. When I need to remember His goodness, I like to read Psalm 103. It highlights some of my favorite truths: *He forgives all our sins.* God loves us so much He forgives our sins completely and wipes them away, so they can never be found again. He doesn't leave our transgressions lying around so He can use them against us. No, He wipes them away, and He does not remember they happened.

An amazing thing occurs when we repent and turn from our sins. God promises to send times of refreshing our way. He also promises to heal all our diseases. Healing comes in many ways. At times God will use our body's natural healing process. On other occasions He uses the invention of medicine or wisdom of medical doctors. Sometimes it is the combination of both. We can say with confidence that all healing power is from the Lord.

If you need healing, I encourage you to read Psalm 103 in its entirety. It highlights how God redeems our lives from destruction, and how He crowns us with loving kindness and tender mercy. It goes on to say that He satisfies our mouths with good things so we are renewed as the eagle. It talks about how our Father executes righteousness and judgment for us against oppression. It is one of the best chapters on healing and divine protection. As you read it, let those words wash over your soul and bring life to you.

Father, help me recall the wonderful provisions
You make available to me each new day.

Karen Brown, Branson, MO

Rise Up

He went up and touched the coffin, and the people who were carrying it stopped. Jesus said, "Young man, I tell you, get up!"
LUKE 7:14 NCV

I love this account of Jesus raising a dead boy to life again. I cannot imagine the pain his mother felt the day of her son's burial. That morning she was scheduled to lay her only son in the grave next to her husband. Alone as a grieving mother and widow, her encounter with Jesus was nothing short of supernatural.

When we face the dark seasons in life, remember Jesus is walking right beside us. He promises never to leave or forsake us (Deuteronomy 31:6). With His strength we can rise up from anything the world throws our way. His word to us is exactly what He spoke to the young man in the coffin, "Young man [young woman], I tell you, get up!" I find it interesting that He didn't offer those words as a suggestion, but gave them as a command.

Today it's time for you to rise up and fulfill the assignment God has entrusted to you. *Rise up* where God has planted you to share your faith with those who don't know Christ. *Rise up* and help your family to know the truth of God's Word. Teach your family how to love one another and create an atmosphere of peace. *Rise up* and discover ways to serve your community. *Rise up* and oppose the enemy when he threatens to destroy your family. Arise and live a healthy, whole, joy-filled life.

Jesus, I ask You to take my hand and give me confidence to arise. Help me arise from any kind of trouble that's been limiting or weakening me. Today I refuse to let the cares of this life bury me, while there is still so much for me to do.

Open Locked Doors

Suddenly there was such a violent earthquake that the
foundations of the prison were shaken. At once all the prison
doors flew open, and everyone's chains came loose.

ACTS 16:26

Sometimes life can hit us hard in ways we've never considered. I found myself exhausted, passionless, and wanting to quit. I was filled with depression and anxiety and felt there was no way out of a situation. I felt emotionally imprisoned. The more my mind magnified the situation, the harder things became.

At some point I had to remind myself that Christ was my strength. He held the power to change negative things going on around me. I knew during my darkest moments, I had the opportunity to worship.

Locked away in prison, Paul and Silas realized they had an opportunity to praise God during adverse circumstances. As they began to sing and worship, their praise unlocked not only their chains but those of everyone else in the prison. That is a good reminder: when we create an environment of worship, everyone has the opportunity to encounter freedom. Who would find encouragement or experience freedom because you choose to worship?

You may not be physically locked up in prison today, but if you find yourself struggling in your mind, heart, or soul, I encourage you to take time to worship the One who can set you free. Praise unlocks closed doors—whether those doors lead to financial freedom, new opportunities, or healing.

Dear Jesus, thank You for setting me free and for
reminding me that I am a prisoner no longer.

DeLana Rutherford, Atlanta, GA

Celebrate the Small Successes

The godly are happy; they rejoice before God and are overcome with joy.
PSALM 68:3 NET

I'm not qualified. I don't have what they have. I can't do it like they do it." We have all compared ourselves to others. Why do we fall into the trap of comparison? Why can't we be more content with our lives?

Society puts so much pressure on us to be "in" with the popular crowd, to be high achievers, to look like fashion models, and to be wealthy. Social media can lead us to make false assumptions that others are living better, if not flawless, lives. When we believe those lies, we discount the good things happening to us.

But if we take time to reflect on how far we have come in our journeys, we would be more content. A simple joy comes in knowing we may not be where we want to be, but we are further down the road than we once were.

When is the last time you took a moment and thought about something you have accomplished? Did that thought make you smile? We can all get better at celebrating the small achievements in life. Maybe you made it through a tough situation you didn't think you could handle. *Celebrate.* Maybe you skipped the frozen yogurt and ran a few miles instead. *Celebrate.* Or maybe you could have gossiped about a good friend but refused. *Celebrate.*

Today whatever the accomplishment, big or small, look in the mirror and say, "Girl, you are beautiful." You are killing the game! Believe it!

Dear Jesus, I pray that my life will be a testimony for
others. Help me celebrate every season of life.

Express Our Affection

Set your mind and keep focused habitually on the things above [the heavenly things], not on things that are on the earth [which have only temporal value].

COLOSSIANS 3:2 AMP

I absolutely love to decorate and shop! I truly believe in retail therapy. In 2013, I finally made one of my dreams come true and opened my first boutique. I will never forget the adrenaline rush I felt the first time the doors opened. I was focused on my customers, making sure every little thing was in place. As I started to figure out what everyone loved and wanted, I was energized to go after my dreams even more.

I found myself spending countless hours searching for the right fabrics, gifts, and décor that would continue to bring people into my boutique. Yet, when I stop to think about how much I enjoy running my company, I can't help but remember how temporal these things really are in comparison to eternity. It is important we don't get so caught up in things, accolades, or passions that we forget to take time to express our love for God. One way we show our love for Him is by spending time with Him.

I grew up thinking my time with the Lord needed to be in a closet or somewhere closed off from the world—that I needed to spend at least an hour praying or He would be displeased with me. Later I discovered that wasn't the case. He wants to hear from us throughout the day and longs to be a part of our lives in the simplest ways. So even as we go about our daily business, doing the things we love to do, let's visit with Him and ask for His wisdom in keeping everything in perspective.

Lord, as I go through today I want to spend time with
You and get to know Your thoughts and ways.

DeLana Rutherford, Atlanta, GA

Shift Your Focus

I will meditate on your majestic, glorious splendor
and your wonderful miracles.

PSALM 145:5 NLT

As soon as I turned forty, everything I read had to be held at arm's length. I was not ready for that sudden change, nor was I accepting it. By not getting my eyes examined right away, I put off the ability to see things clearly. Finally I came across a man in our church who worked for a vision center. I agreed to get my eyes checked and find out whether I would need glasses for close-up reading. All along I was determined that my vision was fine. But when I went in for the examination, the optometrist came out and said, "Yes, you need reading glasses." I knew I had a decision to see clearly or not. I could get glasses and see better, or I could continue in my denial, strain my eyes, and struggle to see.

Isn't that how life goes? Many times we lose our perspective and we stay frustrated when all we must do is make some minor adjustments to see clearly. Life can hit us in unsuspecting ways. Suddenly the clear becomes cloudy and the obvious becomes blurry. But with a subtle adjustment, we can refocus and get back on track. We get this adjustment by meditating on God's Word and, as today's verse says, His splendor and miracles. With a heart trained on Him, we begin to see things anew. And He reveals new things to us as we walk forward into clarity.

Father, I ask You to clear my spiritual vision so I can see things through Your eyes. Shift my focus to the things You see. Help me see the beauty You have set before me.

Thank God in Every Season

Give thanks in all circumstances; for this is God's will for you in Christ Jesus.
1 THESSALONIANS 5:18

What season do you love the most? Where I live, we enjoy the beauty of all four seasons. But if I had to choose a favorite season it would be summer. I love the flowers, the picnics, the water, and all the outdoor things that come with the season. I feel best when I am in the outdoors enjoying the sun and extended hours of daylight.

Although I hate to see the summer end, I know it is necessary to move to the next season. As with seasons in the natural world, our spiritual lives need to experience change. Embracing each season is the key to peace and fulfillment. In the fall and winter everything is cold, there is little movement, nothing blooms, and everything seems gray. Then when the spring and summer come around, everything seems to blossom, kids play outside, the sun shines, and everyone seems happier.

I have learned that God has a plan for each season of our lives. If we look intently, there is always something positive or rewarding to take away from each season. It is up to us to see the beauty and enjoy the journey as He guides us through them. I'm often reminded the best fruit grows in the valley. The same is true in our lives. We often learn the most valuable lessons during the darkest seasons. So let's accept what God is trying to give us. Real maturity will embrace every season as beautiful and valuable.

Father, help me see Your fingerprint in every season. Let
me know I am not alone or forgotten. I choose to face each
day knowing You are working all things for my good.

DeLana Rutherford, Atlanta, GA

Turn Your Worry into Something Wonderful

Now, my dear, don't worry! I intend to do for you everything you propose, for everyone in the village knows that you are a worthy woman.

RUTH 3:11 NET

As moms, wives, friends, business owners, or entrepreneurs, we can easily find something to worry about. Too many questions and demands can have us feeling overwhelmed. If we are not careful, those concerns can turn into worry and anxiety.

Let us be intentional about guarding our peace, so the questions like, "Will this project turn out all right?" "How will I get where I am going?" "Have I made a mistake?" or "Did I invest too much money?" don't leave us emotionally frazzled.

The moment we wake up and our feet hit the floor, the enemy of our souls comes to steal our peace. If we are not quick to get hold of our thoughts, fear and doubt will consume our thinking. Sometimes it is hard to see past the worries, but God promises never to leave nor forsake us. He knows our names; He knows our heart, and He is mindful of us.

Whenever worry tries to take over your thoughts, I encourage you to take a moment to worship. When you worship, wonderful things begin to happen. You can shut out distractions and fill your heart, mind, and ears with God's goodness. Today fix your mind on good things. Write those words out and place them where you can see them. Speak positive words over your situation, and believe them!

....

Dear God, I place my cares before You. I know I am not capable of handling everything on my own.

Approach the Throne of Grace

Let us, then, feel very sure that we can come before God's throne where there is grace. There we can receive mercy and grace to help us when we need it.

HEBREWS 4:16 NCV

*M*any have played the childhood game Father (or Mother) May I? The father stands at one end of the room and the children (the players) stand across the room taking turns asking for permission to take steps toward the father. The first one to reach the father wins the game.

Over the years I held back from running toward my heavenly Father. I didn't understand I had already been given permission to leap into His arms. It took a while for me to see that the Father has given us an irrevocable access pass to come into His presence. The truth is that I allowed lies and condemnation to create a gulf between my Father and myself. How He felt about me and how I thought He felt about me were two very different things. My spiritual feet were chained to the ground as emotional baggage kept me from drawing near. Guilt and shame were holding me back. He wasn't denying me access to His heart; my thoughts and emotions were.

As a result I stood in the same spot for many years. I thought that if I could just perform well, I'd earn the Father's love. When I look back, I see I always had His love.

Thankfully, the Father's love broke my chains. Grace showed up, unlocked my heart, purchased my liberty, and set me free. Every day my Abba, "Daddy" God, eagerly waits for me to come boldly to the throne of grace with my requests. I can't wait to meet Him there.

Father, I receive the fullness of Your grace and run into Your arms.
Help me remember how much You love and adore Your daughter.

Rosalind Booker, Allen, TX

Mercy . . . Hold On

She said, "According to your words, so be it." Then Rahab sent them
off, and they departed; and she tied the scarlet cord in the window.
JOSHUA 2:21 AMP

*T*he alarm didn't go off. Rising in panic, Danielle hurried to get
Johnny dressed, fed, and to school on time. She sped off, only to
hear a loud *boom*!

"Momma, wake up," Johnny said as he pushed his mother's shoulder. As the police and EMTs tried to open Danielle's smashed-in door,
Johnny climbed out of his car seat, unlocked the back door, and let them
in. It all happened so fast. Danielle's only memory was trying to make
a left turn at a stop sign. She and Johnny were taken to the emergency
room by ambulance. In a blink of an eye, her vehicle had been T-boned
by a school bus. Although Danielle was knocked unconscious, neither
she nor Johnny suffered a scratch, broken bones, or injuries from the
accident. Both of them left the emergency room within a few hours of
their arrival.

God's desire is for us to live in peace and assurance knowing His
protective hand will take care of us. When we believe He is taking care
of our concerns, large or small, we will relax and rest in His grace. When
facing adversity or unexpected tragedy, the best thing we can do is stay
calm and reach for peace. Today I encourage you to put an end to anxiety
and worry. Feed your faith, focus on His words, and trust God will watch
over everything that concerns you.

Father, thank You for promising goodness and mercy that will
follow us all the days of our lives. My heart melts knowing
the mission of mercy is to draw my heart to Yours.

Be Rescued . . . Again

Many times He rescued them.

PSALM 106:43 AMP

Thank God! I was rescued . . . again. My faith walk was a complex journey. For years my life was total chaos as I struggled to understand the balance between God's laws and grace. Before I accepted Christ, I did not consider the consequences of making bad decisions. To say it bluntly, I was a hot mess.

After I accepted Christ, it took a while before I realized I had been set free from condemnation and guilt. For a long time I felt like a failure because I was caught up in trying to obey every rule, follow legalistic laws, and never fall short in my perfectionist ways. I was a target for unhealthy people who took advantage of my gifts, talents, and longing to do something great for God. Because I did not take responsibility for my relationship with Jesus, trusting Him to be my spiritual authority and security, I ended up being controlled by people who did not have my best interest in mind.

But then the law of love captivated my heart and showed me grace. Grace was beautiful. Grace knocked the *t* off of *can't* and crossed every boundary to rescue me. Finally I was free.

With the relentless love of a Father, He never stopped pursuing me. In fact He forgave me for all the times I placed things or other people ahead of Him. When I embraced the fullness of His love, everything inside me changed. My priorities aligned and I served Him with a faithful heart. God is pursuing your heart too. Relax in His love, and be rescued.

....

Lord, thank You that I am loved and lovable, and that the price
Jesus paid for me is enough to rescue me . . . again and again.

Rosalind Booker, Allen, TX

Possesses a Humble Heart

Always be humble, gentle, and patient, accepting each other in love.
EPHESIANS 4:2 NCV

*I*t was a mild summer evening at dusk; a ray of sunlight beamed through the trees, stroking Joy's cheek while she and Christina sat on the front porch sharing sentiments. Joy's nature is to be spontaneous, out front, visible, and courageous. She is a natural-born fighter and risk-taker. Christina is quite the opposite—a strategic thinker, gentle-spirited, non-confrontational, and cautious.

During the retreat Joy and Christina bonded in an unexpected way. Joy explained that Christina had encouraged her heart. It was like Christina had been sent from heaven with encouraging words, prayer, and answers to the questions hidden in Joy's heart. Her genuine love, concern, and kindness made Joy feel accepted, relaxed, and as if she were the most important person in the world.

Because of their conversation, Joy felt safe, empowered, and protected. In a loving way, Christina allowed Joy to be free from the pressure of trying to *fix* everything. The walls around Joy's heart dissolved. She didn't need to be right, first, most important, or rewarded. Christina's humble heart showed Joy how to rest and relax in the strength of Jesus.

Like a rudder—small in size, but mighty to guide a huge ship—Christina's humble heart helped steer Joy in a new direction. Where performance and control once led the way, peace now lights the path. When we mirror Christ's heart of compassion like Christina did, we will see an amazing harvest of peace and healing.

....

Dear Lord, clothe me in humility. Let my heart be
satisfied with laboring in love to help others.

Discover Favor in Unexpected Places

The king said to Joseph, "God has shown you all this. There is no one as wise and understanding as you are, so I will put you in charge of my palace. All the people will obey your orders, and only I will be greater than you."

GENESIS 41:39–40 NCV

God's favor goes before those who are determined to do right in unjust situations. When I think about favor, my mind races to Joseph, who was shamefully wronged, mistreated, falsely accused (while living in Potiphar's house), and abandoned by those he loved. But despite the horrible things he went through, he served others with a cheerful attitude, kind heart, and positive work ethic. He was so pleasing to those he worked for that he was quickly appointed to the position of COO and CFO over the pharaoh's house. His optimistic outlook secured his destiny.

Through each trying season Joseph gave the important things top priority in his life. He trusted in the faithfulness of God and kept a tight grip on his dream. Even though he served difficult personalities, Joseph did everything he could to make those he worked for become successful.

In Christ you have the strength to trust God in good times and bad. Often what you consider a difficult season is God's way of positioning you for a divine appointment. Who would have imagined that when Joseph's brothers threw him in a pit, it would lead him to the throne of Egypt after leaving Potiphar's house? Maybe you have struggled to see good in a bad situation. Don't give up prematurely. Let favor go before you and lead you into the most blessed season of your life.

Lord, I believe no external circumstance or adversary can deprive me of Your favor and goodness. Let me love with such a pure heart that Your presence in my life will change hostile environments.

Rosalind Booker, Allen, TX

Cloaked in Compassion

If you return to the LORD, then your fellow Israelites and your children will be shown compassion by their captors and will return to this land, for the LORD your God is gracious and compassionate. He will not turn his face from you if you return to him.

2 CHRONICLES 30:9

*P*ain swelled in my heart. I held back the tears. A day of celebration turned tragic. My mind raced with questions: *How did I get in this situation again? What was I thinking when I made the decision to allow this person in my personal space?* My memory played out like a horror movie as I watched someone I loved turn into someone I didn't recognize.

I needed the wisdom of the Holy Spirit to give me an exit strategy. I've learned God's grace isn't something we can rely on occasionally; we must rely on it constantly. When we call out in repentance to our Father, He sees us through the eyes of compassion rather than error or sin. His grace cloaks us in compassion and wraps us in mercy.

In Exodus we read about the four hundred years God's children spent in Egyptian captivity. Although most of us have never been slaves, we have from time to time been enslaved by our way of thinking. Thankfully God doesn't leave us trapped in our self-made circumstance; He finds a way to lead us out of what has imprisoned our thinking.

I am thankful that His way of thinking is so much higher than our own. Even in my broken state, His love and compassion created a bridge from brokenness to healing and from captivity to freedom. May we remember the power of His redemptive love, and how He died for our transgressions so we could experience freedom.

....

Lord, I am humbled by Your grace and compassion. I proclaim
Christ's compassion, goodness, and unreserved kindness in my life.

Go All In

A poor widow came and put in two small copper coins, worth less than
a penny. [Jesus] called his disciples and said to them, "I tell you the truth,
this poor widow has put more into the offering box than all the others."

MARK 12:42–43 NET

I have many friends who are widowed. Their husbands have died
because of illnesses, car collisions, or unexpected accidents. Though
their circumstances may be different, they've walked through the same
grieving process and have asked similar questions: *Why has this happened to me? Who will take care of me? How will I get through this season
in life?*

For my friends who were stay-at-home moms or did not have an
independent career, there was the pressing question, *How will I manage
the next phase of my life on a fixed income?* The grieving process seems
harder for the widow who has relied on her husband for financial security or who has been married for a long time.

In Mark we read a story of an unnamed widow who had a routine of
bringing her offering to the Lord. This is a beautiful image of trust. Even
though she no longer had a husband to rely on for security, she did not
stop making an offering to God. If anything, she was more committed
to bringing her offering before the Lord. Whatever her thoughts that day,
she came to worship with her offering. She was letting God know she
relied on His provision and trusted Him with her future. Like the widow,
we can trust Him with ours, no matter how unsure our future may seem.

Abba Father, today I place all my worries and concerns in Your
hands. Thank You for being my Rock, my protection, and my peace.
With a joyful heart, I will praise You in every season of life.

Marina McLean, Keller, TX

Please the Father

"Father, if you are willing, please take this cup of suffering away from me. Yet I want your will to be done, not mine."

LUKE 22:42 NLT

*H*ow many times in life have difficult circumstances seemed to swallow up our hope? If you are like me, you can remember moments when negative thoughts tormented your mind. I can recall seasons of crying over an uncertain future. At times I even considered giving up. I admit, there are levels of suffering that will leave us wondering, *Will I survive the season in front of me?*

When we face emotionally crippling moments, it is easy to let fear overtake our faith. During a dark moment a friend asked me to explain what I was feeling or experiencing, and to be honest I had no answer for her. I couldn't put into words what I was feeling. I was strong and weak all at the same time. I was full of faith one moment and sliding down the slope of fear the next.

When I felt as if I had come to the end of the road and there weren't any optimistic choices in front of me, God came through with a miracle. I can't count the number of times I whispered the prayer, "Lord, I trust You are able to do the impossible through me."

In my weakest moments I've learned to rely on the strength of my Father. I now understand when I reach the end of what I can do, He rises to do the rest.

Father, I rejoice that Your strength is available in our weakest moments. I worship You, knowing You walk beside me through every heartache and dance with me during every victory. You alone are worthy of my praise.

Worship God's Way

*"A time is coming and has now come when the true
worshipers will worship the Father in the Spirit and in truth,
for they are the kind of worshipers the Father seeks."*

JOHN 4:23

I love teaching about the woman Jesus met beside the well in John 4. The topsy-turvy relationship she shared with multiple male partners made other women run away. Her bad reputation had made her a social outcast. But that is exactly what makes this story so amazing. Jesus went out of His way, even rearranging His schedule, to meet with the woman everyone else avoided.

In a compassionate way Jesus took time to ask her questions that would uncover the pain hidden in her heart. He opened His life to her so she would open her heart to Him. What began as a debate over *where* people should worship God quickly changed directions, and Jesus began to teach her *how* to worship the Father.

He emphasized that the Father isn't as concerned about where you worship as He is about how you worship. He underscored how the Father is looking for those who will worship Him in spirit and truth. How ironic! The woman many would not consider "worship worthy" was the one Jesus gave a mini-worship seminar to. The woman many would not consider worshipping alongside is the one God wanted worship from. Jesus was very clear: worship from a repentant heart is what pleases the Father most.

....

Today, I worship You not because I have to but because
I get to. Thank You for accepting my praise as an
offering of worship. I give You my heart.

Marina McLean, Keller, TX

Drink Living Water

You, God, are my God, earnestly I seek you; I thirst for you, my whole being longs for you, in a dry and parched land where there is no water.

PSALM 63:1

I have never been to a desert, but our hot Texas summer sometimes makes me feel as if I live in one. On average summer temperatures top one hundred degrees. A few summers ago we experienced an extra-hot snap, when thirty days cleared the 100-degree mark. That summer I learned the importance of drinking excessive amounts of water to stay hydrated. I also made it a point to move slower than normal and spend more time in the shade.

I wasn't the only thing affected by the heat. My beautiful flowerbeds also needed extra care and attention. No longer was a morning watering enough. Due to the escalating heat, high humidity, and absence of a cool breeze, I found that watering my garden again in the late evening would keep my delicate flowers from wilting. Keeping a watchful eye on them, I noticed the extra watering kept the water around the root from evaporating. It was amazing to watch the wilting petals perk up and suddenly return to full blossom.

In a similar way as I worship God in desert-like moments of life, I return to full bloom. When we come into His presence feeling beaten down by the cares of this life, we can water ourselves through the act of worship. Whether we are kneeling in prayer at a bedside or worshipping at church in His presence, we regain our strength.

Dear Father, thank You for watering the dry places in my heart. I praise You for giving me strength to rise above situations that have the potential to wear me down.

Hold Your Head High

Now my head shall be lifted up above my enemies all around me, and I will offer in his tent sacrifices with shouts of joy; I will sing and make melody to the LORD.

PSALM 27:6 ESV

*I*t is never easy to lift your head up after you have been shamed publicly. Maybe you made a huge mistake in the office presentation, and it took you right back to childhood memories. Your coworkers are looking at you with adult eyes, but the expressions on their faces are reminiscent of the ones on your childhood playground. You're embarrassed, but wise enough to pull things into focus. Silently you tell yourself, *You're an adult now. It was just a mistake. Things will get better.*

I share this with you because I was the boss who made a near-disastrous mistake in front of my team. My good-natured team helped me work through the error, and together we recovered from what could have been a sticky situation. I've learned not everyone has a good support system. Sometimes those around us are quick to point fingers and make harsh accusations.

During seasons of failure, we can lose our confidence and fail to move forward. Maybe that is what has happened in your life—you've let one situation hold you back from fulfilling the things God wants you to do. I encourage you to rediscover your courage. Get up and try again. Move forward with that creative project. One failure doesn't mean you won't ever succeed. A wrong decision doesn't mean you're not qualified to lead a future project. Learn to speak to your heart. Encourage yourself through God's Word.

Father, thank You for helping me rise above my mistakes.

Marina McLean, Keller, TX

Crown of Beauty

To all who mourn in Israel, he will give a crown of beauty for ashes, a joyous blessing instead of mourning, festive praise instead of despair. In their righteousness, they will be like great oaks that the LORD has planted for his own glory.

ISAIAH 61:3 NLT

We've all mourned the loss of something we've treasured: the death of a family member, a fractured friendship, the loss of financial security, or the repossession of a home or vehicle. The truth is that recovering from the feeling of loss takes time.

I've been told there are at least seven stages one goes through to process grief: denial, anger, frustration, acceptance, forgiveness, resolve, and goal setting. Sometimes it is hard to work our way through these stages, and they often don't fall in that order.

I want to encourage you, if you are in a stage of grief, God has a way of inviting you into His presence and giving you hope again. He longs to wrap you in the security of His arms and surround you with His peace. He promises to exchange the garment of grief for a coat of hope. As you spend time in His presence, His light will shine through you. Others will begin to see a glow on your face, joy in your step, and a smile that lights up the room.

The fear of never feeling hopeful can be replaced by God's never-ending promises. As you enter His presence, your heart will be filled with the joy of the Lord. Your ashes of pain and grief will be transformed into unexpected rays of hope.

....

Father, I praise You for transforming my grief into joy. With expectation I move forward into the next season of life.

Climb Out

*Who redeems your life from the pit, who crowns you
[lavishly] with lovingkindness and tender mercy.*

PSALM 103:4 AMP

One morning I woke up with an overwhelming sense of panic. The feeling was so strong that for a moment I forgot I was standing in our rundown home in Texas. I knew something had to change. I felt I had to stop and pray, *Lord, please show me how to make this house a home. In faith I trust You have not forgotten us.*

Our family had recently moved from California. My husband was a pastor and felt God was calling us to a new place. I felt sad as we packed our van and waved goodbye to our family and friends. The truth is, I was in a pit of self-pity. I sank deep down into the pit because life had not turned out the way I thought it should.

I felt stuck in the dingy old house the church had us staying in. No one had lived there for several years, and it showed. We were left alone in a rotting house being overtaken by field mice.

That very day a new friend showed up offering to help me paint the peeling walls. We laughed as she boldly threw out the mouse we caught, and together we transformed something bearable into something borderline beautiful. As she was getting ready to leave, she went to her car and brought back a gift bag. Inside the bag was a beautiful new purse. I was overwhelmed by her act of kindness. God used her to answer my whispered prayer.

....

Dear Lord, thank You for tender mercies and
lovingkindness. I am grateful You answer my prayers
and surprise me with abundant provision.

Karen Sebastian-Wirth, Grand Prairie, TX

Be Cradled in Comfort

Heavens and earth, be happy. Mountains, shout with joy, because the
LORD comforts his people and will have pity on those who suffer.

ISAIAH 49:13 NCV

I t was the longest day of my life. It seems as if it were yesterday, even though it has been more than five years. When I woke up, I felt the joy and peace of God's presence. On my way to a training class in Mississippi, I received an unexpected call from my daughter. I immediately cancelled my class and made my way to the airport. Miraculously I could book the last plane out for the day.

That night when I had arrived back at my home, the reality of what had happened began to set in. My mind filled with beautiful memories of my husband, Bill, who passed on to heaven the night before. I felt like I was drowning in a sea of grief. The harsh reality of losing someone you love is hard to recover from. As I sat on the front porch, deep, guttural sobs racked my body. I cried until I could cry no more. Then, when I felt empty inside, God's comfort cradled me in His arms.

After a while I moved inside and sat in my favorite rocker. As I snuggled beneath a blanket, I felt the peaceful presence of the Lord. In a difficult moment I looked for something to be thankful for. My mind drifted to the memory of Bill depending on a machine to provide for his next breath. As tears flowed down my cheeks, I thanked God for giving me breath and courage to trust Him with my future. Our God is our Comforter, and He does not leave those who suffer without hope.

Father, thank You for comforting me in the darkest seasons of life.
Your strength renews and restores the secret places of my heart.

Feel Strong and Secure

*God is the one who saves me; I will trust him and not be afraid. The
LORD, the LORD gives me strength and makes me sing. He has saved me.*
ISAIAH 12:2 NCV

*I*t's hard to say what I missed most about my husband, Bill. Before he
passed away, I had the privilege of being his full-time caregiver for
more than two and a half years. The effects of muscular dystrophy made
it impossible for him to breathe on his own. Though unable to speak, his
eyes spoke volumes and his firm grip made me feel like everything was
going to be okay. I still remember how secure I felt holding his hand.

After his death my heart sank when I looked at our finances and
realized I did not make enough money to make the mortgage payment
each month. Fear gripped my heart as I realized my serious financial
dilemma. I wept at the thought of having to sell our home. I felt helpless
and without hope.

Over time I learned that fear dissipates when we are courageous
enough to face it head-on. I was determined not to panic. I patiently
waited and trusted God to provide for every step of my new journey.
I decided to make a list of people I could stay with for a week or two if
I needed to sell the house. By having an alternative plan, I chose to see
how God would bring me through a difficult season. I am amazed by the
miracles God brought from surprising places to carry me through that
time. He is always there to take His children from insecurity to security,
in the most surprising ways.

Dear Lord, thank You for miraculous provision. Today I cast
my cares on You, knowing You will sustain me. You are bigger
than any problem I face or stormy season I walk through.

Karen Sebastian-Wirth, Grand Prairie, TX

Hope in Your Desolation

"Who cuts a channel for the torrents of rain, and a path for the thunderstorm, to water a land where no one lives, an uninhabited desert?"

JOB 38:25–26

I stumbled out of bed and into the bathroom. Splashing cold water on my face, I noticed bloodshot eyes staring back at me. I was completely exhausted from the daily responsibilities of caring for my mother-in-law who lived with us. On top of that I was dealing with a rebellious teenager, a difficult boss at work, and the tasks of being a pastor's wife. It wasn't long before my body began to feel the effects of stress.

When I went to the doctor, she told me, "Mrs. Sebastian, we are going to have to run some more tests, but your symptoms indicate lupus." As I drove home, I had to pull over as tears blinded me. I sobbed until there were no more tears to cry. Just when I felt hopeless, I noticed a small shaft of light breaking through the dark clouds. One shaft of light burst through, then another. Before long rays of light were illuminating the dark sky. In that moment I began to feel hope.

During that dark season, I asked for help and received the loving support of family and friends. Every time I felt like giving up, I remembered the "hope rays" I'd seen that day. Over time I began to take charge of my life and health. Six months after the diagnosis my symptoms disappeared. Hope had transformed me from the inside out. We can have confidence, when we encounter storms, that God will walk with us and calm our hearts.

Lord, today we rest in comfort, embracing the
rays of hope You put in our path.

Journey with God

The LORD replied, "My Presence will go with you, and I will give you rest."
EXODUS 33:14

When my parents accepted the call to the mission field, we were thrust into a strange new world. I realized what heroes of faith my parents were when they took us on a journey to Latin America.

I remember feeling nervous as Mom, my sister, and I climbed up the steps of the train car. Almost every seat was taken, and Mom pulled us a little closer until we finally found a place to sit for the night. My dad and brother decided to stay on another part of the train to protect our car and belongings.

The train stopped often and every stop guaranteed that street vendors would jump aboard trying to sell us stale food covered with flies. Frightened by my new surroundings, my only security came from snuggling deeper into the arms of my mother. Sometime during the night my brother decided to join us in the passenger area. At one of the stops he got off the train and then had to start running toward us when the train started moving again. I can only imagine the panic my dad must have felt as his seven-year-old son ran next to the train somewhere in the badlands between Mexico and Guatemala. Finally the train slowed and my brother managed to hop on and sit with us for the rest of the night. When asked what he would have done if he had been left behind, he said, "I knew Dad would come find me, so I wasn't worried."

We can have the same kind of confidence in our heavenly Father, who is always with us in seasons of transition.

Dear Lord, when the unthinkable happens, it is comforting to
know we can count on Your presence to give us peace.

Karen Sebastian-Wirth, Grand Prairie, TX

Unwind and Escape

David was greatly distressed because the men were talking of stoning him; each one was bitter in spirit because of his sons and daughters. But David found strength in the LORD his God.

1 SAMUEL 30:6

When I entered the planning meeting for the women's ministry at our church, something felt strange. Abruptly everyone stopped talking, and I wasn't sure why. Later one of the ladies called to share with me what was going on. A group of the ladies were not pleased with my style of leadership, since it was different from the previous pastor's wife.

I shed a few tears of hurt and frustration. When I had my quiet time the next morning, I was still hurting, reliving the unfairness of it all. My daily reading happened to be about David. Yes, compared to David's situation, my story seemed less dramatic. I had women complaining about me; David's men were ready to stone him.

The passage that day contained a very powerful three-letter word: *but*. This simple word turned everything around for David. Despite disappointment, disgrace, loss, and rejection from his own men, David decided to be *better* instead of *bitter*. But this time discouragement came from those he had invested the most in; this time his enemies were those closest to him.

During this time David turned to the only One who could give him strength. David stopped listening to those following him and began to listen to the One who could comfort him.

David inspired me to stop trying to gain affirmation from other people. His story reminds us to look up instead of looking around.

Dear Lord, thank You for strengthening us during our greatest battles. Even when others turn against us, You never let us down.

Live Brave

"I told you these things so that you can have peace in me. In this world
you will have trouble, but be brave! I have defeated the world."
JOHN 16:33 NCV

*B*eing in ministry for more than twenty-five years, I've had the
honor to meet women from all walks of life. Whether a young
innocent teen, an overwhelmed mom, or a prayerful, wise grandma,
they all have one thing in common: a desire to find courage and bravery
to rise above their struggles. I've often sat across the table from a sister
with tears streaming down her cheeks, as she poured out her heart, sharing unexpected betrayal, detours in life, or unfulfilled promises as she
grasped for a glimmer of hope.

A few years ago I found myself on the other side of the table. Over
coffee with a dear friend, I shared about a difficult decision in ministry,
releasing the despair of my broken heart during a distressing desert season. I'll never forget her comforting words that day as she said, "Rachelle,
I'd lay it *all* down."

Her words calmed my fear and helped me to be brave and rise above
my struggle. Even though I was still afraid, I was daily determined not
to allow fear to overtake me. It's not the absence of fear that takes us into
our destiny, but the embracing of courage and bravery.

The Lord became the water in my desert and made me brave in the
most tumultuous time of my life. Because Jesus overcame death, hell,
and the grave, we are promised the same resurrection power to overcome
any circumstance that comes our way. Our peace is found only in Him.

Father, when things look completely hopeless, help me
run to You, the One who defeated the whole world.

　　　　　　　　　　　Rachelle Fletcher, Haslet, TX

Inspire Those Around You

The LORD gave this command to Joshua son of Nun: "Be
strong and brave, because you will lead the people of Israel
to the land I promised them, and I will be with you."

DEUTERONOMY 31:23 NCV

O ne of the most powerful things we can do is encourage others to
pursue the plans God has for their lives. God will orchestrate the
most complex situations to ensure that we are at the right place at the
right time to carry out His divine purpose, and those around us may
need someone to lead them deeper into their calling.

Inspired by Moses, Joshua was a loyal follower of God and an
incredible leader. He was Moses' assistant for forty years, traveling with
the murmuring Israelites in the wilderness. Yet he was the one called to
take them into the promised land.

God exhorted Joshua *three different times* to be strong and courageous. At this point Joshua was ninety years old. Crossing the Jordan
seemed like an insurmountable task. Notice how many times God had
to remind him to be strong!

It's important to note that his success was measured not by his lim-
itations, but by his willingness to follow God who had promised the
inheritance for his generation.

While Joshua was fulfilling his purpose, he helped the Israelites fulfill their destiny. He gave voice to the kingdom seed that was already
inside them.

Lord, help me be a loyal follower, a humble servant, and a brave,
strong leader like Joshua, inspiring others to live out their God-given
destiny with Your promise of always being with us wherever we go.

Pray Risky Prayers

LORD All-Powerful, the God of Israel, you have said to me, "I will make
your family great." So I, your servant, am brave enough to pray to you.

2 SAMUEL 7:27 NCV

My husband, Bill, announced he felt the Lord's calling to go into
full-time evangelism with the Goodness Project, a nonprofit
ministry we birthed while pastoring a church in a working-poor community. While raising our two young daughters, we'd been building the
ministry together for five years and finally had security, something every
woman desires. I was shocked when he told me he wanted to give it all
away, but told him I would take it to the Lord in prayer.

The Lord gently reminded me of the power of agreement and how He
would increase our sphere of influence. Often, when we get comfortable,
the Lord will challenge us to move to the unknown, but always for the
purpose of advancing His kingdom. I made agreement with my husband's risky prayer, and as a result, thousands of people received Christ
over the next five years as we provided resources and food, partnering
with churches and communities across the United States and Canada.

In today's verse, God had been behind all of David's successes, and
now promised him an even greater glory and eternal kingdom through his
bloodline. David found the courage to ask the Lord to allow *him* to be the
one to build His house. Even though his son was the one who would build
the temple, he was brave enough to make the request. With a humble heart
David changed his petition to line up with the will of God. Praying risky
prayers births heavenly strategies that lead to the perfect will of God.

Father, I want to hear Your voice as You strengthen
my faith to pray risky prayers.

Rachelle Fletcher, Haslet, TX

Wait with Courage

Wait for and confidently expect the LORD; be strong and let your
heart take courage; yes, wait for and confidently expect the LORD.

PSALM 27:14 AMP

*H*ave you ever longed for something deeply but wondered why
it took the Lord so long to fulfill the desire of your heart and
answer your prayer? Maybe you've never been able to take your family
on a vacation or you've asked God to give you a perfect job that matches
your level of passion.

Let's go deeper: What about waiting on the Lord as you cried out
for the salvation of your child, or healing a loved one's struggle with
cancer, or provision for your family? Waiting on the Lord is not easy and
requires you to resist the flesh by saying no to your impulsive nature and
instead saying yes to living in active submission to His will. His promise
is that He *will* renew your strength as you wait on Him.

As we allow our hearts to trust the Lord's sovereignty, we create an
atmosphere of faith. We may be tempted to think, *I'm not going to expect
anything so I won't be disappointed.* Expectation requires courageous
thinking and then moving into action with our words.

God has given you authority over the atmosphere of your home.
There you turn your petitions into declarations, believing what God has
already promised. Once you believe it and speak it with courage and an
expectant heart, you will see the mountains you've been facing melt like
wax. Courage defies fear and wins the battle.

Lord, I live in great expectation of Your mercy and grace
as I walk in the confidence of Your living Word, allowing
my heart to take courage as I wait patiently on You.

Expect Favor

Joseph from Arimathea was brave enough to
go to Pilate and ask for Jesus' body.
MARK 15:43 NCV

*J*oseph from Arimathea was an important part of the Jewish council and a disciple of Jesus. After Jesus was accused of treason and then brutally crucified, Joseph was bold enough to go directly to the Roman governor, Pilate, and ask for the body of Jesus. What a brave soul!

Like many others he was awaiting the kingdom of God, but for fear of the Jews, he was secretly a disciple of Jesus. How many times have we missed out on something beautiful by giving in to the fear of man?

Something happened to Joseph on the day of the crucifixion: courage was stirred and passion and justice awakened. When he saw with his own eyes that an innocent man had been scorned and put to death, he knew he could no longer remain silent. He became the guardian of Jesus' sacred body, and the cross laid bare the heart of Joseph.

When we speak up for those who have been wrongly accused, oppressed, or murdered and step into the courtroom of the heaven, which trumps all other judicial systems, we can expect immeasurable favor from the Lord. As we speak from His heart, He gives us an anointing to have influence with those in places of authority over our land.

The cross is a wondrous magnet, drawing others to Jesus as we draw closer to His heart.

Lord, I step out in bold faith declaring Your Word will bring
divine favor from those in places of government. Allow me,
like Joseph, to be the voice to the oppressed, vulnerable, and
voiceless, as You enable me through the power of Your cross.

Rachelle Fletcher, Haslet, TX

Journey Somewhere New

Whether the land is rich or poor; and whether there are forests there
or not. Be of good courage. And bring some of the fruit of the land.
NUMBERS 13:20 NKJV

J'm blessed with two beautiful girls, and I remember when they
each learned how to walk. They loved hearing their daddy cheering
them on as they bravely charged toward him and then suddenly fell. As I
watched my precious daughters, I noticed something. They *never* fell on
the first step. Never. It was as they attempted that second step that they
became full of caution and doubt, giving in to an invitation to fear. But
the more steps they took, the less fearful they became.

In today's passage Moses sent twelve spies into Canaan to investigate
land promised by God as their inheritance. Each brought back impres-
sive reviews of the area, and some grapes the size of plums! But after
seeing the multitude and strength of those occupying the land, fear
entered their hearts. This dangerous journey would require that they
resist the temptation to give in to fear, unbelief, and doubt. They would
need to embrace courage and trust God wholeheartedly.

From their first excited steps out of Egypt to the promised land, the
Israelites, sadly, gave in to fear and proverbially fell down many times.
It was a challenging, dangerous journey they were on—one filled with
fear and excitement. Yet around every bend in the road, from the parting
of the Red Sea to the crumbling walls of Jericho, God proved Himself
faithful.

Father, when I journey somewhere new and fall, help
me get back up and bravely walk toward You one
step at a time. Thank You for cheering me on.

Be Rewarded for Dark Days

"Then young women will dance and be glad, young men and old as well. I will turn their mourning into gladness; I will give them comfort and joy instead of sorrow."

JEREMIAH 31:13

I was excited to take a new step in life and pursue a master's degree in professional counseling. I began my three-year journey with the hope of one day starting a private practice, helping people, and becoming financially independent. During my second year of graduate school, I became aware of my heightened anxiety. I began to seriously question if I had made the right decision. My inability to cope with my anxiety left me feeling paralyzed on the inside. My confidence slowly faded. I felt lonely, heartbroken, bitter, and angry. The excitement I enjoyed a year before was replaced with a dark feeling of frustration. Before long, my joy turned into depression and excitement to anger. The girl known for not giving up was slowly slipping away.

Did I eventually earn my degree? Yes. But along the journey I received something more than letters beside my name. I learned that some of life's greatest rewards are discovered in our darkest moments. When the pain felt unbearable and sufferings seemed too great, the grace of my Father showed up. His mercy found a way to reach my soul.

If you are in a situation that is swallowing up your faith, reach for God's goodness. He is closer to your hurts than you think. I encourage you to reach up from the low place your heart has fallen, and allow Him to pick you up. Rest in His embrace. And pass it on.

Today I choose to believe You are with me. I make myself available and say yes to being used to show others Your love even in my darkest hour. You are my reward.

Lacey Mings, Kansas City, MO

Exit a Bad Season Blessed

The LORD had made the Egyptians favorably disposed toward the people,
and they gave them what they asked for; so they plundered the Egyptians.

EXODUS 12:36

I arrived at my office earlier than normal. This was the last day of my first dream job. My heart was pounding; internally I questioned, *Where do I go from here?* I felt as though my life was moving forward; the only problem was I didn't know if I was going to like where it was taking me. It is a strange thing to feel completely confident one moment and rocked by doubt the next. My situation led me to a state of panic. I felt like I was walking through life without a compass. The truth is, I was finding it hard to navigate through life with peace being my only guide.

Many times we find ourselves in what appears to be a bad situation full of inconvenience, rejection, family conflict, or worn-out relationships. The ability to lay down what we have, what we know, and hand it over to our Father takes courage. Maybe you're searching for supernatural peace. If so, I encourage you to begin taking small steps of courage.

You may be struggling to find a way to exit a bad season. It may be a situation at work you need to let go of, a wrong relationship you need to leave behind, or a bad memory you need to release. When you are brave enough to let go of what is wrong, God will lead you to what is right. I believe you will rise, move forward, and leave behind the things that hurt you. We are promised deliverance from our enemies, provision, protection, and the comfort of God's presence to lead you somewhere new.

....

Father, I trust You to go before me and lead me into new things. I know, with You, I am safe and protected. In Your arms I find rest.

Pass Down a Blessing

"Through your descendants all the nations on the earth will be blessed, because you obeyed me."

GENESIS 22:18 NCV

God has blessed me with extraordinary mentors who have imparted spiritual wisdom and guidance to me. In return I try to find ways for God to use me to help others. In the same way, God has allowed me to pour into the lives of others by leading worship. There was a time, however, when I took a season of rest from reaching out to others through music. I no longer felt I had the energy to lead others in worship. I wanted to sit and rest for a while. The problem was that God was calling me to lead others even when it wasn't what I wanted to do.

One Sunday I arrived at church and felt empty inside. I went to play the keyboard, but my hands felt numb and I couldn't remember the words to the song. Fear and frustration consumed me. For a second I considered walking off the stage. I had to choose between obeying God or caving into my fears. Silently I prayed for strength and slowly my confidence returned. The blessing of doing what I knew God wanted me to do that morning led the way for others to receive joy and healing.

God's heart is for you to experience the rewards of obeying Him even when you don't feel like it. Each time you follow God fully, you position yourself to receive God's blessings. Maybe God is asking you to do something you don't necessarily want to do. Do it anyway. Watch and see the goodness of God's grace fill your life.

Father, I rest my heart in the quietness of Your love. Thank You for providing grace to carry out Your purposes for my life. Make my life a blessing to others as I do what You have called me to do.

Lacey Mings, Kansas City, MO

Reap a Supernatural Harvest

Isaac planted [seed] in that land [as a farmer] and reaped
in the same year a hundred times [as much as he had
planted], and the LORD blessed and favored him.

GENESIS 26:12 AMP

I was in my twenties when I began my academic journey at my dream
college. It would take years of hard work before I finished my master's degree. Every day I was more afraid to check the balance of my bank account than I was to check my most recent test score. My college experience was far from what I imagined. There was no comfort-spending money, no expensive nights out with friends, and name-brand makeup was replaced with whatever got the job done on a budget. I was thankful sweatpants and messy buns were considered stylish. Every day felt long, I slept less, and long hours of studying never seemed to be enough.

To find encouragement I attended various church conferences during this time. The message I heard always seemed to confirm what I felt God was calling me to do. It was invigorating, mind-blowing, and terrifying all at the same time. In my lowest moments I found God's prophetic word was still reaching out to me.

During this season of life God demonstrated His commitment to help me become what He desired. I learned patience, the beauty of surrendering my will to His, and the importance of submitting to His timing. Maybe, like me, you are going through a season when God is stretching your faith. I encourage you to rest in His strength. His love for you is immeasurable; reach out and receive it.

God, today I surrender all I am to You. The timing
of my life is safely held in Your hands.

Transform Disgrace into Something Beautiful

"The Lord has done this for me," she said. "In these days he has shown his favor and taken away my disgrace among the people."
LUKE 1:25

*R*ejection. Even as I type the nine-letter word and say it silently, I feel its sharp points pierce my insides. Can I let you in on a secret? Rejection has been one of my greatest fears.

At one point it seemed everyone I knew had grown up and moved on in life. I began to lose my place. I was now the single misfit. It's hard not to compare your life when you leave your friend's baby shower or a wedding only to return to a closet full of bridesmaid dresses. If you have felt the wound of rejection, most of us would agree, we never want to experience it again.

Holding on to the lies of rejection makes it almost impossible for you to experience true love and a healthy sense of belonging. The truth is, you are worthy of all your desires. Let that sink in. Yes, you might feel disgraced for being the single twenty-eight-year-old who's still patiently waiting for Prince Charming, the one who has been abused, overlooked, and forgotten. But you are worthy of God's goodness.

Today if you are striving to fit in because you have placed your strength in shallow things or people, I encourage you to reach out to God and place all misplaced affections in the arms of the Father. Let His love fill your heart.

Father, thank You for the finished work of the cross that guarantees the repair, renewal, and transformation of my heart. Only You can turn disgrace into something beautiful.

Ask for What You Wish

Queen Esther answered, "If I have found favor with you, Your Majesty, and if it pleases you, grant me my life—this is my petition. And spare my people—this is my request."

ESTHER 7:3

Growing up, I fell in love with the Christmas season. It was a magical time of year. Most of my childhood dreams came true, gifts were handpicked, and things we probably couldn't afford were bought and wrapped with love. Looking back, I can still remember the enchantment of Christmas morning.

Although my wish-list items have changed, my hope of receiving good things in life has not diminished. Toys have been replaced with a desire for a thriving career. Games have turned into a drive to find true love and carve out the perfect summer-ready body. We love receiving those kinds of gifts. But what about when life sends us something less desirable? When love fails or dreams turn into disappointments?

Years ago I learned to stop praying small prayers. My heart found courage to ask God one more time for reconciliation and restoration, for provision, for breakthrough, and joy. But if we're honest, the boldness to ask for what we wish seems impossible when faced with unexpected detours in life. It makes it hard to ask for anything.

Is there something you've stopped believing God for? Ask Him anyway. Ditch the small prayers and confidently approach God with big requests. He desires to give His children good gifts (Matthew 7:11). He cares about the smallest and biggest details of our lives.

Father, I trust in Your abundance to provide everything I need according to Your riches.

Find Beauty in Brokenness

*Strength and dignity are her clothing and her position is strong and secure;
and she smiles at the future [knowing that she and her family are prepared].*
PROVERBS 31:25 AMP

*A*s a mom of three boys, I worked with my sons to move them from bikes with training wheels to bikes with two wheels. I remember holding the back of wobbly bikes while they tried to reach new levels of childhood freedom. Sometimes they succeeded; other times they took tumbles. Whether it was the boldness of boys or sheer will, they brushed themselves off from the fall and climbed back on. In the same way as we pursue personal dreams and newfound freedoms, we will encounter the occasional bump, sideswipe, or collision as we reach out of our comfort zones. The important thing is not to let setbacks detour us from trying again. It is often in our most difficult moments when we will hear our heavenly Father whisper, *Try again.*

Getting back up when you feel like you've failed, broken your dreams, or lost your way reflects our faith in your Father. Today let Him take you in His arms, dust you off, and reposition you for success. Trust that He will never let go until you are fully prepared to take on the next season in life. Remember, in our brokenness we discover strength to go somewhere we have never journeyed before.

Lord, I give You my broken places and pain. I choose
to hear You whisper words of encouragement so I can
walk forward in the beauty of brokenness.

Tonya Hubbard, Fordyce, AR

Witness the Splendor of Creation

I will praise You, for I am fearfully and wonderfully made;
marvelous are Your works, and that my soul knows very well.

PSALM 139:14 NKJV

After the chaos of packing and planning, we loaded the car and began our road trip from Arkansas to Arizona. Mile after mile the scenery changed from the tall green pines and hills of Arkansas, to the plains of Texas that stretched as far as the eye could see, to the red rocks reaching to the heavens in Arizona. There was enchanting beauty all around us.

The majesty and artistry of the land we drove though left us breathless at the creativity of our heavenly Father, who with only His words crafted these inspiring horizons. Imagine: in six days He created all this imagery. Our cameras were snapping pictures of the exquisite sights surrounding us. As creation revealed His glory, I watched people stand in wonder of these beautiful views.

Our lives, intricately formed and designed by the Master's hand, are His masterpiece. Each of us was formed by the hands of the One who created the mountains, canyons, and plains. The creativity of the Master has been placed within our being. As His most personal creations, we reflect His glory in the simplicity and artistry of our own lives. We reflect the same majesty, because He has created us not only by His hand, but in His image.

Lord, I thank You for the sheer genius of Your creation.
Help me remember my place as Your creation as well,
and show me how to reflect Your beauty.

Unwrap Hidden Blessings

We have this treasure from God, but we are like clay jars that hold the treasure. This shows that the great power is from God, not from us.

2 CORINTHIANS 4:7 NCV

*C*hristmas is my favorite time of year, and giving is one of the things I enjoy most. I often use old paper and cardboard boxes, and even small appliance boxes as gift boxes. Imagine the letdown my children felt when they saw a toaster box on Christmas morning! More than one Christmas gift was misunderstood because of the outside of the box.

Can you relate? Imagine you open a gift, and the box is quite different from what you imagined. But when you discover what's *in* the box, you find it was much more than you anticipated. You were expecting the box to show you what was on the inside.

Sometimes we look at ourselves and see nothing more than a recycled cardboard box. When we see our weaknesses, our faults, and our struggles, we see vessels made of clay in today's verse. Focusing on the box we sometimes stop looking for the gift. God sees beyond the outside and looks to the heart. He has put a special gift inside each one of us, and He longs for us to discover it. We cannot risk only looking at the outside box and tossing it aside. It is up to us to move past any underwhelming packaging and enjoy the gift He has given us.

Lord, I pray I will seek to see the gifts You have given me.
I ask You to help me see beyond the box of my insecurities
and faults as I walk into all You have created me to be.

Tonya Hubbard, Fordyce, AR

Accept the Mystery of Grace

With great power the apostles gave witness to the resurrection of the Lord Jesus. And great grace was upon them all.

ACTS 4:33 NKJV

Many days I have watched my mom struggle to remember who I am, who my children are, or even who her husband of more than fifty years is. She has been overcome with grief from feeling left alone by her parents, who left this earth many years ago. She remembers few moments of her life and even fewer people. This once beautiful woman, full of life and hope, now wrecked by years of disease plaguing her mind and her emotions, is a shell of who she used to be. But then we witness a moment of recollection beyond her human ability, as she rises to sing the anthems of her life. "He Set Me Free," "I'll Fly Away," and "Amazing Grace" are the melodies that echoed through the halls of her home, her car, and even the grocery store. No matter what has left her life through the effects of this disease, she, through no power of her own, holds on to the power, the promise, and the message of the cross.

The grace that doesn't let my mom lose the one thing she holds the dearest, her Savior and King, is the same grace that holds us when we cannot rise above the situations that cause us to feel as though we have been left alone. This grace sustains and overcomes no matter what. This grace continues to tell the story of Jesus when there are no more stories to tell.

Lord, I pray that as I give You the struggles that are greater than I am, You will empower me with Your grace to overcome.

Find Mercy When You Fall

Though he brings grief, he will show compassion,
so great is his unfailing love.

LAMENTATIONS 3:32

*L*ife was good for me. I was running the race with hope and expectation, but then the rough terrain of life invaded my path, and all the sudden I felt myself slipping from the solid pavement beneath my feet. My hopes, dreams, and expectations were crushed as I lost my footing and fell. Faithfully, I had been running strong from the beginning, keeping pace with all God's promises. I was full of hope and vision for the future and racing toward all He had planned for me to become. Then somewhere along the way something tripped me and I fell. With my focus misplaced, I lost sight of what God had called me to do and be. Undone, I waited for my wounds to heal and searched for a reason to hope again. Every time my footing failed to keep me upright and on the right path, I was left feeling as if there was no way to recover.

God in His mercy sees our failures and faults. He sees our faltering steps; and although we feel there is no chance of us finishing the race with victory, He compassionately helps us back to our feet and back into the race.

Inspired by His love and tenderness, I see the hope of His tomorrows. Rising to take my place back among the racers, I know failures will come in my life, but the mercy I receive from the Father is what has inspired me to keep going. Failure isn't the end, and it isn't final unless I allow it to be. With the race before me, I will run to victory.

....

Lord, wrap me in Your arms of forgiveness.
Help me get up and run again.

Tonya Hubbard, Fordyce, AR

Heal from Hurtful Words

I kept very quiet. I didn't even say anything good,
but I became even more upset.

PSALM 39:2 NCV

A s I stood there, shocked by the hateful words being spoken over me, every word I tried to speak seemed to give my accuser more ammo to fire at my heart. So I chose to stay silent in hopes of silencing my accuser. With insults flying at me from a trusted friend, all I could do was stand there. The person she described was completely different from who I am at the core. Again and again she lashed out at me, degrading the very person God has created me to be. It wasn't a spiritual rebuke prompted by the Spirit. These were hate-filled words, threats, comparisons, and curses. Moments passed, and I felt empty and hated. Silent, I stood there confused, hurt, and slandered. The words I had spoken had been twisted and turned into something they were never intended to be. So I resolved not to speak again.

We have all stood in those moments when we feel if we speak, we would only make things worse. Our heartache and anger could taint our words and make them hurtful. So we hold our words, and we keep the hurt inside, but it only becomes a greater heartache. God never intended us to carry all the burdens and wounds inflicted by others or by circumstances. He longs for us to give Him our frustration, our anger, and our heartache. He has never wished for us to hold on to what bothers us. He burns to liberate us from the harmful words and actions of others.

Lord, I release into Your hands those who have hurt me.
Please take my hurt and frustration and give me peace.

Experience Sweet Surrender

I heard him speaking, and as I listened to him, I fell
into a deep sleep, my face to the ground.

DANIEL 10:9

*A*s we walk the journey of life, it is important to listen to the heart of God. Sometimes in our busy pursuits we tend to over-plan and miss the purpose of what God is asking us to do. We fill our lives with things that are unnecessary and overlook God's calling entirely.

I remember as a child singing the song "I Surrender All." The truth is, although I was sincere in singing the words, I really didn't understand what fully surrendering to God's plan meant. As I matured, my life became overwhelmed with details of everyday living and ministry needs. I soon hit a speed bump in life and realized we cannot do God's will our way. To be effective we must surrender to His timing, directions, and instructions.

As an architect designs blueprints, so God fits together the master plan for our lives. He knows how to lay the proper foundation and construct the weight-bearing walls. It would be a mistake to build a beautiful home without creating a strong structure. In the same way it would not be wise to try and build our lives without the input of the Master Designer.

When I learned to yield my plan to God, I began experiencing miraculous moments. Faith replaced worry as I grew to trust God fully. When we place our plans in the hands of our Father, He does for us what we cannot do for ourselves.

Lord, I understand surrendering doesn't diminish
my plans but enlarges Yours.

Brenda McClintock, Springfield, MO

Let God Fight the Battle

The LORD will fight for you while you [only need
to] keep silent and remain calm.

EXODUS 14:14 AMP

I can recall a time I wanted to defend myself and say something that would have probably made a bad situation worse. While my heart was hurting and the idea of being misunderstood seemed so unfair, I knew I needed to rest and let God take care of the matter.

Was it easy to let someone off the hook? No. I wanted to speak my mind and set the record straight. But there was another part of me, a deeper part, that knew I needed to keep silent and trust God to defend me during this time of testing. It wasn't easy, but I chose to lay down my pride and let Him make things right.

With tears flowing down my face, I fell to my knees and began to pray. Like melting wax, my emotions tumbled out as I shared my hurt and heartache. I prayed until the heaviness was gone and I felt assured God would take care of the things causing me pain. That is exactly what happened.

Even though that relationship was never reconciled, I embraced this situation as a learning experience. I came to realize God is faithful to His word. He works all things to our benefit when we trust fully in Him. Today, if you are in a situation that seems unfair or unjust, I encourage you to lean on the Father. In His arms you are safe and secure.

....

Heavenly Father, I trust in Your strength and wisdom concerning every situation I go through. I hide in the shelter of Your embrace.

Please God

Without faith it is impossible to please God, because anyone who comes to him must believe that he exists and that he rewards those who earnestly seek him.

HEBREWS 11:6

The journey of life can make us feel as though we are on a winding if not dangerous path. At times our emotions can be shaken by what we see. This is especially true when our circumstances seem to be going in the opposite direction of our dreams.

I cannot count the number of times when life has had me running into the arms of my Father. It is when I am nestled close to Him that I am comforted by the assurance that nothing can uproot me from His hand. My everyday connection with God builds a strong resolve that flows into every part of my life. The increase of joy, peace, wisdom, and understanding becomes fuel for my soul. When I seek His heart, I uncover His will. The more I love Him, the more rest I find for my soul. It's a full circle of worship that never stops, and the benefits of spending time with Him are extravagant.

The enemy seeks to destroy our destiny by causing us to doubt the promises of God. Living in doubt and fear doesn't draw us near to our dreams; it pushes them further away. We only move forward when we take the next step in faith. Today come into agreement with God's Word that no miracle is too hard for Him to perform. There is no problem He cannot solve. Challenge yourself to walk in complete assurance that He will do more than you ask, think, or imagine (Ephesians 3:20).

Today I stand firm believing in the promise and plan You have for me. May my life bring You great pleasure!

Brenda McClintock, Springfield, MO

Know God Is Listening

*I will provide for their needs before they ask, and I will
help them while they are still asking for help.*

ISAIAH 65:24 NCV

*H*ave you ever been in a conversation with someone only to discover her attention has drifted somewhere else? You try to reclaim her attention but realize she is not interested in what you are saying. Soon the conversation moves to another topic and you feel as if you've been ignored.

The good news is that God never ignores our needs. He is always attentive to the call of His children. In fact no one understands us like our Father does. Many times we look for a friend to understand our heart, but no one can comprehend the depths of what we are feeling like God can.

When we face mountain-like moments, it can be hard to see that God is already working on the other side of the mountain. I remember when my daughter was in a medically induced coma for six days. She suffered from oxygen deprivation, causing massive brain trauma. My heart was torn in a million pieces, and I knew the only thing that would help my hurting heart was God's grace.

On the seventh day we received a call from the hospital with the news: her eyes had opened and her health was stabilizing. Though many tests were yet to come and grim news would be given, we trusted God would hear our prayers. He remained faithful to our family, and He will to yours as well.

*Father, You hear my prayers and see every need in
my life. Nothing is outside of Your reach.*

Take a Walk with God

The man and his wife heard the sound of the LORD God as he
was walking in the garden in the cool of the day, and they
hid from the LORD God among the trees of the garden.

GENESIS 3:8

It was five o'clock in the morning, and I was wide-awake. I felt an unexplainable need to walk around the neighborhood and spend time with the Lord. Everything seemed special. The dew on the flowers, the birds singing, and the early morning sunrise refreshed my spirit.

When I arrived home, I spent time on the back deck and began working on a new recording project. Words and lyrics poured out of my spirit and onto the paper. The time alone was exactly what I needed before going into the studio that week. When I glanced up from my work, I noticed a beautiful white dove sitting on my privacy fence. In awe of its beauty I studied it closely. Before long the noise of the morning traffic came by, and the dove flew to a quieter place in the yard.

The dove was a gentle reminder of how God longs for us to engage with Him. His heart longs to spend time with us without the surrounding noises of our busy lives. In the quiet moments we will hear His voice most clearly.

Our Father is ready to share His songs, instructions, and thoughts with us. The question is, will we take time away from our busy schedules to hear what He is saying? Intimacy with one another and with God begins by making time to get to the heart of what the other is saying.

Lord, here's my heart. I open myself to You. Look deep inside and speak to me. Walk with me in this journey, and order my steps.

Brenda McClintock, Springfield, MO

Redemption

"I have blotted out, like a thick cloud, your transgressions, and like a cloud, your sins. Return to Me, for I have redeemed you."

ISAIAH 44:22 NKJV

*I*n my early teens I experienced times of being distracted and distant in my relationship with God. While singing songs of worship at church, I was withholding pieces of my life that I wasn't willing to give up. I remember trying to find excuses to justify my behavior even though deep down inside I knew God was not pleased.

During this time I found it hard to resist the calling of God. When I lay down at night, I would be reminded of the wise words my mentors had given me. Prophetic words spoken over me would come to my mind, and I knew the whispers of the Holy Spirit were keeping me from ensnaring situations. Having been raised in the ways of the Lord, I knew I was at a crossroads in my faith. I felt an urgency to stop playing games.

One Sunday morning I made the decision to surrender completely to the loving guidance of the Father. Repenting with my whole heart, I made a fresh commitment to live for Christ. For the first time in a long time, I felt free. I went home that morning with a fresh expectation and readiness to embrace the good things God had in my future. As I returned to the heart of the Father that day, I no longer desired the past. Maybe you are walking through a season of feeling uncommitted to your faith. I encourage you to return to the arms of the One who loves you. It's not too late. God is standing ready to receive you.

Lord, You see where I am on the path of life. Forgive me my sins. Cleanse me. Redeem and reclaim my heart. I will serve You the rest of my life.

Rise Above Our Excuses

Then I heard the voice of the Lord saying, "Whom
shall I send? And who will go for us?"
And I said, "Here am I. Send me!"

ISAIAH 6:8 NIV

My husband is a pastor, and I absolutely love being a pastor's wife. But when it became apparent that I needed to be more visible in ministry, I was nervous and reluctant. I have always been a comfort-zone person with many reasons (excuses) why I couldn't do certain things. You know, "Someone else could do a better job" and "Surely there are more qualified people than me." But God really started to deal with me about my ministry. As I spent time in prayer, I truly began to trust God, knowing He wouldn't call me to do something if He hadn't prepared me to do the job. It was time for me to rise above my excuses.

I have been through a season of stretching and growth, which hasn't been easy, but it has been rewarding. I am enjoying teaching with my husband on occasion and leading our women's group. If I can grow past my excuses, so can you.

Today maybe you are finding it difficult to reach for something new. The truth is you will never know what you can do until you try. I encourage you to step out of what feels comfortable and let God empower you to do something you've never done before. Rise above your excuses and embrace His invitation to move into unfamiliar territory. Start the business you've always dreamed of. Take a new class. Discover a new path. Enjoy the journey.

Father, I am ready today to lay down my excuses and say, "Send me!"

Crystal Murray, St. Simons Island, GA

Do Something Extraordinary

Noah did everything just as God commanded him.
GENESIS 6:22

Ten years ago my husband and I felt God was calling us do something new. Mike was the worship pastor at our church, and we led marriage classes together. For two years we prayed for direction, shed tears of frustration, and had many sleepless nights. We were transitioning into a new season. It was an odd time. We felt restless where we were, but we didn't feel confident it was our time to move on to something new. The only thing we knew to do was remain faithful to the things we were doing.

A short time later God opened the door for Mike to submit his resumé for the position of senior pastor at a church in our fellowship. Before the interview we were both nervous and excited. We felt confident we were doing what God wanted us to do next. A few minutes into the interview, Mike was asked to be the new pastor of the church. We knew deep in our hearts that this was God's will. Humbled and thankful, we accepted the position and began a new journey of faith.

Following God's leading isn't always easy. Sometimes it feels more comfortable to stick with what is familiar, to stay on the well-traveled path, and to do what others are doing. But comfort never brings about extravagant rewards. Some blessings come only with doing something daring for God. Are you willing to follow God's commands and allow Him to take you on an extraordinary journey?

Dear Father, help me know that I can do extraordinary things in Your name. Help me keep my eyes on You and walk in daily obedience.

Laugh in Adversity

Sarah said, "God has brought me laughter, and everyone
who hears about this will laugh with me."

GENESIS 21:6

A few years ago my husband and I answered a call every parent dreads receiving. The person on the other end of the call informed us that our son Josh had been in a life-threatening four-wheeler accident. At that moment they weren't sure if Josh was even alive. We were devastated. We felt every ounce of energy drain from our bodies. We had no strength of our own; God had to be our strength. Josh had multiple injuries, required surgery, and was in a wheelchair for three months following the accident. Despite this he completely recovered and is now in perfect health, married, and the father of two children.

In the time Josh was going through surgery and slowly recovering, we never expected to experience joy or laughter. But even during days of frustration and pain we could keep our focus on God and the miracle He performed by saving Josh's life. Though the days were tough and the nights long, we discovered bright spots where we could laugh and enjoy the goodness of God.

Are you walking through a hard situation? Do you feel as if everywhere you turn you are facing adversity? I encourage you to look for and embrace moments of joy. When you start your day, no matter how you feel or what things may look like, refocus your thoughts by embracing something good. Sing a favorite song. Enjoy a happy memory. Call someone you love. Most important, ask God for moments of laughter.

Jesus, be the center of my joy. Remind me when I walk through
times of adversity that I can find joy in every season.

Crystal Murray, St. Simons Island, GA

A Better Plan

"For my thoughts are not your thoughts, neither are
your ways my ways," declares the LORD.

ISAIAH 55:8 NIV

A few years ago our daughter Jordan was diagnosed with a brain tumor. The words "Your daughter needs emergency brain surgery" stopped us in our tracks. The doctors offered little hope and said if Jordan survived the surgery, she would have memory loss and would possibly never be the same. We prayed in faith, asking God to heal Jordan and to make the tumor dissolve. Instead of doing this He allowed Jordan to go through surgery. It was a long and risky surgery, but God brought her through it and gave her a perfect recovery. Her doctors were amazed by her progress, and we were thankful for a miracle. Jordan is now healthy, married, and a mom.

Sometimes things don't turn out the way we want or expect they should. I thought the simple solution to this situation was for God to completely heal Jordan. It wasn't my plan for her to go through surgery. But God not only wanted to do something *for* us, He wanted to do something *within* us. His plan was for us to trust Him. Because of Jordan going through this situation, our faith was stretched and grew in an unexpected way.

Do you struggle allowing God's plan to be your plan? It's easy to feel discouraged when things don't happen on your timetable. But in those moments when your faith level seems low, you can have faith that God has something good in store for you.

Father, I submit my life to You. Help me walk out Your
plan for my life. I surrender my will to Yours.

Know You Are Forgiven

*He chose us in him before the creation of the world
to be holy and blameless in his sight.*

EPHESIANS 1:4

*S*ome days I feel as if I say all the wrong things, I am irritable and overly sensitive, and I snap at the ones closest to me—even my spouse. Similarly I have days when I don't have a right attitude with God, days when I'm not completely obedient when He prompts me to do something for someone, give something to someone, or spend time with Him in fasting and prayer. On those days I am so grateful that God is a loving and forgiving God, even when I selfishly have a bad attitude. It is so freeing to know that when I repent of my sins and disobedience, God will freely and lovingly forgive me.

When God asks us to do something, we tend to disobey and go in the opposite direction. Don't miss God by overanalyzing His instructions. If we think about things too much, we will miss out on the opportunity to follow God fully. If He asks you to forgive someone, don't ask, *Why should I?* Instead thank Him for giving you a tender and loving heart.

When you are quick to obey the voice of God, you will experience the best life has to offer. Know that you can go to God in confidence, pour out your heart, repent of your actions, and receive forgiveness. God chose you, and if you choose to live for Him, you have assurance that you are forgiven.

....

Father, thank You for loving and forgiving me. By Your
grace I am confident my sins have been forgiven. Wash
me. Transform my heart. Renew my mind.

Crystal Murray, St. Simons Island, GA

Exchange Your Weakness for God's Strength

For Christ's sake, I delight in weaknesses, in insults, in hardships, in persecutions, in difficulties. For when I am weak, then I am strong.
2 CORINTHIANS 12:10

*F*our months before I married my husband, Mike, he had a heart attack. After undergoing many tests, Mike's team of doctors told him that he would never work again. They went on to tell us his life expectancy was three to five years. We didn't know how to react to that kind of news. We felt totally devastated. Our lives seemed to spiral out of our control. The only thing we knew to do was trust in God. We spent much of our time praying, fasting, and confessing the promise of God's Word.

Looking back, I see God was our strength and confidence. Over the years through God's healing power and the wisdom of doctors and medicine, Mike is thriving and strong. It has been thirty-four years since that initial report, and his doctor is amazed by how well he is doing. He calls Mike "Miracle Man."

Today no matter what difficulty you are facing, choose to activate your faith. Though you may start out weak in faith, His power will strengthen you. Be determined to face every day with a good attitude and optimistic outlook. Allow His power to overtake your situation.

Dear heavenly Father, when I am overwhelmed and weak, help me remember I don't have to be strong on my own. Help me to stand on Your promises. Through my weakness I am made strong in You.

A Fresh Start

God remembered Noah and all the wild and tame animals with him in the boat. He made a wind blow over the earth, and the water went down.
GENESIS 8:1 NCV

When I was a young woman and didn't know the Lord, I felt as though hardships would never end. I was divorced twice, worked two jobs, was in an abusive relationship, and felt older than I was. One day at work I was crying into my cup of coffee. I questioned, *How much stress can one person handle?* That day I felt I would never be happy again. I had no idea how quickly things would change. Two weeks later I met a man who would lead me to Christ and later would become my husband. Twenty years have passed, and my life has never been the same.

Tucked away in the book of Genesis is the story of Noah. If you've read today's passage before, you know his family watched as water flooded the earth for more than 150 days. I'm sure at times they wondered, *Will things ever get back to normal?* Maybe you've had a similar thought: *Has God forgotten me? Can God see the mess I'm in?* Just as God remembered and rescued Noah's family, God will remember you. He sees the situation you are in. His heart is to give you a fresh start and turn your heartache into joy. I assure you, troubles won't last forever. There is a new season ahead. Let God wash away the tears from your eyes and lead you somewhere new.

Today, Lord, I refuse to stay stuck in discouragement. I will not let disappointments overshadow my joy. Thank You for seeing my situation and rescuing me from pain. My heart and eyes are fixed on You.

Kerrie Oles, Colleyville, TX

Beautiful Seasons

He has made everything beautiful in its time.
ECCLESIASTES 3:11 NKJV

Growing up I used to sing along to the song "Everything Is Beautiful." Upbeat and positive, the words made me smile. But the truth is, life is not always blissfully happy. God didn't promise every day would be beautiful. He promised to make everything beautiful *in its time.*

The words *anaphylactic shock* had worked their way into my vocabulary. From his hospital bed my eleven-year-old weakly asked, "Why is this happening to me?" After all the treatments and tears, we were still trying to find out what triggered his violent reaction. Grabbing his hand I gave the only answer I had: "I can't answer that question, but I know God is here."

As my child fell asleep, I felt the enemy of our souls delight in my feeling overwhelmed and defeated. Staring out the window, I caught a glimpse of other hospital rooms and began to wonder what kind of heartache others were going through. Silently I prayed for their needs as I prayed for mine. That night I began to sing and worship the Lord. I felt a calming peace and discovered that worship drives our worries away.

We all experience seasons of pain and heartache. Today you may be struggling to find peace, struggling with needing a new job, fighting back feelings of loneliness, or experiencing a health crisis. I want to encourage you to keep pressing forward during the tough times. I promise you, there is victory on the other side of your darkest season. Our Father will take the bad things you're going through, turn them around, and in the right season He will use them for His good.

Father, help me learn to praise You in every situation, good or bad.

Unfailing Hope

*If a tree is cut down, there is hope that it will grow
again and will send out new branches.*

JOB 14:7 NCV

I never thought I'd be at the prison again, but I was. I spent most of my childhood visiting my brother who was incarcerated. I promised myself, *When I am older, I will never go back to that place.* I had no idea God would lay it on my heart to return to the prison system and bring words of life to women who were serving time.

As I met with these women and learned more about their stories, I developed a deep compassion and drive to see their lives turn around. One day a woman let me know, "I just gave my life to the Lord, and I will be out of here in seven days." I smiled with excitement, but she looked sad. Confused by her expression, I asked what she was feeling. Her response made me stop in my tracks. She said, "I have served seven years in the system, but I don't want to leave. Out there I don't know how to stop being me. And I'm so afraid I will fall back into my old habits."

Her words affected me so much because I struggled with those same thoughts after giving my life to the Lord at age thirty. I was excited to be a part of God's family, but it would take a while for my thoughts and behavior to line up with God's Word. I needed healing in my heart and healing from past situations. Over time that is exactly what happened. I began to think pure thoughts. My actions and reactions began to reflect those of Christ. The same will happen for all of us when we place our lives in the hands of the One who makes all things new.

....

*Father, I release my past to You. I wrap myself
in the goodness of Your grace.*

Kerrie Oles, Colleyville, TX

A New Name

He took twelve stones, one stone for each of the twelve tribes, the
number of Jacob's sons. (The LORD changed Jacob's name to Israel.)

1 KINGS 18:31 NCV

*M*y son asked me a surprising question: "Mom, do you ever wonder what your life would've been like had you not made the
mistakes you've made?" I stopped to think my answer through before
responding.

"There was a time I thought God had only one plan for my life and
that I had messed that plan up. It took a while before I discovered God's
grace gives us the opportunity to make something good out of our
messes."

For years I struggled to feel worthy of the good things God had for
my life. I felt that the bad decisions I made in some way disqualified me
from God's goodness. I believed the lie that I was unworthy of His grace.
This way of thinking warped my identity. For a period of time I lost my
identity as God's daughter and took on a false identity of shame.

Maybe the enemy has lied to you as well. Don't let those negative feelings strip away the promises God has for your life. Embrace His mercy.
God doesn't throw your dreams away because your life gets off track.
His plan is for you to succeed. If the mistakes of your past have left you
broken, if you are wearing a label God never gave you, take it off. God
will give you a new name. He calls you forgiven, righteous, redeemed.

Today, Lord, I release the negative labels of doubt and
shame. I ignore critical voices telling me I am not good
enough. I choose to find my identity in You.

Keep Climbing

Then the LORD said to Moses, "Why are you crying out
to Me? Tell the sons of Israel to go forward."

EXODUS 14:15 NASB

O ne afternoon at the arcade park my teenage son asked if he could climb the rock wall. He wanted to know if I thought he could make it to the top. Being supportive, but feeling somewhat doubtful, I assured him he could do it. Feeling this was a good opportunity to encourage him, I offered to scale the rocks with him. I'm not sure why I suggested; the truth was, I didn't believe I could make it to the top either.

As I slipped on the harness, I felt the Lord whisper, *Kerrie, you can do all things through Me.* I had an inner peace that He was asking me to turn my *I-can't* mind-set into an *I-can* way of thinking. I laugh now at how God uses everyday circumstances to build our faith.

Did I make it to the top? No, but I made it halfway up! And I felt good about my efforts to try something new. I was surprised by how far I made it up the makeshift mountain.

If you're facing something that makes you fearful, don't abandon your faith. Take a running leap, and keep moving toward things you never thought you could do. Believe me, when you extend your faith and try your best, God will infuse you with courage. You are equipped to accomplish more than you've imagined. Stop settling for situations that make you comfortable. It's time for you to bravely break through walls of self-doubt.

Father, teach me to be brave. Encourage me when I feel
weak. Show me how to embrace new opportunities.

Kerrie Oles, Colleyville, TX

Follow the Father

"That the world may know that I love the Father, and as the Father gave Me commandment, so I [talk with you]. Arise, let us go from here."
JOHN 14:31 NKJV

*E*ven though we want the men in our lives to act like superheroes, we must remember that every superhero has a weakness. Watching the recent release of *Superman* reminded me that even though he could move mountains with his strength, a moment or two with kryptonite would strip away his power.

In a similar way, my dad was my superhero. His inability to express his love or affection was my kryptonite. In my heart I hoped he loved me, but I was never certain, because he never told me he loved me. For a long time I believed the lie that he didn't love me. The longing to receive something he didn't know how to express left my heart in shambles.

Unrealized expectations can take hearts down dark, lonely roads. Maybe you feel less than loved by someone you care deeply for. I discovered that sometimes the greatest way to receive love is to teach others how to love. This means loving without the expectation of receiving love in return.

Jesus didn't tell us to love those who love us. He challenged us to love the unlovely, to reach out to the bitter, to help those who are hurting. In doing so we set ourselves up to feel the love of the Father. What are ways we can teach others how to walk in love? Maybe they have never received love, so they don't know how to give it. Be the one who shows them how to follow the Father and love like Christ.

Father, thank You for loving and accepting me. May I learn how to express unconditional love. Make my heart more like Yours.

See God's Purpose Is Better Than Our Plan

You will find favor and good success in the sight of God and man. Trust in the LORD with all your heart, and do not lean on your own understanding.

PROVERBS 3:4–5 ESV

Our plans, though well thought out, always seem to be shortsighted and often miss the target we anticipate. We strive to fill the void in our lives with plans that keep us busy and consumed with a hectic lifestyle. But the void is only filled when God's purpose in our life is made complete.

I have a dear friend who is a very loving, caring person whose purpose in life is to show love and compassion to others. I can often tell when she is trying to fulfill a plan instead of her purpose. Her actions become agitated and her disposition changes to one of being discontent with life. She immediately goes into a reactive, self-defense mode instead of her usual loving demeanor. Our discontent and agitation with life is often our first sign that we are seeking our self-made plans instead of the destiny God has in store for us.

God's invitation is simply to trust Him, even though we cannot see His plans and often must trust Him to take just one step at a time. But as we begin to move, God brings peace into our hectic plans. And with each step closer to God, we rely less and less on the ill-fated plans we have made and more on His faithfulness.

Father, I accept Your invitation to trust You with each new step. I will pursue Your plan and not my own. I lay aside the heaviness I have carried and trust You fully.

Kristy Thomas, Valley Springs, AR

Walk on Waves

Mightier than the violent raging of the seas, mightier than the breakers on the shore—the LORD above is mightier than these!

PSALM 93:4 NLT

*H*ave you ever felt that if one more thing went wrong, your heart would burst into a million pieces? We've all felt the overwhelming urge to run and escape to a safe place.

When the news came that my second-born baby girl would not be born healthy, I almost crumbled. My heart broke when they told us her organs were not developing, and that if she survived, she would be severely disabled. In that moment life seemed to stand still; I felt it no longer held any meaning. But the Holy Spirit within me would not let me simply slip into a fog; instead all I could do was cry out to the Lord for help. As the days passed and the impending appointment with the specialist arrived, everyone advised us to be prepared to abort the baby. We knew God had heard our prayers, and soon the doctor and everyone else would know God had a plan for our daughter. All tests came back and said our baby girl was healthy. She is now a vibrant, beautiful, healthy teenager with an amazing voice, who loves to sing and praise the Lord.

Mightier than the waves that are raging in your life, mightier than that which threatens to break you, is the God who is! He will stand for you when you cannot find the strength to stand for yourself. Cling to His Word when everything else seems to fail you, cling to His name when you cannot even form a prayer to describe your anguish. Cling to His everlasting arms when you have nowhere else to turn.

Father, thank You for caring for me and walking
with me when the storm rages.

Cultivate What Was Planted in Faith

*Let us hold tightly without wavering to the hope we affirm,
for God can be trusted to keep his promise.*

HEBREWS 10:23 NLT

*I*t is easy today to become discontent with our surroundings, and to desire something new and exciting. We long for something better, for an adrenaline boost, for excitement in every area of life. I've noticed the price of constant excitement is often an uneasy heart. The desire for more and better can overwhelm every area of our lives.

Being raised on a farm I learned rather quickly that anything worth having usually requires patience and hard work. If you wanted a good garden, you planted and waited; if you wanted a good herd, you had to be patient and take care of what you had. Being raised around grandparents who lived in the same house for more than sixty years showed me consistency. But my grandmother always told me that I had inherited a free spirit. In other words, I liked change; I liked to be in different places and experience different things. It never seemed like a bad quality until I found myself constantly asking the Lord for change in my life.

But just as God is faithful, He is quick to let us know when our lives become unbalanced. The best way to keep order in our lives is to have a consistent relationship with the Lord. In all our fast-paced living, let us remember to make sure that burdens, frustration, and stress do not grow inside us. If we keep our minds focused on His plans, our plans and dreams will stay in the right order.

Lord, make my roots grow deep, that I may be steady and secure.

Kristy Thomas, Valley Springs, AR

Begin Again

"See, I am doing a new thing! Now it springs up; do you not perceive it? I am making a way in the wilderness and streams in the wasteland."

ISAIAH 43:19

*I*t's hard to think that after we have dedicated years to a career, marriage, family, or even a church, God would ask us to start over. But often, due to loss, change, desperation, or heartache, we find ourselves in a season of starting over.

I remember watching my daughter be overcome with emotions as we moved our family to start a new chapter in our lives. As a mother, it was heartbreaking to watch our child struggle with trying to fit in, be strong, and hold on to faith. No matter how hard she tried or how involved she was, I could still see the longing in her eyes—; she just wanted her old life back. It is easy for us as parents to want to step in and make everything better. But sometimes it is better for our children to journey through a new season in faith and see the rewards of God doing something fresh.

Starting over, even for the best of reasons, comes with challenges, doubts, and fears. But during our self-doubt, fear, and adversity, God still promises to do a new thing. The courage to begin again takes faith, determination, and trusting God one step at a time.

Is God doing a new thing in your life? Is He stirring you to trust Him in this new chapter? Just as my daughter trusted that we were doing what was best for her (and is now a very happy young woman), trust in the Lord that His plan is the absolute best for your life. Face your new beginning with boldness, strength, and anticipation as God's new thing unfolds. Simply trust God's plan.

Holy Spirit, give me the courage to begin again.

Obey Without Questioning

Jesus replied, "But even more blessed are all who hear
the word of God and put it into practice."

LUKE 11:28 NLT

God told Abram, "Go." And Scripture tells us, "So Abram went" (Genesis 12:1, 4). A simple command and a simple act of obedience. Or so it appears. We are not told the prayers Abram prayed, nor do we know the details surrounding why God chose Abram. But we do know God is the Master at using ordinary people in ordinary places to bring about extraordinary outcomes of faith.

How do we model the faith of great men and women we read about in the Bible? How did they come to have such great faith? Were they born with great faith?

The truth is that in obedience they took small steps of faith that eventually became life-journeys of faith. Small acts of obedience—getting into the boat and going to the other side, trusting God at each turn in life, listening—that bring supernatural results.

At the time of this writing, to trust Him and step into full-time ministry alongside my husband. We have always been a team in ministering together, but for the past eleven years I have worked in a full-time position outside our ministry. Our desire to obey the Lord's calling at this point makes us feel as if we are stepping into thin air and trusting there will be a solid rock under our feet—even though we do not see it. Just as it was with the men and women we read about, we too must be obedient to accept God's perfect will. Learning to obey God without question will take us that much closer to His plan for us.

....

Father, turn my small steps of obedience into giant leaps of faith.

Kristy Thomas, Valley Springs, AR

Experience Faith Without Anxiety

*Anxiety in a man's heart weighs it down, but a
good (encouraging) word makes it glad.*

PROVERBS 12:25 AMP

We have faith that can move mountains . . . for everyone else's lives, or so it seems. We dig deep and speak encouragement, we pray, and we believe the Lord will do great things in their lives. But what about ourselves? Where is that great faith when it comes to us? Where are the words of encouragement, the words of authority, the unshakable faith that we so easily demonstrate for others?

Years ago my husband and I promised the Lord we would always follow after peace. Little did we know that peaceful did not always mean easy, or even without some form of major difficulty. Peace did not always look like what we thought it would, but deep down inside it was a peace that we could not explain. So with each road of ministry the Lord has led us down, we have asked Him to provide His peace. At times, peace did not come automatically, and often we prayed for months and even years for the pieces to come into place so we could make the right decision.

Our faith is not in our faithfulness, but it is ultimately in the faithfulness of the Lord. It's in His ability. It's never a question of if He can; it's a question of if it's His will. And with His will comes His peace.

The strife and anxiety that wage war on your mind and lay heavy on your heart can only be calmed by the peace of God that surpasses all understanding. Resolve today always to follow after the peace of the Lord in every area of your life.

....

Lord, please grant me Your peace, and remind
me to seek it along with Your will.

Live an Extraordinary Life

To Him who is able to do exceedingly abundantly above all that
we ask or think, according to the power that works in us.

EPHESIANS 3:20 NKJV

*F*ew things in life are as sweet as a spring afternoon spent enjoying time with your family. My three-year-old daughter and I were in the front yard playing with sidewalk chalk when a mockingbird landed a few feet away from where we were drawing. She quickly dropped everything and hopped to her tiptoes, anxious to sneak up on the "birdie." Her sneaking skills were as inconspicuous as an elephant's, causing the bird to quickly take flight. Her little arms reached as high into the sky as was humanly possible while she jumped and bounced and leaped in every attempt to catch the bird. Realizing it was gone, she sunk her head and came back to finish drawing.

Moments later a plane flew overhead, and she once again jumped to her feet and began reaching to catch and hold it. In her sweet, innocent mind, she could not understand why this was not possible.

It's incredible to me the limitless imagination that a child holds. What if we, as adults, could allow our minds to dream bigger, to believe bigger, and to live bigger? What if we reached for our wildest dreams as she reached for that plane, with every belief that God can do in our lives "exceedingly abundantly above all that we ask or think" (Ephesians 3:20 WEB)? While my daughter is unlikely to grasp a bird or a plane in her sweet little hands, our Father wants every good thing for His children. May we all have child-like faith and imagination as we reach for what He holds for us.

Thank You, Lord, for the extraordinary life You have planned for
me. You promise to give me a life greater than I can imagine.

Rachel Price, Bentonville, AR

Diminish Doubts

For God alone my soul waits in silence and quietly
submits to Him, for my hope is from Him.
PSALM 62:5 AMP

*T*he signal had been given, and the room was so quiet you could hear a pin drop. The crowd waited in anticipation, hoping for their chance at the weekly atmosphere award. This group of children was accustomed to the rules of the weekly contest. They knew that after cheering as loud as possible, the first group to be completely silent when given the signal would win. They waited in complete silence and obedience, hoping for the coveted award.

As followers of Christ we are offered a much greater reward. We are promised a hope that is unfailing and absolute, a promise of eternity with our Lord. If we will wait in silence, quietly submitting to Him, we can let go of our doubts.

On our journeys to live extraordinary lives, one of the many obstacles we must overcome is doubt. We are each affected by it to varying degrees. Some face doubts about their marriages, their kids, their careers, or their finances. Still others may have doubts about their faith, their future, or their abilities. Doubt is a common thing, but not a God thing. When we place our faith in an unfailing God rather than an ever-failing world, our doubt is outweighed by our faith.

....

Dear God, thank You for the unfailing hope I find in You.
Remove any doubts from my heart, and help my faith to be
the overwhelming factor of my life rather than my fear.

Be Led by the Spirit

If you fully obey the LORD your God and carefully follow
all his commands I give you today, the LORD your God
will set you high above all the nations on earth.

DEUTERONOMY 28:1

I am inspired as I observe a visually impaired person being led by a sighted person around new territories. When being shown through hallways, up stairs, and around rooms, he must both trust and obey his guide. When told to turn left, he did not turn right. When advised to step up, he acted accordingly. An important principle lies in his actions: to be led, we must first be obedient. Not only do the blind trust their guide to lead them, they also follow their exact directions, despite not being able to see where they are going. If we want to be led by the Spirit, we must trust and follow Him even when we can't see what's ahead.

As we strive to live extraordinary lives free of doubts, we are reminded to fully obey the Lord and follow not just some but all His commands. We won't always know where God is leading us, but we can count on the fact that when we obey, we will be blessed beyond measure. God's Word reminds us, when we follow His leading, blessings will overtake us. Not only will we receive the blessings of God; they will overwhelm us.

Father, thank You for being the guide I can always trust. Help me listen
for Your voice, and give me a heart that is ready to follow You.

Rachel Price, Bentonville, AR

Prepare for Promotion

Do you see a man who excels in his work? He will stand
before kings; He will not stand before unknown men.
PROVERBS 22:29 NKJV

Whether you are a businesswoman, a stay-at-home mom, or a girl just trying to find her place in this world, it is easy to get caught up in the daily grind. From going to the office after a sleepless night with a sick child to folding laundry, doing dishes, taking kids to practice, writing a book, and getting lunches packed, I have done it all. (And that was just yesterday!) Sometimes we get so focused on our task list for the day that we forget God has a task list for our tomorrows.

It's hard to see past today's chores and expectations, but we must stop long enough to remember that everything we do is part of God's plan and should ultimately serve to glorify Him. We can change the world by changing diapers. There is no limit to what God can do with a person who is fully committed to Him. We may stand before kings, but someday we will stand before the King of kings. Stand in His presence having lived a life with no regrets.

Make the most of every moment, knowing that He has given you this moment for a reason. Know that He wants to give you more, and prepare yourself to receive what He has in store. Promotion requires preparation.

God, I thank You for the opportunity I have to serve You today. I recognize that everything I do today is just in preparation for where You are leading me tomorrow. May You be glorified through it all.

Know God Is Exceedingly Good

The LORD your God is bringing you into a good land—a land with brooks, streams, and deep springs gushing out into the valleys and hills.

DEUTERONOMY 8:7

While I am not a sports fan, the men in my family are total enthusiasts. Football is their favorite sport, and I enjoy listening to them cheer on their teams. I can always tell when the referees have made a bad call—the guys go crazy yelling at the screen. I am fully convinced that they believe the coaches can hear them through the satellite feed. I can also tell whether they feel the coach is doing a good or bad job by the way they cheer or complain.

We tend to treat God the same way. When things are going great, we give Him praise. But as soon as trouble comes, we are back to questioning God, asking why He let negative things happen to us. Reading in Deuteronomy, I am reminded of God's faithfulness to the Israelites despite their reckless behavior. They had a very consistent history of loving God, hating Him, living for God, and then acting against Him. Yet despite their actions, His love and mercy endured. He continued to provide for and bless them when they turned their hearts back to Him.

Maybe you have been inconsistent in your walk with God. Know that His desire is to have your full heart, to walk with you every day. You don't have to have a perfect history. But you do need a willing heart to walk out God's purpose for your life. God's plan for you is exceedingly good, because God is exceedingly good.

Lord, I know You are exceedingly good. I trust You in every situation.

Rachel Price, Bentonville, AR

Imagine

As it is written: "What no eye has seen, what no ear has heard, and what no human mind has conceived"—the things God has prepared for those who love him.

1 CORINTHIANS 2:9

Our imagination is powerful. When God created us, He filled us with creative thoughts and ideas. But many times the imaginative part of our mind gets tripped up by negative thoughts and skewed thinking. God's Word makes it clear that we are to take control of our thoughts and lead them rather than allow them to lead us.

Our enemy loves to twist our thoughts. It can only take a small seed of doubt or confusion for our minds to run wild. Before we know it, we begin imagining terrible scenarios: tragedies within the family, financial battles, career failures, health struggles, and more. If we give the enemy control, we can see an array of things going wrong in our lives and fall into a prison of paralyzing fear. We must fight off the attack against our minds and use our imaginations for God's glory. We must dream big, because we will never out-dream God. What He has planned for you goes far beyond what your mind can conceive.

The creativity of God is all around us. My eyes have seen the crystal-clear waters of Cozumel. My ears have heard the thundering roar of Niagara Falls. My mind has meditated upon the splendor of God's faithfulness. Yet in all this, His Word reminds me, no eye has seen, no ear has heard, no mind has conceived what God has prepared for us.

....

God, I want to experience everything You have for me. I want to live an extraordinary life; help me dream extraordinary dreams.

Leave It at the Altar

"Whenever you stand praying, if you have anything against anyone, forgive him, that your Father in heaven may also forgive you your trespasses."

MARK 11:25 NKJV

*H*ow can I forgive . . . again? I just want to pull the covers over my head, wrapping myself in its comfort, as my heart aches in utter disappointment. The sting of betrayal has once again found its way into my heart. I muster through my pain as the whispers to my heart say, *Be still . . . everything will be okay.*

Unforgiveness is the thief of all peace. We get caught up questioning *why, how,* or *what if I only knew this was coming?* Our hearts begin to collide with what is right and what we should do: forgive. But we lose control of our emotions. We crawl into our beds defeated by the pain of disappointment.

We aren't responsible for how others treat us, but we are responsible for how we respond. Is it fair? Sometimes it's not. But we aren't asked to do what is fair; we are asked to do what is right. To forgive as our Father in heaven has forgiven us. We are asked to become an imitator of Christ, forgiving even when it hurts the most.

It would be remiss of me to say, "Let it go. Sweep it under the rug and trust God." Instead I charge you today to take it out from under the rug. Look at it. Hold this painful moment along with your emotions for just a moment. Then turn and leave it at the altar—at the feet of Jesus.

Father, I come boldly to Your throne and ask You to take unforgiveness from my heart. I choose today to release my pain and hurt to You, as I leave it at the altar.

Christine Martin, Chicago, IL

Break Free

Let them give thanks to the LORD for his love and for the miracles he does for people. He breaks down bronze gates and cuts apart iron bars.

PSALM 107:15–16 NCV

When tough circumstances arise, and our hearts become overwhelmed, our initial thought is often to simply escape. Escape from the chaos and heartache. Escape from our circumstances. We just want to break free. I recall so many moments in my life when I felt I just couldn't do it anymore. I was desperate for a breakthrough. I'll never forget the awakening that followed my near-death car accident. It took this near-death experience for me to break free.

Maybe you have found yourself struggling to find freedom in a certain area. You're seeking a way just to break free. You may be a mother of young children who is overwhelmed. You may be struggling with the heartache that comes from the loss of a loved one, a marriage that ended in an unwanted divorce, or the loss of a job. Life throws you many variables, but your circumstances don't have to hold you captive.

When we desperately need a breakthrough, we crave freedom like a rich, decadent dessert. We long for the moment we can savor freedom. This desire to break free is the heart of God wanting us to have total freedom. We desire the richness of our heavenly Father's freedom from the suffering we have endured for far too long. We must align ourselves with the heart of God by declaring our freedom—*before* we see it. The moment we decide to believe His truth above our feelings and declare we are *already* free, we will truly break free.

Father, I come before You, releasing every situation and circumstance, as I declare this my break-free day!

Embrace Redemption

"Say to the children of Israel: 'I am the LORD; I will bring you out from under the burdens of the Egyptians, I will rescue you from their bondage, and I will redeem you with an outstretched arm and with great judgments.'"

EXODUS 6:6 NKJV

Rejection, self-regret, insecurity, and unforgiveness all create bondage that holds us back from living the life God intended for us. We yearn for freedom from those very chains holding us captive. We seek to be rescued. We plead desperately to embrace freedom—to embrace redemption.

I remember it like it was yesterday—a time when the burdens of my past weighed heavily upon me. I felt like a prisoner trapped in feelings of shame, guilt, and regret. I began to muster up my praise and to look past my weaknesses. I asked the Lord to search my heart and reveal the root of what had me in bondage all those years. The moment I surrendered my past hurt and pain to the Lord was the moment I was released from the chains holding me back.

I was reminded of God's great love. The love of God that has come to set the captives free. The love of God that says He has come "to bind up the brokenhearted" and give relief to those who are bound (Isaiah 61:1).

When we allow Jesus into our pain and surrender the bondage that has been holding us back, the Spirit of Truth will overtake us. We break free from the chains of captivity. We begin to walk in extraordinary freedom, encompassed by exceptional joy.

....

Lord, thank You for bringing me out from under my burdens. Today I declare redemption over everything the enemy has stolen from me.

Christine Martin, Chicago, IL

Come Out of Darkness

*He brought them out of darkness and the shadow of
death, and broke their chains in pieces.*

PSALM 107:14 NKJV

*F*eeling alone, unloved, and isolated can leave us wanting to run away from everything. We hide from the world, trapped in our darkness. All we want is to sneak off from the crowds and just sit in solitude where no one can see us falling apart.

I'll never forget that cold wintry day when everything around me seemed insurmountable. All my worries and cares about this world had overcome me. I found myself trapped in a deep, dark place. I had allowed myself to fall into a pit of feeling isolated. I knew God's Word said, "He brought them out of darkness and the shadow of death, and broke their chains in pieces," but I just couldn't see that. I cried to God, "*God . . . pieces?*" I was the one in a million pieces! I needed God to take me, in all my pieces, and give me His peace.

It was as if I were hiding in a dark closet in a great big house, where no one could find me. I had pulled away from everyone because I believed in the lies from the enemy. But God called me out. He reached in with one hand and said, "My daughter, you are loved, and it's time you come out of darkness into the light."

The moment we reach for God's hand, He pulls us out from believing in those lies, from the fear, rejection, shame, guilt, or those toxic emotions that plague us. Only then can we see with eyes of faith who we truly are.

....

Father, I thank You for every chain broken. Today I take a step
of courage as I come out from darkness and into Your light.

Walk in Wide-Open Places

When hard pressed, I cried to the LORD; he brought me into a spacious place.

PSALM 118:5

*L*ife's circumstances or our own false beliefs can lead us to feel constrained and hard-pressed. We begin to feel limited and restricted by what we can and can't do. When we allow life's situations to constrain us, we essentially are putting limits on God and what He can do for us.

When I began to feel the stress of being hard-pressed, I cried out to the Lord. I saw that God didn't want me limiting myself and placing restrictions on His calling. When I did that, I found God led me to a spacious place, a wide-open place—a place where all my worries and fears were whisked away in the wind.

Maybe you have found yourself hard-pressed by life's circumstances, by debt, divorce, a stigma you put on yourself, or a label you branded yourself with. My dear friend, do not conform yourself to your circumstances. Ignite that spark within you. That spark that will release you from the restrictions that have confined and restrained you.

When we walk with a mind-set of "wide-open spaces," we enlarge our capacity to believe that anything is possible. We remove the limits we placed on God, and we can now see the vastness of what God has for us. Creativity begins to flow, and we no longer feel confined or constricted. We feel that sense of worth and calling once again. Go ahead and enter that wide-open place God is leading us to.

Father, thank You for leading me to walk boldly into wide-open spaces, where all things are possible, where I have clarity, wisdom, and peace.

Christine Martin, Chicago, IL

Released from Infirmity

When Jesus saw her, He called her over and said to her,
"Woman, you are released from your illness."

LUKE 13:12 AMP

Sometimes what we are walking through requires not a spiritual healing, but a physical healing instead. We can struggle with difficult emotions that arise from an infirmity. Often, these struggles bring doubt—doubt that there will ever be a release from the ailment.

At one time in my life, doctors said I was unable to produce children. As devastating as hearing this was, I believed faithfully that God could turn my circumstance around. In time God gave my husband and me a miracle! God not only healed my womb from this infirmity, but He set me free from drugs and alcohol. If that wasn't enough, God also set me free from the emotional infirmities I suffered from. And not long ago God cleansed my body from an infirmity that seemed never ending. I was the modern-day woman Jesus had released from her illness.

You may be suffering from an illness right now, or perhaps you have a loved one who is battling with a sickness. You might be overwhelmed with hopelessness and questions about why all of this is happening. Your heart's greatest desire is to get relief and be whole again.

I encourage you to speak words of divine reversal for healing and release from all infirmity. When you do, you will shut the door to those feelings of hopelessness, discouragement, and complaining, and open the door to the power and presence of Jesus as it heals you.

....

Father, thank You that according to Your Word You are
releasing me from this infirmity. I know that with one word
spoken, I am healed and made whole once again.

Make Your Mark

[David said,] "The LORD who saved me from a lion and a bear will save me from this Philistine." Saul said to David, "Go, and may the LORD be with you."

1 SAMUEL 17:37 NCV

I recently had a conversation with a friend about our pregnancy stretch marks. *Yuck.* I hated the sight of them in my swimsuit. I mentioned to my friend I was interested in having surgery to remove the stretched, scarred skin, but I was having second thoughts. After all, as much as I don't like the scars, they remind me of something I love deeply: my baby.

As I looked at my scars, they brought back memories of the baby born after a previous miscarriage. My second pregnancy went perfectly, until birth. Our newborn stubbornly refused to take his first breath. Seconds seemed like hours until he let out a cry. Those scars also remind me of my third pregnancy. The doctor had told us this child was too big for me to deliver. Not only was it a healthy birth, but the easiest delivery I experienced.

Those unsightly marks are evidence of God's miracle power that changed my identity. I am a mom—a mom empowered by a supernatural God. I watched God perform miracle after miracle in our family. He will do the same for you. Scars, like trials, tell your story and the unending goodness of God's grace. The tough situations you are going through today may be a sweet reminder of God's faithfulness down the road. Scars are not left to remind you of pain, but are a signature of God's goodness.

Father, may I walk in confidence knowing that the same faithfulness and power that has always saved me in trouble will show up today.

Kelly Parish, Eufaula, OK

Exhale Fear

"Don't worry, because I am with you. Don't be afraid, because
I am your God. I will make you strong and will help you; I
will support you with my right hand that saves you."

ISAIAH 41:10 NCV

*M*iracles come in many forms. Mine came wrapped as a ten-thousand-dollar check. It was a generous gift to help with the expense of my first worship album, *Drenched*. As I held the check, I was in awe of the goodness of God. I was nervous, excited, and amazed all at the same time. Recording in a professional studio was a lifelong dream. I had spent years writing songs and preparing for this moment.

My first day in the studio, I felt fear come over me. I knew I needed God to fill me with courage. Standing at the studio desk I whispered a prayer. I asked God to steady my nerves and give me a brave heart. He did. At that moment, I felt a wave of peace come over me. I could feel the Holy Spirit standing in the room with us. The feeling of knowing He was right there with me pushed any lingering fear right out the door.

Exhaling fear is an exercise of trust. It is easy to trust God with the day-to-day things. But what happens to our faith when we must face a new challenge? Do we trust Him to fulfill His promises? Do we pull back our dreams? Or do we step into our future knowing He holds us in the palm of His hand?

....

Today, I believe Your promises are greater than my fears. You are
not a Father who goes back on His word. I choose to I rely on
Your strength and know Your promises are true. I exhale fear.

Be Confident Enough to Ask

With God's power working in us, God can do much,
much more than anything we can ask or imagine.
EPHESIANS 3:20 NCV

Recently my husband encouraged our congregation to ask God for extravagant things. He used many examples of how God performed great miracles when His people were brave enough to pray crazy prayers. Our youngest son must have been paying attention that Sunday. It was December, and like most young boys he was preparing his Christmas list. As we read over the list, we expected to find items like toys, games, electronics, or sporting equipment. What we didn't expect to find were the words, "Rolex watch, a million dollars, and a baby brother." Although we couldn't get the things on his list, you have to appreciate his ability to dream wildly.

Though it made me smile, the more I read over the list, the more challenged I was to ask God for extravagant things. I realized I had put limits on God. If we have full confidence in our Father, we will not feel afraid to ask Him for anything. It's easy to ask Him for things we can achieve on our own, but it takes confidence to ask for something that would leave us failing without His help.

Asking reveals the level of confidence we have in the One we are praying to. The things we are willing to ask for reflect how much we know Him. We serve a great God. If we take the limits off, He will blow our minds.

Father, in confidence and bold faith I ask You to do extravagant
things in my life. I lay down small thinking, doubt, and fear
because I know how great and powerful You are.

Kelly Parish, Eufaula, OK

Lead the Cause

Stand up, for it is your duty, and we will be with you. Be brave and act.
EZRA 10:4 AMP

I have always believed if you see someone in need, it is a divine opportunity for you to reach out and help that person. We notice something isn't right or needs attention because we know we can make a difference. When a book falls off the shelf, we reach down and pick it up. Why? Because we know the floor is not the proper place for the book. The same principle applies to life. When we see people fall, we should help them find healing for their hearts and restoration for their dreams.

When it comes to fulfilling our dreams, we often find ourselves waiting for someone to come along and help us carry out our plans. The question is, why do we sit back and expect another person to fill a need or take on the vision God has entrusted to us? Maybe we are afraid to step out. Or maybe we struggle to feel worthy of God using our gifts and talents. Our fear could be rooted in many things.

The truth is that we cannot expect others to fulfill our vision. God gave it to us for a reason. He knows the calling on each of our lives. When we follow Him fully, He can take us further and faster than we could ever imagine. We may experience a few setbacks. Everyone does. What is there to fear? Let the Holy Spirit breathe life into our dreams. We can do all things through His strength.

....

Lord of hosts, You are my Shield and my Strength. I move forward and trust You with every step. I will be brave and act. Let's do this.

Do Mighty Things

With God we will do valiantly, for it is He who will trample down our enemies.

PSALM 108:13 AMP

When I think of mighty things, I automatically think of people who go into dangerous places to preach the gospel. Maybe you have always wanted to do something extraordinary for God but feel what you are doing is small. On days when I don't feel I am doing enough for the Lord, He reminds me, *I don't just take pleasure in what you do, but in the heart behind what you are doing.*

When our middle son was a baby, we noticed a bump on the side of his neck. It was small, but it stuck out enough that we could see it clearly. We wanted the doctor to look at it right away. Concerned it was something serious, we felt relieved to discover it was an extra lymph node. He told us this would be a very healthy boy. He was right. Our son is now fourteen years old and has never taken an antibiotic. Sickness that affects others skips right over him. What is inside of him makes him different and healthy.

Like our son, each of us has something that makes us unique or causes us to stand out in some way. The temptation to be average goes against the very thing God will use to make us great. Our lives should stand out as extraordinary not because of us, but because of the God who lives inside us. We have talents and abilities that God has placed inside us, which allow us to do wonderful things. He has something for you to do that no one else can accomplish.

....

Mighty God, help me not to settle for average. I will rise up and do mighty things because You have conquered every enemy.

Kelly Parish, Eufaula, OK

Become a Woman of Excellence

*My daughter, do not fear. I will do for you whatever you ask, for all
my people in the city know that you are a woman of excellence.*
RUTH 3:11 NASB

*T*here will always be opportunities to take the easy road. I know it
may look more comfortable—no stones, smooth surface, one-way
traffic—but where does the easy road lead? The road most traveled may
be easier in the moment, but to choose a more excellent way will open
the windows of heaven over your life for generations to come.

In the story of Ruth we see a woman known for doing everything
with a spirit of excellence. No matter what life threw at her, she was willing to do something out of her comfort zone and take a risk. Abundant
provision in the form of a wealthy husband, land, and a family was
afforded her because she was known for doing everything with a spirit
of excellence.

Like Ruth, we must be faithful in everyday assignments and daring
enough to step out of our comfort zones to take risks that will unlock
extraordinary blessings. Society has grown comfortable with expecting to do little but gain much. If we want favor and blessings to chase
us down, we must be willing to do the uncomfortable and irrational.
Following God takes risk, but with risk comes great reward.

What reward has God hidden for your future? What difficult path
are you willing to journey down to discover something good?

Father, I choose to live in a spirit of excellence. As I step out of my
comfort zone, I invite Your extraordinary favor to overtake me.

Be Wiser Than Your Adversary

Your commands are always with me and make me wiser than my enemies.
PSALM 119:98

Many years ago I walked through a devastating situation. A close friend and confidante suddenly turned against me. I never saw her actions coming. Shocked and emotionally shattered, I tried to make sense of the act of betrayal. For weeks I tried to process how things had gone horribly wrong. Feelings of rejection and pain hurt my heart in ways I cannot fully express.

During my prayer time I felt the Holy Spirit say, *Grab a journal. I'm going to reveal Myself to you through this disappointing situation.*

With the journal in my lap I sat quietly and waited to hear from the Lord. He began to whisper words to my heart. He didn't reach out to me about my pain or feelings of rejection. He took a different approach entirely. Through love He dealt with me about my character and spirit. No harsh words. No finger pointing. In the sweetest way He reached out to me with love and gentleness.

As the Lord poured His words into my heart, I penciled them in my journal. Before long I filled pages full of God's purpose for the pain I was experiencing. Most importantly, I learned much about His love for me.

That journal is a treasure to me. I keep it in a special place where I can quickly reach for it and remind myself of the wisdom captured there. It serves as a constant reminder that God takes the pain of our experiences and heals us with His Word. He is faithful.

Father, help me be sensitive to Your Word. Let me lean in to
Your strength when I feel weak and uncertain. Thank You
for taking care of me when I feel rejected by others.

Susan Nordin, Houston, TX

Wait Patiently

Though the fig tree may not blossom, nor fruit be on the vines; though the labor of the olive may fail, and the fields yield no food; though the flock may be cut off from the fold, and there be no herd in the stalls— Yet I will rejoice in the LORD, I will joy in the God of my salvation.

HABAKKUK 3:17–18 NKJV

Hearing the door open, I glanced up to see my friend Kathy walk in my office. Though she was usually smiling, today tears fell from her face. After giving her a quick hug I asked, "Are you okay?" She wasn't. Her marriage was a mess. Her husband was threatening to leave. She feared the worst. Her family was falling apart. My heart broke as I watched my good friend walk through this dark season. I wanted to ease her pain and bring hope to her heart. It can be hard to know what to do when those you love experience pain. I decided to reach out, suggesting that we fast from lunch each Wednesday and meet to pray for her husband.

As planned, we met each week. During our time together we laughed, encouraged each other, and believed God would speak to her husband's heart. Over time our faith grew. Our prayers became bolder and stronger. We looked forward to those Wednesdays together. They were a source of emotional strength for my friend, and along the journey I experienced a deeper understanding of the faithfulness of God.

One Sunday I noticed Kathy's husband was sitting with her in church. A huge smile flashed across her face, and I could see hope in her eyes. At the end of the service, her husband went forward for prayer and invited Christ into his heart. That day we witnessed the fulfillment of our prayers. Patience produced amazing fruit.

Today, Lord, I choose to wait patiently on Your promises.

Guard Your Words

*My mouth will speak words of wisdom; the meditation
of my heart will give you understanding.*

PSALM 49:3

Fear tolerated is faith contaminated. My husband spoke those words during a message he gave on faith. As I heard those words leave his lips, I knew they were what I needed to hear. I had allowed my faith to become contaminated with fear, doubt, and unbelief.

At the time we were facing a major financial crisis. Having taken on the financial responsibility of a piece of property from a family member, we found ourselves in a difficult situation. Not long after we acquired the property, the bank called in the entire loan. We received notification that $490,000 was due immediately.

To be honest, I was angry with my husband for getting us into this mess. I questioned, *How could he put at risk everything we have worked so hard to build?* It appeared we were trapped in a hopeless situation.

After my husband concluded his message, I found a place to pray. I repented of doubt and disbelief and looked for my husband so I could make things right with him. That day, our family decided we would agree in prayer, each week, declaring the property *sold*.

Weeks went by with no further word from the bank. One day, driving home from work, the wind blew a sign lying in the road right in front of my windshield. I stared in shock. The sign read *Sold*. I felt strongly this wasn't accidental but a sign from God. Holding on to that word in prayer, we saw the property sell within weeks, and the bank note was settled.

Today, Lord, no matter what my circumstances look like, I choose
to speak words of life, laced with expectation of good things.

Susan Nordin, Houston, TX

Benefit from Discernment

Let Pharaoh look for a discerning and wise man and
put him in charge of the land of Egypt.

GENESIS 41:33

The door opened, and my friend extended her arms toward me. Earlier in the day I had called and asked if my husband and I could stop by for some tea and quiet time. We needed a safe place to share our hearts and shed our tears. Having experienced a disappointing turn of events, we needed comforting words of wisdom. We thought God's direction was taking us one way, but due to the decisions of others, our lives took a radical turn. Our emotions were shaken and our faith rather shaky.

Feeling fragile, I asked my friend and mentor for advice, prayer, and wisdom. She gently led me to the living area where we sat and I poured out my bitterness and anger. She listened quietly without judgment or condemnation. She let me cry it out and say exactly how I felt. Once I finished, she stood up and told me she would be right back.

I expected her to agree with me. I was sure she would take my side. She had been my mentor for twenty years. She knew my heart was in the right place and everyone else was wrong. Right?

She handed me a book on forgiveness. With kindness in her eyes she suggested, "Go home, read this with an open heart, and do what it says."

While my husband and I drove home, tears began to flow as I read words of redemption. I received revelation my heart needed for the journey toward healing. Seeking out discernment brought new hope and strength as we faced our problem.

Today, Lord, help me choose healthy friendships that will help
me serve Your purpose for my life. I trust You to lead me.

Be Stable

He will be like a tree firmly planted [and fed] by streams of water,
which yields its fruit in its season; its leaf does not wither; and in
whatever he does, he prospers [and comes to maturity].

PSALM 1:3 AMP

*L*ate one Saturday night we received a heartbreaking phone call. Elaine's voice broke as she informed us the hospital had called to let her know her husband, Hugh, was being prepped for surgery. She pleaded for us to meet her at the hospital as quickly as possible. The doctors had been alerted there was an opportunity for Hugh to receive a heart transplant, but timing was critical.

Quickly we made our way to the hospital to meet with Elaine and pray for Hugh during his surgery. Our prayers worked, and God performed a miracle.

Thinking back over Hugh's miracle, I remember how Elaine responded to a difficult season. I had admired the way she walked out her faith openly and without reservation. Every time we visited Hugh, she expressed complete trust in God. She believed he would receive His healing.

During his hospital stay, she kept his room filled with worship music and played an audio recording of healing verses. When the doctors came to give updates on his condition, in a kind way, she asked them to step outside the room to share the results of his tests and blood work. She only wanted faith-filled words in Hugh's room. Elaine is an incredible example of what it looks like to trust in God's Word. She teaches us how faith can frame a miracle.

....

I will live each day with peace as I rest in Your protective arms.

Susan Nordin, Houston, TX

Calm the Storm

He caused the storm to be still, so that the waves of the sea were hushed.

PSALM 107:29 NASB

I hurried up the steps of the courthouse in an attempt to reach Karen before the verdict was handed down. I found her sitting in a side office, shaking with the realization that today she would know her daughter's fate.

Karen's daughter had been involved in a tragic accident that had taken the life of another person. The court wanted to hear Karen's testimony regarding her daughter's struggles with drugs and alcohol.

As I reached Karen's side, I quietly prayed for God to give her comfort and strength. "You can do this," I reassured her. At a loss for what to say, I thought, *No mother should have to walk this difficult journey.*

I felt that the Holy Spirit wanted me to give Karen the necklace I wore. The message on it simply said, "Be Brave." In a small way I sensed it would remind this precious mom that somehow God would turn this horrible moment into something good. She simply needed to stay calm and trust Him.

The sentence given was twenty years. Karen quietly sobbed as her daughter was escorted from the courtroom.

Karen experienced unexpected joy some months later when she had her first phone visit with her daughter. She received the report her daughter had been attending Bible study and growing in faith, and it brought her great comfort. Though it wasn't the vision this mother had for her daughter, she learned to trust in God during a very dark season.

....

Holy Spirit, thank You for working on my behalf
even when I can't see the result.

Encounter Grace

"Truly I tell you, if anyone says to this mountain, 'Go, throw yourself into the sea,' and does not doubt in their heart but believes that what they say will happen, it will be done for them."

MARK 11:23

My husband, Asa, and I have always enjoyed driving through neighborhoods looking at different styles of homes. Many years ago, before we built our dream home, we were driving through a subdivision in a neighboring town, when Asa suddenly stopped in front of a lovely home. I looked at him and said, "That's it, isn't it?" We had found what we wanted our future home to look like. He pulled into the driveway, rang their doorbell, and asked them about the house plan they'd used. I was a bit jealous when they invited him in and gave him a tour!

We *knew* that was our house plan. This inner knowing is exactly how we should feel about our faith. We know that we are saved by grace, but we only know it by faith. If we truly know something, we can never doubt it. When you get to know God, you won't doubt His promises. You'll know you can ask anything of Him (according to His will), and He will do it! Today, you may be believing for something just outside your reach. I encourage you to pray before you push aside the idea. Our initial reaction was that we could not afford this type of home. However, because God led us to it, we knew it was possible. Our faith moved that mountain, and we have lived here more than twenty years! God wants to lavish good things on His children. He will move your mountain too.

Father, just like the disciples said in Luke 17:5, we say, "Increase our faith!" May we *know*, so that we stand firm until the promise is given.

Be Raised Up

The king loved Esther more than all the other women, and she obtained
grace and favor in his sight more than all the virgins; so he set the
royal crown upon her head and made her queen instead of Vashti.

ESTHER 2:17 NKJV

*T*here is perhaps nothing I am more passionate about than the role of
women in God's kingdom. Esther was raised to the highest position
in the land, but she didn't come from a prestigious family. In fact she
was an orphan taken captive for King Ahasuerus's pleasure. Esther had
to have been terrified. Can you imagine being forced to compete to be
married to the king of your enemy?

Still, as bad as Esther's situation was, she was immediately shown
favor. God sent people to assist, train, and develop her. She received
everything she needed to please the king. As a result the king chose
Esther to be queen above all other women.

Just like Esther, when we commit to preparing ourselves for our
godly assignment, God will provide the favor necessary to place us in
positions of influence. Who would have thought that an orphaned
Jewish girl could be queen? Esther's assignment was so important that
she needed to be in the highest position in the land. The amazing thing
is that God will do that for us too. If we need training, finances, or even
an encouraging word, God will send these things. Never expect the ordinary, because as a loving Father, God wants His daughters to flourish.
We may not all be queens, but we all are chosen "for such a time as this"
to fulfill a God-given assignment (Esther 4:14).

Father, thank You for raising up an army of godly women whose
assignment is to influence the nations of the world for Your glory.

Act with Expectant Faith

Now, Lord, for what do I expectantly wait? My
hope [my confident expectation] is in You.
PSALM 39:7 AMP

*M*y husband had just gone into full-time ministry, and finances were always tight. Often we were not able to get our boys the things they needed, and certainly almost never the things they wanted. As a mom, it was hard to see our boys hurting because we could not afford to bless them as we wanted to.

One day we were busy doing our daily schoolwork when I suddenly felt the Lord impress upon me that I should tell them that we were going to a popular amusement park. I listened as they expressed their doubts, then I explained what we were going to do. I told them we could expect God to provide everything we needed; after all, it was His idea for us to go. I saw them perk up a little, but they still weren't sure about it.

We made a faith list of all the things we would need to make the trip: money for the tickets, gas, food, and spending money. I asked them not to share our plan with anyone, but if any of us received unexpected money, we would know it was God providing our way. Right away God began to supply, and we checked off every item on our list. I saw their faith building as God provided for each category of need. We enjoyed a fabulous trip; but most importantly, our children learned to step out in expectant faith. They will forever know that nothing is impossible if we wait on God!

Father, develop in me the heart to know that all things are possible for those who wait on You and expect You to move on their behalf.

Debbie Dockery, Ellijay, GA

Find Unexpected Wisdom

Wisdom will make your life pleasant and will bring you peace.
PROVERBS 3:17 NCV

*I*t's funny; I can't even remember what the question was now. I had been asking the Lord for an answer to it for some time, but He had never given it to me. One day my husband, Asa, and I were in his church office with a sweet couple who had come for counseling. They needed answers too. I'm sure I had a strange look on my face when one of them asked us the exact question that I had pleaded with the Lord to resolve. I knew that neither Asa nor I had the solution. Nevertheless, to my utter amazement, out of my mouth came the answer! I don't know if I was happier about receiving the answer or knowing that I had heard from God.

I have often said, "Wisdom is better than experience." I continually ask for it. I do not want to have to go through the process of gaining it through experience. God gives wisdom, knowledge, and happiness to those who please Him. Oh, how I want to please Him!

Proverbs 29:11 says that the wise will bring calm, and that is exactly what happened in the office that day. God's wisdom brought peace to the situation the couple faced. Solomon asked God for wisdom, and He gave it to him. Likewise He will give you wisdom for the friend who has a wayward child or the person you work with who has a problem at home. God's wisdom led Solomon to becoming an inventor, a songwriter, and even a king! What can it lead you to?

Father, Your Word says that if we lack wisdom, we should ask for it, and You will give it liberally. I ask that Your wisdom give me the power to heal, deliver, set free, and bring peace.

Develop Gifts with Grace

[He did this] so that in the ages to come He might [clearly] show the immeasurable and unsurpassed riches of His grace in [His] kindness toward us in Christ Jesus [by providing for our redemption].

EPHESIANS 2:7 AMP

*T*he Israelites thought they wanted out of Egypt; their desire was to be an independent nation. They started the journey, but quickly found that freedom has responsibility. It was hard out there in the wilderness, so they decided they wanted to return to Egypt. Can you imagine being so discouraged that you'd rather be a slave than be free?

Unfortunately, most of us act the same way the Israelites did. I have often wandered in the wilderness because I let doubts and fears hinder my journey with God. Even when I was reassured by high school teachers and college professors, and even given a dream, I did not seriously pursue one of my God-given assignments.

Nevertheless, when I asked Jesus to be my Lord, God showed me His kindness by setting me free from the grip of Satan. His grace toward me is immeasurable and unsurpassable; with that much grace I can do anything He asks of me!

God placed a gifting inside each of us that is impossible to do on our own. It can only be developed with grace. What gift has He given you that only He can open for you? Step out in faith to develop it. Don't let negative thoughts pull you away from freedom. God will guide you and open doors. Trust Him to lead you safely out of the wilderness.

....

Father, I pray that each of us comes to realize the immeasurable and unsurpassable grace we have been given. May I have the courage to use it to become all You have destined me to be.

Debbie Dockery, Ellijay, GA

Decide to Forgive

Be kind and helpful to one another, tender-hearted
[compassionate, understanding], forgiving one another [readily
and freely], just as God in Christ also forgave you.

EPHESIANS 4:32 AMP

I remember exactly where I was when it happened. I was sitting at a restaurant drive-through. I had been studying spiritual authority, and I said, "God, You want me to act just too much like Jesus. I can't do it!" You see, God wanted me to take responsibility for my actions in a situation where I had been wronged. Someone had done some hurtful things to us. But I didn't want to see that person, and I refused to go anywhere he might be. God explained to my heart that his actions were not my responsibility, but mine were. God asked me to forgive him because He had forgiven me; I had not even realized that I needed to ask for forgiveness. He was wrong, not me. Nevertheless He made me call him and ask forgiveness for my reaction to the wrong he had done!

Forgiveness is a decision, not necessarily a reconciliation with the person who wronged us. I made the decision to forgive, and God gave me the grace to do it. Guess what? I was free! It no longer bothered me to see this person. In fact I sat next to him at a dinner and was not bothered at all. Why? It was because I had gotten things right between God and me. It was a valuable lesson. I must show tenderness and compassion to people, no matter what they have done to me. I *can* act like Jesus after all, and so can you!

....

Father, convict my heart where there is unforgiveness and
give me courage to forgive others quickly. Help me be like
Jesus—tender, compassionate, merciful, and forgiving.

Miracles

You know about Jesus from Nazareth, that God gave him the Holy Spirit
and power. You know how Jesus went everywhere doing good and
healing those who were ruled by the devil, because God was with him.

ACTS 10:38 NCV

I remember praying for a man who suffered with debilitating multiple
sclerosis. As he sat in his wheelchair, surrounded by family members, we agreed for a miracle. As we prayed, in my mind I heard these
words: *Tell him to say, "I am healed," and he will receive his healing.* I hesitated for a moment because the instruction was so specific. I wondered,
*What if these words are just thoughts from my imagination? What if this
man doesn't receive his healing?* But I went ahead and asked him to say
the words *I am healed* out loud and believe for a miracle. Though I could
visualize him walking free of pain, we saw no proof our prayers had been
answered. I walked away wondering if I had said what the Holy Spirit
wanted me to say. A few days later the man showed up at my house, walking and pain free! We rejoiced in his healing and gave thanks to God.

Through that experience I learned many valuable lessons about
prayer and faith. On this side of the miracle I wonder, what if I hadn't
been faithful to listen to the Holy Spirit? What if I had stopped short in
following a divine instruction because I was second-guessing my faith?
The truth is that God has given us a spirit of courage. When we follow
His leading, miracles will happen. We have nothing to fear when God
is with us. Today, step out in faith. Your obedience could be the link to
someone's miracle.

Lord, increase my faith, and remind me to believe in miracles.

Tammy Cooper, Kinsey, AL

Have a Soft Heart in a Hard World

Suppose someone has enough to live and sees a brother or
sister in need, but does not help. Then God's love is not living
in that person. My children, we should love people not only
with words and talk, but by our actions and true caring.

1 JOHN 3:17–18 NCV

*A*s I walked across a dark parking lot, a young woman timidly
approached me. I knew what she wanted before she asked.
Although I needed to get home, I took time to hear her request. In a soft
voice she explained how she and her three children had lost their home.
Pulling back her sweater she revealed her baby bump; number four was
on the way. With her head hung in shame, she asked me for money to pay
for a hotel room. In the back of my head, I was thinking, *This is probably
a scam of some kind.* But after hearing her desperate plea and looking into
her tearful eyes, I knew I had to do something to help her out.

Before I could take the situation in, I made the decision to give her
the remaining cash I had in my purse. She was very grateful and thanked
me. I prayed with her and asked the Lord to bless her, meet her needs,
and give her peace. Then I hugged her and drove away.

We live in a harsh world. Let us choose to love people the way we
want others to love us.

> Lord, I give You my heart. Shape it into what You
> want it to be. Let me recognize opportunities to show
> Your love through my words and actions.

Highlight Love, Not Hate

*Above all, love each other deeply, because
love covers over a multitude of sins.*

1 PETER 4:8

*H*as a situation wounded you so deeply you feel there is no hope of healing or restoration? Maybe someone you loved betrayed you or a good friend has taken credit for your work. Or maybe the angry words of a teenager broke your heart. Or, even worse, you might have experienced tormenting flashbacks of being physically assaulted.

There are levels of pain. Sometimes emotional pain hurts so deeply it causes a physical reaction. Even though others try to bring us comfort, their words fall short of easing our pain.

I know what it is like to wrestle with feelings of hurt, anger, bitterness, resentment, and even hatred. I've even wondered, *How do I overcome my feelings and forgive this person? Can my heart heal and love again?*

In times of great heartache, I've learned to linger in the presence of Jesus. When our souls are overwhelmed, those private moments of prayer and worship bring healing to our hearts.

Your hope is renewed as we believe and trust in the Lord. He is your Comforter, Refuge, and Strength. If situations have robbed you of your peace, be intentional about resting in His grace. As His love fills your soul, He will give you strength to forgive and love deeply. Grace will replace anger as His love overshadows their actions and allows your heart to heal.

Lord, thank You for forgiving my sins. Help me to forgive (name of person). Give me the ability to forgive others as You have forgiven me.

Tammy Cooper, Kinsey, AL

Lavish Honor

Be devoted to one another in love. Honor one another above yourselves.

ROMANS 12:10

*A*t the lake on a warm summer day, a family enjoyed time relaxing in the sun. The kids laughed as they splashed water on each other while their parents caught up on the events of the week. Out of the corner of her eye, a mom watched her son go under the water; then he bobbed back up shouting something she couldn't quite make out. At first she thought he was playing around, but as she continued to watch she noticed he was in trouble. Within seconds she leaped into the water only to watch him go down again. Lunging forward she grabbed him and pulled him to the shore. He was coughing, but to everyone's relief, he was unharmed. Later that night the son came to his mother with his most precious toy. With his hands outstretched he said, "Here, Mom. This is for saving my life." He put aside one of his greatest loves to honor his mom.

Our Father in heaven gave His best when He sent His only Son to die for our sins. The temptation must have been great to reach down and rescue His Son from death. But just like the little boy, God put each of us above what He treasured most so we could have eternal life. He saved our lives, and the best way to show our gratitude is to lavish Him with honor.

Lord, thank You for giving Your best to me. My heart seeks to spend time with You, knowing the very best gift I can give You is me.

Love Like It Is the Only Language

These three remain: faith, hope and love. But the greatest of these is love.
1 CORINTHIANS 13:13

*H*ave you ever been to a foreign country where you didn't speak or understand the common language? Without an interpreter, situations can get sticky. I've found it's easy to use the wrong word and end up looking foolish. Trust me, a compliment can come out as an offensive remark if we don't have thorough understanding of the language.

I experienced this challenge while speaking at a women's conference in Central America. Throughout the week we were fortunate to have an interpreter translate our sessions. But on the last night of the conference a group of ladies traveled a great distance to give us a gift. The only problem was, we didn't have anyone who understood the dialect the women spoke. As they presented very delicate, hand-painted plates for each of our team members, we could not understand what they were saying. But what we could not understand through words, we interpreted through their tears. We couldn't speak their language and they couldn't speak ours, but we didn't need words as we embraced and wept. An interpreter wasn't necessary because we spoke the language of love.

Whether through words, gifts, actions, giving of your time, or a gentle touch, you can speak the universal language of love. Make it your goal to learn the language of heaven and speak it fluently.

....

Lord, thank You for loving me. May I learn to be kind to others, compassionate, and forgiving. Teach me to master the language of love.

Tammy Cooper, Kinsey, AL

Unpack Someone's Pain

So we say with confidence, "The Lord is my helper; I will not be afraid. What can mere mortals do to me?"

HEBREWS 13:6 AMP

*T*oday is just another day for everyone else, but not to a grieving daughter. Drinking her coffee, she remembered sitting beside her father's hospital bed waiting for the inevitable to happen. She watched as his chest rose and fell, wondering if the next breath would be his last. In her heart she longed for one more conversation with him.

Though her father loved his family, he didn't really know how to express his feelings. Having grown up in a home where affections were rarely shared made it hard for him to say, "I love you." Looking back, she couldn't remember him saying "I love you" one time. He wasn't good at expressing his affection with words, but he would do it with small acts of kindness. He was faithful to bring home gifts and small surprises. After his passing friends told stories of times he proudly pulled worn pictures of his children, grandchildren, and great-grandchildren from his wallet and boasted of each one's accomplishments. He was proud of them and loved them, but he never told them.

As his sickness grew worse, he knew he might not have another chance to express his feelings verbally. He finally said the words she longed to hear, "I love you."

Feeling loved is important and something we all need, but when it becomes a guessing game it causes pain. We can break the cycle and unpack the pain of others by making sure they know how much we genuinely care for, love, and support them.

....

Lord, show me how to share love.

Remain at Rest

You only need to remain calm; the Lord will fight for you."
EXODUS 14: 14 NCV

As I travel throughout the United States, I encounter women from every walk of life. I cannot count the number of times I have met with women privately, listening to their stories of heartache and pain. Although many of them have been through unique situations, their stories are unified by their resolve to overcome the things that have tried to destroy them. Their brave hearts find the strength to pick up the broken pieces and move forward.

Maybe you went through a season of depression and found it hard to climb out of bed each day. Or maybe you've been through a financial crisis, bankruptcy, foreclosure, or job loss. Others may have experienced declining health, long-term illness, or a bout with cancer. With whatever you are dealing with today, I encourage you to reach out and embrace hope. Let Christ give you supernatural strength and courage.

Maybe you are still holding on to things that have brought you great pain. Perhaps you spent your childhood without one of your parents or a spouse walked out of your marriage. When you go through difficult times, the enemy will often tell you, *You'll never be happy. You'll never find someone who will love you and won't leave you.* Those aren't facts; they are lies. Know God has laid out good plans for your life. It's only when you release the pain of your past that you can move forward to something better. Today choose to let go of things you cannot change. Trust the Lord to heal your broken heart.

Father, heal my broken heart. Mend my pain. With joy I
look forward to the blessings that are coming my way.

Marsha Bilderback, Fayetteville, AR

Accept God Has Something Greater

*Since God had planned something better for us so that
only together with us would they be made perfect.*

HEBREWS 11:40

*A*lthough heaven is our ultimate destination, God has things for us to do on the earth. He has kept many of us from dangerous situations that would have destroyed our earthly assignments. If we look back over our lives, we can remember moments that could have altered our lives forever. For some it was a near-fatal accident, serious illness, loss of income, or harsh betrayal. But somehow God kept us from ultimate destruction.

With all the chaos in the world, it is easy to feel overwhelmed. In fact one of the enemy's greatest schemes is to use distractions to pull us away from the assignment God has for our lives. Don't fall into that trap. Speak the words of truth over your discouraged heart. Remind yourself of what God has called you to do. Meditate on the promises He has given you. Write out Scripture verses that build up your faith. Most of all surround yourself with people who will encourage you to follow God fully.

What do you believe God has called you to do? Does it seem impossible? Have you considered quitting or thought about doing something different? At some point everyone has felt that way. But those who don't quit are those who embrace God's grace. His grace reminds you that God is the one who will complete His word in your life. Grace gives us hope that there is something great in your future. When you fall into the pit of discouragement, grace takes you by the hand and keeps you moving in the right direction.

Father, lead and guide me today. I refuse to give up on Your
assignment for my life. I will push back the distraction of the
enemy and fulfill the calling You have entrusted to me.

Be Unafraid

"Do not fear, for I am with you; do not be dismayed, for I am your God. I will strengthen you and help you; I will uphold you with my righteous right hand."

ISAIAH 41:10

*B*ecause I allowed hesitation to hold me back, I was robbed of my dreams. Timidity kept me from stepping out and grabbing God's promises in faith. God never designed us to live captive by fear. It is time we rise up and embrace the promises of God. We must trust in His Word and align our words with His divine promises. Our words set the course for the direction of our lives. What we believe, we will put into words. Let's use our words to shape the futures we want to experience.

As daughters of God we have been set apart and chosen to do great things. When we believe He has good things in store for us, we will use our faith and move toward those purposes. In fact, when we surrender to God's plan, the thing the enemy used to set us back, God will use to propel us forward. Stay focused in faith. Our dreams are worth fighting for.

Father, help me cast off fear and embrace every
good thing You have for my life.

Marsha Bilderback, Fayetteville, AR

Feel Secure in an Unstable World

*We are persecuted, but God does not leave us. We
are hurt sometimes, but we are not destroyed.*

2 CORINTHIANS 4:9 NCV

*H*ow can we feel secure in a world full of chaos and confusion? On every news channel we hear reports of destruction, lies, trickery, and deceit. It's hard to stay positive when the world tries to convince us everything is falling apart. I understand we all face difficult times. Occasionally everyone goes through a season when everything feels as though it is coming unraveled. Friendships fall apart, family members do unexpected things, or someone we respect has a moral failure. These things can make us feel emotionally unstable.

I've learned when problems and trials arise to take my issues straight to the Father. For too long I reached out to others who only made a negative situation worse. When I quit reaching for negative-thinking people to be my confidants, my emotions began to change for the better. Now I take the things that would have overwhelmed me straight to the One who can solve them. I know God will lift me up and encourage me.

Our strength can only be found in the Lord Jesus. He is our Deliverer, Savior, Healer, Confidant, Dream-Giver, and Protector. That is the reason the enemy seeks to separate us from the presence of the Lord; he recognizes our source of strength comes from spending time with our Lord. It is there no weapon can harm us. No lie can withstand truth. Chaos cannot contend with the peace of His presence. Today let each of us take time away from our schedules to enjoy time with our Father.

Father, help me be strong in an unstable word. I place
every battle in Your hands. I rest in Your presence.

Be Refreshed

Not that I speak from [any personal] need, for I have learned to be content [and self-sufficient through Christ, satisfied to the point where I am not disturbed or uneasy] regardless of my circumstances.

PHILIPPIANS 4:11 AMP

*T*en years ago I felt the Lord wanted me to spend time alone with Him. In my mind I felt the mountains would be a good place to pull away and relax in His presence. I didn't know how I was going to carve time away from my family for this private retreat with the Lord, and I certainly didn't know anything about the mountains. A few days later I received an email from a friend who told me she had a place in the mountains of Georgia. As a gift she wanted to bless me with this getaway.

I took a flight to Georgia, where my friend picked me up and took me to my lodging. I was excited to get away and meet with the Lord. For three days I fasted, drinking water only. Every day I enjoyed the view from my scenic balcony. I took time to breathe in the mountain air and thank my Father for the beauty of His creation.

One night a storm knocked out the electricity. All I had was the light of my cell phone. (Talk about a new level of rest). During this time I was reminded of the importance of resting in Him. It felt good to rely on Him. It was also good for me to work through past hurts from things I had kept buried in my heart. By the time I left, I was refreshed, renewed, and ready to go on to a new season in life.

Even if you can't get away to somewhere beautiful, make an effort to schedule time to be with Him. You'll be glad you did.

....

Father, help me find time to be with You.

Marsha Bilderback, Fayetteville, AR

Be Fruitful in Every Season

"Blessed is the one who trusts in the Lord, whose confidence is in him.
They will be like a tree planted by the water that sends out its roots by the
stream. It does not fear when heat comes; its leaves are always green.
It has no worries in a year of drought and never fails to bear fruit."

JEREMIAH 17:7–8

When I was growing up, my mom and dad planted a garden every year. My dad's job was to till the dirt, and my mom would plant the seeds. I can remember sitting in the garden, eating fresh tomatoes.

Both my parents were good at expressing their love for each other and worked hard to take care of our family. Mom loved to pray, and my dad insisted she take me to church every week. Our faith was simple, but looking back I see how God honored our small faith in big ways.

There were often financially lean years for our family. In fact I can remember during years of drought praying and asking God to send us rain. The miraculous thing was that at times it would rain over our garden, but not anywhere else in the neighborhood. I smiled, knowing God heard our prayers. They weren't dramatic, loud, boisterous, or complex prayers, but they were heartfelt, sincere, and honest. God honors genuine acts of faith. Whether it is a young girl writing letters to God or a soldier bowing on the battlefield, our Father looks at the condition of our hearts.

No matter what you are going through today, trust God. Don't get caught up in comparing your faith with someone else's. Praise God out of a pure heart and willing attitude.

Father, help me have faith for every season of life. Let
me serve You and others from a heart of humility.

Dream Impossible Dreams

To Him who is able to [carry out His purpose and] do superabundantly more than all that we dare ask or think [infinitely beyond our greatest prayers, hopes, or dreams], according to His power that is at work within us.

EPHESIANS 3:20 AMP

*T*hrough social media, conferences, and groups I get to know women who have great vision for their lives but feel lost in how to push forward and act on those dreams. Some feel they have too many responsibilities or fight feelings of depression and hopelessness. Recently a young woman shared with me that she didn't feel worthy of God's help with her dream. She went on to explain she felt foolish for dreaming such a big dream, that with her limited finances she couldn't imagine how a dream like hers could come to pass.

Although we may never *feel* as though we can accomplish much, the truth is that with God leading the way, we can fulfill every dream and experience victory in places we have felt discouraged. We simply must push past how we feel and take steps of faith to discover God's vision for our lives. I assured my young friend that God places desires in our hearts because He believes they will come to pass. The dream God plants in our hearts is far beyond anything we can achieve in our strength.

Have you laid down a dream because of tough times or difficult challenges? Has God ever showed you something that at the time seems unlikely to happen? The Lord has promises for us, and if He speaks to our hearts and we follow His plan, those promises will come to pass.

Father, today I push forward in faith, knowing if You have called me to action You will give provision for the journey ahead.

Kezia Alford, Mableton, GA

Crush Your Comfort Zones

*The Spirit God gave us does not make us timid, but
gives us power, love and self-discipline.*

2 TIMOTHY 1:7

I was invited to take a trip to Nashville, Tennessee, to share my gift
of singing and writing with total strangers. I had no clue where I
was going or what I was in for. I just knew I had to challenge myself to
do something I had never done before. I thought, *This is an awesome
opportunity to record in Nashville.* The truth was, I didn't know anyone
who lived in the city. But I prayed God would connect me with the right
people. I was scheduled to sing and present my songs to some of the most
well-known producers in the industry. Since I had little experience in
this area, I thought this would be a good time to gain knowledge and
discover new things in the industry. I prepared my heart to hear con-
structive feedback on how I could better use my gift.

It's hard for me to explain how nervous I was that day. I was totally
out of my comfort zone, placing my talents in the hands of strangers.
After much prayer I steadied my nerves and did what I came to Nashville
to do: record and meet incredible new friends. Since then I've cowritten
a song with another writer I met there and have been invited back as a
featured vocalist. I am so glad I stepped out of my comfort zone and
allowed God to take me somewhere new. I encourage you to do the same.

....

Father, I break loose of the things that have kept me back from
achieving my dreams. Today I invite You to do a new thing in my life.

Be Bold Enough to Stand Alone

Therefore, since we have such a hope, we are very bold.
2 CORINTHIANS 3:12

Years ago I hosted a conference for women. I was very young at the time but felt strongly I was to follow God and host this event. I was new to ministry life and did not have many spiritual friends or mentors to rely on for advice. But by faith I moved forward and made plans to host the event. To be honest, I wasn't sure if anyone would show up. I remember looking at my watch and then glancing at the doors in the back of the room. I started to worry, questioning, *Did God really call me to host this event?* Then I calmed my emotions and made an internal decision: *If no one shows up, I will preach and speak anyway.* Before long I could hear women starting to come in. I looked around, and there were almost one hundred women in attendance. They showed up ready to worship and hear from the Lord.

I met so many wonderful women that day who are now my close friends. It's hard to imagine how differently things would have turned out if I had not chosen to follow God's direction. Years later women are traveling from all over to meet with us in our conferences.

Sometimes God will ask us to take bold steps of faith and begin the journey alone. We can take comfort knowing He'll never leave nor forsake us (Deuteronomy 31:6). When we make the first step of hope and follow through with God's plan, we will see God perform miracles because of our obedience.

....

Father, give me bold, audacious faith to follow Your instructions.
May I choose to take risks, knowing that You walk beside me.

Kezia Alford, Mableton, GA

Learn You Are Wired for Success

"Keep this Book of the Law always on your lips; meditate on
it day and night, so that you may be careful to do everything
written in it. Then you will be prosperous and successful."

JOSHUA 1:8

When I was young, I heard my grandmother talk about the importance of being a virtuous woman. She explained to me that virtue comes from setting aside time for prayer, leaning on God for strength, and making time to meditate on His Word. She also taught me that true success comes from listening to and obeying the voice of the Holy Spirit. Because of her influence, I can attribute many wonderful opportunities back to her shared wisdom.

Later in life as I began reading the Bible, I stumbled upon verses about the virtuous woman my grandmother so vividly described. As I read about this woman in Proverbs 31, I noticed her many successes could be linked back to her committed prayer life. That is one reason I make prayer a priority. I've learned very little gets accomplished until we are willing to put our prayers into action. Prayer, praise, and worship are three powerful things that position us to lead successful lives.

When we are committed to obeying the Word of God, we will be successful at what God has chosen for us to do. Our Father is faithful, and to get to the promises He has for us, we must read His Word, meditate on it, and apply it to our lives.

....

Father, thank You that when You see I am faithful in the small things,
You make room for me to enjoy much larger opportunities.

Trust Your Instincts

God is within her, she will not fall; God will help her at break of day.

PSALM 46:5

At the time I recorded my first album, I didn't have enough money to cut a high-quality product, but felt confident God would use the lines and lyrics of the songs to change lives. When I cut the album, a professional told me the quality wasn't up to par to play on the radio and that even if somehow it made it on air, people would listen to it and would never buy a copy.

Even with the negative feedback, I knew God had a plan for this recording. After many months passed, I received an e-mail that said, "I want you to know, your song drew my heart back to Christ. I am in the military, and I am battling depression and wanting to take my life. I miss my family and feel so alone. . . . I'm not sure how I came across your music, but I am thankful I did because the words to your song saved my life."

I am so glad that the soldier reached out and shared his thoughts. Just as my song had been an inspiration to him, his words brought new life to me. His e-mail confirmed what my heart already knew: when it comes to the dreams God places in our hearts, we need to obey God rather than listen to the opinions of others.

I encourage you to trust the Holy Spirit to lead and guide you. He will align you with good opportunities. Remember, He is working in ways you cannot see.

Father, thank You for filling me with Your gifts and talents. May I use them to glorify Your name. Make my heart one with Yours.

Kezia Alford, Mableton, GA

Plug into Power

Jesus said to her, "I am the resurrection and the life. The one
who believes in me will live, even though they die."
JOHN 11:25

J once went on a fast and prayed daily because I wanted to be used by God. As I prayed, I asked God to give me opportunities to share His love with others. One morning my friend called and asked me to go with her to a school function. When we arrived at the venue, I saw an older lady slumped and not moving. I went to check on her and found she was not breathing.

Even though my initial reaction was fear, I stopped to pray over her. As I prayed, I called life into her body. She needed a miracle, and outside the healing power of the Lord there was no hope for her.

As I relied on the Holy Spirit, I continued to pray in faith. Even though I don't remember all the words I prayed, I know the Holy Spirit was praying through me on her behalf. Before long I could see her body slowly regaining strength. Her eyes finally opened and gazed into mine. When she was once again alert, she asked what happened. I explained how through prayer she received healing.

True to the prayers I had prayed earlier that week, God gave me the opportunity to be used by Him. He longs to use you as well. Others need the treasure God has placed within you. They need your strength, boldness, prayer, and wisdom. You must have your eyes and hearts fixed firmly on our Father. When you focus on His will, He will do great works through you.

Father, help me be sensitive to Your voice. Fill me with wisdom and revelation. Let me look for opportunities to be used by You.

Be Yourself

I can do all things [which He has called me to do] through Him who strengthens and empowers me [to fulfill His purpose—I am self-sufficient in Christ's sufficiency; I am ready for anything and equal to anything through Him who infuses me with inner strength and confident peace.]

PHILIPPIANS 4:13 AMP

J can't believe I said yes. Now I was grappling with the *how*. How would I be able to do this big thing I had said yes to in faith? For a moment my heart was filled with fear. I was so sure what I committed to was a God-granted opportunity, a call to do something so much bigger than myself with so much more of a challenge than I had ever faced before. That's God, isn't it? He brings His God-sized challenge to our incapable hearts and says, *I will do this through you, if you will let Me!*

Fear had been a prevailing struggle in my life. So many times I was absolutely sure that I didn't have what it took. But over time I allowed God to transform my fearful steps into leaps of faith. In the darkest seasons of wondering if I could rise to the challenge, I heard the Lord whisper to my anxious heart, *I didn't place you in this position for what you could do for Me, but for what I can do in and through you. I'm placing a demand on what is in you, and I* AM *in you!* His Word infused me with strength and confidence as I realized that He had already prepared me for this opportunity.

If you feel challenged beyond your comfort zone, I encourage you to rest in His strength. He has equipped you. He has called you. Rise up in confidence.

Father, help me accept the challenges of doing something new. Bless me with Your favor. Infuse me with courage.

ReGina Johnston, Temple, TX

Release What Is Weighing You Down

Show me what I should do, because my prayers go up to you.

PSALM 143:8 NCV

*H*ere I am again, Lord. Show me what I need to do to fix this mess."
I was on my knees before God—again. I had been there so many
times, trying to find something new to do or say that would fix this relationship. I felt helpless in my attempts to bring restoration to this situation.

I've been accused of being just a little obsessive-compulsive.
Sometimes the accusations came from my sons, who simply did not want
to clean up their rooms. Other times the accusations held some truth.
I admit I like things neat and orderly . . . and preferably all wrapped
up with a nice little bow, fixed, and working wonderfully. That kind of
desire comes with just a small issue: control.

Control issues are really trust issues. Where am I placing my trust?
Am I placing my confidence in God's plan or my own? Am I trying to
juggle the things that are overwhelming me or am I relying on God's
strength to carry me through?

That day when I was praying over the things that were broken, I surrendered my will to the Father's. I spoke my confession aloud: "I cannot
do one more thing to fix this. God, the work of restoration is Yours. I give
up!" Every time the pain shadowed my heart, I said the words again. "I
give up, God. It's Yours!" No need to step on a scale; I knew I was lighter.
Not by pounds, but by worries. I was lighter.

I encourage you to release the things that have weighed you down.
Surrender them to God and don't pick them up again.

Father, I refuse to let situations that are out of my control
steal my joy and peace. I give them up to You.

See Suffering Is Only Seasonal

We have small troubles for a while now, but they are helping us gain an eternal glory that is much greater than the troubles.

2 CORINTHIANS 4:17 NCV

S he stood at the doorway of her bedroom knowing she must go forward, and going forward meant walking into that bedroom and crawling into that same bed. The same bed where hours earlier her husband's heart had stopped beating.

She told herself she must go forward. She told herself she would make one decision at a time. And at this moment she forced herself to walk into the bedroom, put on her pajamas, and crawl into that same bed.

My mom's life was challenging. I watched her make these hard life adjustments more times than I can remember. I also knew she depended on God for her strength. How could she make such resolved decisions during such hardship? Perspective.

Perspective challenges how you see everything. Imagine placing a quarter right in front of your face. All you can see is the coin. But pull it back a few inches and you will be able to see the quarter in relationship to other things around it. In fact the circumference of the quarter appears much smaller.

Learning to look at grief through the lens of eternity takes courage. Maybe you haven't been separated from someone you love, but other things have wounded your heart. I encourage you to move the thing blocking your vision back into the context of God's faithfulness. Your heart will begin to heal when you see things from an eternal perspective.

....

Father, adjust my perspective. Let me look at life through the lens of faith.

ReGina Johnston, Temple, TX

Walk with Confidence

You will walk on your way [of life] securely and your foot will not stumble.
PROVERBS 3:23 AMP

She knew the Lord, all right. Though there had been proving times, she had obediently followed Him. Her way was established . . . somewhat. However, she was unsure of her place. She was hesitant to pray aloud and was soft-spoken when asked to share. "Sweet and beautiful" would have described her, but not "bold and daring," not in the things of the Spirit.

This day was different though. It was as if a switch had been flipped. To our sweet surprise she was bold, uninhibited, and confident in declaring the Word of the Lord. The change was transformational. When asked what made the difference, she said the change took place when she recognized the anointing of God on her life. From that day forward she lived out her faith in a bold and confident manner.

Proverbs 3 is written to a son and encourages him to walk in the anointing of God. Knowing the son was destined to be king of their nation, the writer admonishes him to place his confidence in the Lord, to make wise decisions, to honor God with his wealth, and to respond to correction with a submitted heart. He is exhorted to be merciful, to be kind, and to walk in the ways of truth to attract the favor of God and man. And he should fully trust in the Lord in every situation, good or bad.

Whether you are a woman needing to embrace a new level of confidence or a mom trying to shape the lives of your children (or both), recognize God's anointing and walk in His supernatural strength.

Thank You, God, for establishing me with confidence.
Today I step out of my safe zone to follow You fully.

Receive Restoration

Jesus said to him, "I will come and heal him."

MATTHEW 8:7 AMP

I survived many years of meal preparation using a small handheld mixer with the mind-set that I didn't need one of those countertop, space-hoarding mixers. When a friend received a beautiful, high-end mixer as a wedding gift I thought, *Well, I've made do with much less!* Then I stopped and considered my warped way of thinking. Those words *much less* did not describe a mind-set I wanted to hang on to.

As I stared at my mixer, I noticed each part had its own locking mechanism that required proper positioning for the mixer to work effectively. Proper positioning consisted of turning this part or that until it came to just the right spot, and then locking it into place.

In Matthew 8, a soldier came to Jesus asking Him to heal his servant. Immediately Jesus agreed to heal him. That's it! A request followed by a *yes*. So simple, but how? Positioning! Why was Jesus so willing to help the soldier? The simple answer is the centurion positioned himself under the authority of Jesus.

What if our miracle moments were contingent on how we position ourselves to receive? What if our dreams depended on us to think differently? Would we be willing to adjust our thinking or change how we do things?

Do not choose to *make do*. Find the place of belief that agrees with the truth of God's Word and lock it in so you are positioned to receive the restoration God has for you.

....

Father, thank You for helping me align my thoughts with
Your Word, positioning myself to receive restoration.

ReGina Johnston, Temple, TX

Realize You Are Incomparable

*Each person should judge his own actions and not compare himself
with others. Then he can be proud for what he himself has done.*
GALATIANS 6:4 NCV

I oversaw creating bows for pretty packages. I made sure I measured
the first ribbon just right before cutting the rest of the roll. Wanting
to do a good job, I cut each strand by hand and compared it to the previous one. But with each new bow, the design began to be less perky.
And the next was, well, just downright floppy. By the time I worked on
the fifth package there was just too much ribbon to make a perfect bow.
With each new piece I had somehow cut longer lengths. My measure-
ments ended up being way off the mark.

I love today's passage in the book of Galatians because it challenges us
to stop comparing ourselves with others. Taken in context, this Scripture
verse speaks of judging another's behavior that is not considered sin but
a matter of conviction, and then comparing ourselves in righteousness
to our brother or sister. There is nothing wrong with righteousness—
nothing at all. But Christ is our measure. Compared to Him, the Bible
says, our righteousness is as filthy rags.

As pastors of a church, we have often been asked, "How large is your
church?" Knowing this question can arouse a *less-than* or *more-than*
attitude, I have often answered, "Between two and three thousand members." Usually my answer is met with a knowing smile, and I'm allowed
off the hook. Size doesn't matter when Christ called us to go into all the
world (Mark 16:15).

Jesus, You are my example of righteousness. As You transform
me, I take confidence in who You designed me to be.

Remain Silent at the Right Time

Joshua had commanded the army, "Do not give a war cry, do not raise your voices, do not say a word until the day I tell you to shout. Then shout!"

JOSHUA 6:10

When God brought Joshua and the army of Israel to the city of Jericho, their cause seemed hopeless. The large walls surrounding the city made entrance to the fortress look impossible. But under the careful instruction of Joshua, the people were challenged to walk around the city for seven days without saying a word. Can you imagine how foolish the army looked to the people of Jericho? Who goes to battle without saying a word? Who confronts an enemy in silence? Joshua understood how influential words are and refused to let his army speak words that would give the enemy an advantage. After circling the city thirteen times in silence, he gave the order: the nation of Israel shouted and the walls of the city fell flat.

What words have you confessed over your life today? Are they words God would speak over you? Every word is a seed. God has given you a mind to envision your future and words to bring those thoughts into fruition. To think one way and speak another is to be double-minded.

Words have creative power. Today make a point to speak positive words over your future. Ask for supernatural favor. Declare ideas, increase, breakthroughs, and opportunity over your life. Most importantly, believe you will receive what you request. Don't draw back in fear. You are blessed. You are equipped. You will succeed and not fail.

....

Father, give me discernment about when to speak
and when to hold my thoughts in peace. In times of
confrontation I will stay calm and remain in faith.

Tracey Mitchell, Dallas, TX

Gaze at the Big Picture

God led Abram outside and said, "Look at the sky. There are so many stars you cannot count them. Your descendants also will be too many to count."

GENESIS 15:5 NCV

*N*ot long ago I spent time on a beautiful island in the South Pacific. Impressed by the exquisite greenery and waterfalls, I asked the biologist who was with us, "Has it always been this beautiful?" I was shocked when he replied, "No! In fact this was once a barren, uninhabitable island. The beauty of what you see now was formed out of volcanic rock." Confused, I followed up with, "Then how was all of this created?" He said, "Over time the wind would transfer soil from neighboring islands, and birds migrating from thousands of miles away would inadvertently drop seed onto the island. Eventually enough seed and soil combined to create this environment."

As I walked around gazing at the beautiful land, I gave serious thought to those words. If seed could transform volcanic rock into lush, green lands, how much more could the seed of God's Word work to transform the barren places in our lives into something beautiful?

You may be worried over things that have caused you pain. Maybe you've received a health report that doesn't sound good, or the company is considering letting you go, or a friend has betrayed your trust. Whatever the medical report says, no matter what your finances may look like, or who conspires against you, I want you to trust in the power of God's Word. There isn't a situation too hard for Him to turn around. There isn't heartache so deep that He cannot heal it. Trust in His promises. Allow His peace to speak to your heart. Lean on His strength.

Father, orchestrate my life. Place me where You need me to be.

Embrace a Better Plan

I say to myself, "The LORD is my portion; therefore I will wait for him."
LAMENTATIONS 3:24

While I was watching a documentary, my heart went out to the undiscovered amateur athlete featured in the film, who had enormous talent but no media exposure. Nothing could be more disheartening than to have your talents go unrealized. But those thoughts faded as the documentary went on to highlight the backstory of a professional athlete who had been sidelined by a potentially career-ending injury. One athlete questioned, "Will anyone discover me?" The other questioned, "Will everyone forget about me?"

Every dream will encounter a season of frustration. Where you allow that frustration to take you will determine what becomes of your dream.

Did the injury end the professional athlete's career? It closed the door for him as a player but opened the door for him as a commentator. Frustration doesn't have to be fatal. Sometimes the thing we are trying to hold on to is the thing we need to let go of if we are to enter the next season of life.

I've learned that how we handle what looks like a delay or setback will often shape what our destiny looks like. When we wake up each morning, we should approach the day with confidence, knowing God will never let our gifts or talents go to waste. Keeping a positive attitude and optimistic outlook will help us discern the good things in our future. Remember, our Father will never let an opportunity or experience go to waste. He uses every situation, good or bad, for our advantage.

....

Father, open my eyes so I can see the good things You
have in my future. I trust You with my dreams.

Tracey Mitchell, Dallas, TX

Stay on the Right Path

The word of the LORD came to him, saying, "Go
away from here and turn eastward."
1 KINGS 17:2–3 NASB

The other day I was driving in Dallas with my friends. Having picked up a friend from the airport, we tried to make our way through the city to a scheduled appointment. On top of running late for the appointment, we experienced trouble locating the building.

Believe it or not we had three GPSs trying to give us directions. We all typed in the same address, but at every intersection each GPS would give a different audible instruction. One would say, "Turn right," the other, "Turn left," and the third said, "Recalculating. Make a U-turn." We ended up driving in circles, each of us certain that our GPS was giving accurate information. What we did not understand was, because we were near each other the satellite signals were bouncing off one another. Therefore no one was receiving the correct information. My friend almost missed her appointment because too many people in the same environment were providing her with inaccurate information.

Getting to our appointed destination in life can be complicated. Having too many people give us advice can create confusion. Whenever I feel overwhelmed by having to make decisions, I ask myself these questions: *Am I moving in the direction God has instructed me to go? Am I going with the flow of the crowd or am I following a divine course?*

Each day we need to take time to unclutter our minds and quiet our hearts. As we focus on hearing from God, we will instinctively know which path to take next.

....

Father, show me which path to take.

Recover All

David and his men wept aloud until they had no strength left to weep.
1 SAMUEL 30:4

*C*an you imagine coming home to find all your possessions, everything sacred to you, everything you have worked hard to build, taken and destroyed? That is how David and his men felt when they returned from the battlefield. The grief of losing their homes, wives, children, and possessions was too much to take in. They likely thought, *Had we not been out fighting for others, we could have defended ourselves from the enemy.*

Have you been through a difficult season and wondered, *If I had been at the right place at the right time, could crisis have been avoided?* Maybe you are struggling with guilt, feeling as though you missed opportunities to avert a crisis in the life of someone you love. The truth is, we can be doing all the right things and crisis can still invade our lives.

In the middle of a mess, David hit the emotional pause button and asked God what to do next. God responded to David's prayer by instructing him to pursue their enemies. He assured David, if he pursued, "You will certainly overtake them and succeed in the rescue" (1 Samuel 30:8).

During tragedy David refused to magnify his hardship; rather, he asked God to be victorious. Boldly pursuing those who had plundered them, David and his men took back everything the enemy took from them. I don't know what the Enemy has taken from you, but I do know the heart of God is for you to recover all. Not some things, not a handful or a portion, but all; if not in this life, then in the life to come.

Father, give me the courage to reclaim what has been stolen.

Tracey Mitchell, Dallas, TX

See an Enemy as an Opportunity

He went away a second time and prayed, "My Father, if it is not possible for this cup to be taken away unless I drink it, may your will be done."

MATTHEW 26:42

*H*ow we respond to our adversaries will determine whether we conquer crisis or crisis consumes us. Jesus had enemies. He identified them and at times used their actions to accomplish His work on the earth. The truth is that enemies are valuable. They force us to analyze our motives and to be mentally and emotionally aware. They identify disloyal friends, and their resistance validates our dreams' potential. Most importantly, God will use those who work against us to position us to fulfill His purpose.

More than anyone Jesus understood the old principle "Our enemies will do for us what our friends and family never will." Jesus talked about rejection and criticism because He understood the depths of being misunderstood and falsely accused. Prophets rejected Him, kings threatened Him, disciples betrayed Him, and those from His hometown doubted Him.

But Jesus came through each situation victoriously. He understood the pain of betrayal and gave a blueprint on how to overcome it. When Judas came into the Garden of Gethsemane to betray Jesus, Jesus did the unthinkable and let Judas get away with it. Why? Because Jesus understood Judas's rejection would position Him to go to the cross, where He would experience victory by redeeming humanity. Rejection positioned Him to do the will of the Father. How can your enemies work for you?

Father, use my enemies to position me for success. Give me
insight and fortitude to carry on despite resistance.

Contributors

Recording Artist, Singer, Songwriter, Founder of P31 Power in Purpose
Women's Conference, Speaker, TV Host, Keziaalford.com.

Christian Music Artist, Women's Conference Speaker, Co-Pastor of Living
Word Christian Center, TV Host, CEO and Business Owner.

Founder of Unlocked Women's Conference, Conference Speaker,
Recording Artist, Author of Multiple Books including *The Jezebel Spirit*,
Ordained Minister, Co-Pastor of Praise Churches of Louisiana,
TV Host, BilboMinistries.com, PraiseChurchofLouisiana.com,
facebook.com/BeverlyGormanBilbo.

Church Planter, Lead Pastor, Creative Arts Director, Speaker, Co Author of
the Constant Friend, crosschurchhouma.com.

Pastor's Wife, Soprano Singer for The Bilderbacks, Preacher, Writer,
thebilderbacks.org.

CEO, Arbook Realty, Speaker, Women's Ministry Leader, Worship Leader,
Music Artist of Gospel CD, Roz, Evolution of Me, ArbrookRealty.com.

Teacher, Biblical Counselor, and Executive Administrator of Strength &
Wisdom Ministries, www.strengthandwisdomministries.com,
www.Facebook.com/KarenBrown91.

Notes

WEEK 26
1 Beth Moore, *Praying God's Word: Breaking Free for Spiritual Strongholds* (Nashville: B&H Publishing Group, 2009), 5758.

WEEK 27
2 http://articles.latimes.com/print/1995-06-22/news/mn-16046_1_oldest-people

Scripture Index

Scripture Index